BREAKING WITH THE ENLIGHTENMENT

BREAKING WITH THE ENLIGHTENMENT

The Twilight of History and the Rediscovery of Utopia

RAJANI KANNEPALLI KANTH

HUMANITIES PRESS
NEW JERSEY

First published in 1997 by
Humanities Press International, Inc.
165 First Avenue, Atlantic Highlands, New Jersey 07716

© 1997 by Rajani Kannepalli Kanth

Library of Congress Cataloging—in—Publication Data
Rajani Kannepalli Kanth.
    Breaking with the Enlightenment : the twilight of history and the rediscovery of utopia / Rajani Kannepalli Kanth.
       p.   cm.
    Includes bibliographical references and index.
    ISBN 0–391–04012–X (cloth : alk. paper).—ISBN 0–391–04031–6 (paper : alk. paper)
    1. Utopias.   2. Dialectical materialism.   3. Eurocentrism.
I. Title.
HX806.R36 1997
321'.07—dc20   96–30252
                    CIP

All rights reserved. No part of this publication may be reproduced
or transmitted, in any form or by any means, without written permission.

Printed in the United States of America

10 9 8 7 6 5 4 3 2 1

This book is dedicated to the women of this world, who have sustained and succored the civilities of social life for aeons; it is their millenium—they, who must emancipate humanity from its self-imposed cruelties.

More personally, I salute the extraordinary women I know (or have known) best: Kesavan Kesari, Antara, Indrina, Malini, Anjana, and Cory. This world were safe, were it to rest solely in their gentle hands!

I'd rather be a Pagan suckled in a creed outworn;
Or might I, standing on this pleasant lea,
Have glimpses that would make me less forlorn;
Have sight of Proteus rising from the sea;
Or hear old Triton blow his wreathed horn.

W. Wordsworth

Contents

Acknowledgments		xi
Preface: The Epoch of Uncertainty		xiii
1	The Ancien Régime: The Roots of Modernism	1
2	The Emergent Imperium: of Conflicting Corporatisms	16
3	A Critique of Political Economy: On Elisions in Materialism	57
4	Capitalism and Socialism: The Twin Faces of Janus	82
5	Against Eurocentrism: Breaking with the Enlightenment	94
6	Alternative Visions: Toward Conviviality	116
7	The Reveille of Emancipation: Toward Volition	129
Postscript		161
Bibliography		163
Index		169

ACKNOWLEDGMENTS

The twentieth century marks the grand culmination, and lofty ascendancy, of the high modernist impulse set in motion by the remarkable forces, both material and metaphysical, unleashed by the European Enlightenment of the eighteenth century. Pockets of resistance aside, the Great Crusade has, apparently, been won—or so the storytellers would have us believe; at any rate, a certain kind of history has been made by some, inevitably, at the expense, of various others. This book provides a searing account of the myth and reality of *modernism*, and its victorious planetary agenda, incorporated in the so-called New World Order—*but counterposed vividly against the emergent, and largely unsuspected, challenges to this new epoch*—in effect since the collapse of the USSR, though in the making for decades prior to that signal event. The triumphalist revival, resurgence, and re-establishment of the capitalist mode of production, after surviving the many challenging uncertainties of the century, including socialism, the depression, and fascism, is of course, part and parcel of contemporary folklore. What it calls for, on the 'Left,' though—a fact not always fully appreciated—is a fundamental re-examination of its alternate, but related, visions of liberation, particularly its inescapable heritage of *Eurocentrism*, which continues to define human/social behavior in linear, reductionist, monist, materialist, and universalist abstractions, not far apart from the canonical prejudices of traditional economics. This text offers a critique of the ideologies, and the metaphysical underpinnings, of both capitalism and socialism—the *psyche* of modernism generally—aside from pointing to a vitally organic, historically revealed, and radically contrasting, docket of values to both of these Eurocentered visions of society.

As such, this work runs on a *dual* track, first arguing with traditional categories, and then subjecting these categories to a scathing critique. To facilitate ease of reading, the two tracks have, for the most part, been separated and placed in different chapters (although some reference to the critique to come is available throughout the text). The critique of Eurocentrism offered here has been the result of many influences, perhaps the most important of which has been the discovery of the potency of *culture*—as a survival kit—while living as a disenfranchised third world subject-citizen, albeit in an entirely *voluntary* exile, of the appropriately deculturalized hegemonic leader of the first world.

Other than the pedagogy implicit in this ontological condition, teaching revelatory courses in race, culture, and gender studies, and supervising emancipatory dissertations of some powerfully committed graduate students in this area, has provided the necessary goad, stimulus, and imperative, to my own continuing education. Friends, family, and comrades (distinctions that, happily, fade with time), at another remove, have also helped to keep the intellectual and moral fires burning at times when the deep freeze of fell circumstances seemed all but impossible to foil. While a full listing of such fellow travelers is out of the question, I must name a few (in no particular order), comprising both intimates and distal compeers, who either marched alongside, or provided necessary philosophical nourishment quite unknowingly, one time or another, in this long and arduous trek: Roy Bhaskar, Noam Chomsky, Roger Owen, Robert Heilbroner, Bill Brugger, Paul Sweezy, Paul Feyerabend, Sai Baba, Harry Magdoff, Paul Auerbach, Mark Blaug, Boudhayan Chattopadhyaya, Peter Bell, Tony Brewer, Wolfram Elsner, Ali Shamsavari, Sudipta Kaviraj, Samir Amin, Andre Gunder Frank, Vandana Shiva, Chandra Mohanty, Warren Samuels, Barbara Thayer, Janeen Costa, Kamal Chenoy, Shaun Lovejoy, David Gordon, Paul Hanson, Tim Wonderly, Janaka Bmanwila, and Janet Darley.

Thanks are also due to an anonymous reviewer, courtesy of Humanities Press, whose gracious criticism helped to redirect my own attention toward strengthening the basic theses being advocated here to the relative neglect of a host of quite secondary, and ancillary, arguments that otherwise might have obstructed them; indeed, an entire new chapter was later added on, in direct consequence of his/her suggestions. I need also express gratitude to several editors of Humanities Press who patiently sustained my excesses of form and style.

Finally, I must note that this work is not intended as yet another offer of abstractions in an already over-theorized world, but as a manual for *engagements* (moral, spiritual, political, etc.—but in the lower case), pointing the way to struggle as an inescapable condition, and emancipation as an unavoidable goal, of a human society; unavoidable, because the passion for freedom (from arbitrary, and unfamiliar, restraint) is arguably the only universal impulse shared by humankind across time and space. It is, by far, the only *episteme* that does not, and cannot, change; it is what still stands between us and a complete capitulation to the dictates of modernism. As such, the most predictable thing about the New World Order (to come) is that it will be, inevitably, the product of our own sustained determinations (or lack of them) to fashion an easeful, more sensual world.

Preface: The Epoch of Uncertainty

We are, in the current period, in a state that physicists might call a *singularity*, where conventional wisdom (whether expressed in the form of 'laws,' or 'models,' or not) breaks down. The collapse of the Soviet Union, though eagerly sought by both the Right and many variants in the Left, came as a complete and total surprise to *all* of the pundits of determinism (doing more damage, actually, to vulgar *Marxists* among that roster). Neither capitalist cold war political propaganda, nor socialist rhetoric, anticipated either the collapse, or—more to the point—the astonishingly effete manner in which it was actually accomplished. That a complex social system, embodying an elaborate power structure, could self-destruct, more or less peaceably, stood all varieties of political science, bourgeois and putatively Marxist, on their head—suggesting, simply, that social science even today is more pretentious than it is prescient in matters involving an understanding of the dynamics of power and social change. At any rate, after generations of tug and tussle, drama and debacle, the twentieth century has provided the modernist ambition, that began its sweep of the world about the time of the European Enlightenment, with a near-total victory over an apparently prostrate world.

In mainstream physics, singularities tend to be abhorred because of the sway of the rabid *anthropocentrism* (the so-called 'anthropic' principle) that refuses to accept any phenomena as beyond the pale of human understanding, as though the universe were created explicitly for human comprehension (arguably axiomatic in most of Judeo-Christian discourse). A similar orientation subsists in the social sciences (social science abhorring a vacuum even more than nature) in both the rationalist and materialist streams, deriving from the European capitalist Enlightenment dating from the eighteenth century. In this context, suffice it to say that *social science remains, today, more of a self-glorifying datum, to be critically examined, than a reliable instrument to decipher the nature of reality.* The fatal flaw here is the materialist *reductionism*, inescapable attribute of the modernist temper, common to bourgeois theory and vulgar Marxism alike—a reductionism that derives human conduct from material motives, as a sort of a radical *a priori*, instead of viewing it only as a *hypothesis* to be tested against actual, concrete experience. In this sense, the obliteration of state socialism has at least provided the shock waves necessary to re-evaluate, also, socialist agendas and Marxian theory, presenting therefore a unique opportunity to explore what is to be *undone* in these areas.

At any rate, it is quite imperative now, at this juncture of both exploded and exulting visions, to critically re-examine the received views of the two dominant European models of society, that have almost completely monopolized the critical idealism of several generations (in both the European and non-European world), as though the future of humanity was completely rendered permanently hostage to either capitalism, or its dual, socialism. Stated simply, human history has always been an almost unfathomably rich treasure trove of societal modes, and the customary liberal-radical penchant of digging no further, nor deeper, than the European sixteenth or seventeenth century for institutional innovations, betrays only a stunning want of intellectual responsibility, to say nothing of imagination.

Today, given the fairly deep and widespread disenchantment with socialism, all paths seem, inevitably, to lead to the inviting abyss of high capitalism. As such, it is one of the tasks of this book to break the near-fatal, hegemonic spell of late European ideology, and its demotic idolatry—to point, instead, to the pleiad of pristine, lush, and opulent, founts of the human genius, in the sphere of societal relations, that have almost been completely overlooked (for being overrun) by this form of monist thinking, that has trapped humankind as the benighted victims either of an omnipotent market (read capitalism) or an omnipotent state (read all forms of 'actually existing' socialism). Stated simply, the ideological conceit that leaves us with only this hopelessly sophistical 'choice' between Tweedledum and Tweedledee is, as Marx might have put it, a sheer libel upon the human race. As such, consigning the last three hundred years of 'modernist' European ideologies to the rubbish heap of history may be but the necessary first step in the rediscovery of utopia.

However, to suspend the sway of received 'reason,' to break out of the trance of everyday life, to snap out of what Gaston Bachelard called the near-sublime state of soporific '*reverie,*' that blindly legitimizes the status quo, requires a form of emancipatory shock therapy that necessarily is apart from the work of ordinary persuasion that we employ, to deservedly dull effect, in the stolid routines of 'normal' science. Accordingly, a work of this nature has some (but obviously) self-conscious defects that the sophisticated reader is expected to take in her stride. Perhaps less obviously, the greatest of its defects are likely to be the ones of *heroic aggregation*; which— a fact we don't always appreciate—is, of course, simply another term for *theory*. Indeed, this matter is important enough to deserve some overstatement. The urge to totalize is understandable, and heroic aggregation is quite class neutral in its incidence, shared by capitalist and socialist theorist alike. However, without the ever present reminder that, in crucial regards, the whole is not just more than the parts, but is also *less*, the enterprise is likely to go awry. Theory misses detail *ab initio*; worse, theory usually appropriates macro phenomena, and is less sensitive, if not altogether blind, to micro phenomena; and finally, theory can be, and is, refuted by unfolding realities. All these considerations impose a deservedly heavy weight of modesty upon the theorist, and upon theory.

As such, the spirit in which these reflections are offered is one that Marx, in his better moods, would have appreciated (it was, by his own confession to his daughter, his favorite motto—though subsequent Marxists would seem to have completely forgotten it): *De Omnibus Dubitandum*. It is also important to note that I claim no apodictic certainty, drawn from either science or theology, for my theses; conceived in the fervid vortex of feeling, and reared in the silent cloister of observation and reflection, they are offered in the spirit only of free, passionate, and moral *Argument* with which people of sincerity and learning (similarly motivated) can disagree quite legitimately without bloodletting, in the full realization that in a human society, it is not so much reason that struggles against unreason, nor truth against error, but rather that it is values that clash with values and interests with interests. It is indeed high time that independent, unattached scholarship (of the, now near-vanished, kind that marked the Enlightenment before the corporate organization of the production and dissemination of knowledge) shed the constricting crutches of corporatist paradigms, tied to the newest fashion of academic respectability, to perform the simple, but signal, intellectual service required of a scholar—of *thinking for oneself*.

The moral failure of socialism, adventitiously, predated its material collapse (some such fate, I will argue, lies also in store for capitalism); as such, this book also represents a long drawn struggle to *emancipate the idea of emancipation from the old-style emancipators*. It is possibly no accident that this work, conceptually, originated in New York, while being completed in Utah; the opportunity to review both ends of the (unpromising) scale of capitalist evolution must have had something to do with the project (paralleling my own personal displacement from the third world to the first, in another evolutionary leap—*backwards*). I believe we are poised, on the eve of the twenty-first century, on the brink of a resumption of an old parity between east and west, rudely sundered by the sudden, meteoric blaze of European capital that, much like Hamlet's uncle, envenomed the non-European world as it lay, peacefully, in deep slumber. Today, the Asian giants are fitfully awake with the possibility of a *polycentric* world, though regrettably united presently only in sharing a common philosophy of greed, once again on the cards. The inevitable outcome of this stark monism of the modern world—despite, and because of, the triumph, in the high modernist crusades of the twentieth century, of *one* warring tribe of modernists—is likely to be the grand revival, and resuscitation, of age-old *precapitalist* endowments of social wisdom, both European and non-European, carrying with them the continent promise, and charter, of a more convivial world to come. In this very preliminary work, I have tried only to prepare the ground for the necessary, even vital, philosophical *retooling*. The spirit of this book, quite naturally, is premised, precariously perhaps, upon that promise, and only events and processes, as yet incipient, can show whether this optimism is (or was) ahead of its historical time.

Finally, a quite necessary note on the mode of exposition of this book. The first two chapters carefully situate and 'construct' the present, but only in the light of past history, 'materially' (and, on the whole, quite conventionally) at the level of system and society, in the upper case. Chapter 3, and beyond, begin the long, unwinding process of *critique*, as 'deconstruction,' proceeding ultimately, in a steady 'downward' spiral, pointing to the irrelevance of aggregate (material) forces and analyses (at the level of 'nation,' 'State,' 'economy,' etc.) when the objective, precisely, is human emancipation from such imperatively coordinated entities. For the impatient reader, anxious to 'get to the point', *I suggest starting with Chapter 5, where the analytical exegetics of the principal thesis are made succinctly available.* This methodological feint, of the disparagement of aggregative analyses, is premised on the 'realist' insight that societies and individuals are separated by what might be termed an *ontological hiatus*, existing as they do at different levels of being and functioning; most European emancipatory discourse has taken the 'social' (material) moment as the effective point of intervention, both theoretically and practically (e.g. socialism)—here, I focus on its exact antipode, the (ideal) 'individual' as an equally critical social 'moment' of transformation: indeed, far more so, since the individual, ultimately, is also a human end, and not just a 'moment' in some suitably satisfactory analytical scheme. *Ultimately, it will be apparent, however, that in convivial social forms, the wholly modernist antagonism between individual and society is entirely illusory and chimerical.* At any rate, it is high time, I think, that dreams of amelioration were gently *microcosmic* in their practical propensities; if nothing else, in contrast to the received history of social engineering to date, their frequent failure(s) would at least be proportionately less cataclysmic and damaging to human existence.

As I see it, the immediate, consummate, emancipatory challenge facing humankind today is the annulment, and abolition, of the ruling modernist paradigm of social relations inherited by all of us, by dint of force, from the all-consuming world trajectory of late European history. The truth will appear to be heresy; but *modernism is the distinctive malaise afflicting us all* —it is time to understand, and excise, all its vaingloriously epideictic cant that has held us in thrall for centuries. As yet, on the threshold of this Great Rejection, we may lack the articulated vocabulary, perhaps even the rhetorical tropes, to sacralize this monumental revolution in human affairs, though the premonitory *practices* outlining this resolve are already actively extant in various novel, subaltern struggles gradually gathering force across the world. I have taken but the first, precursory step here in detailing the driving inspiration(s) of this spiritual revolution whose time, I am convinced, is abundantly come; up to others, now, to make of it what they will—this book is but a token offering, by way of valediction, to that Stygian scourge of humankind.

1

THE ANCIEN RÉGIME: THE ROOTS OF MODERNISM

CLASSIC COLONIALISM

Colonialism was the material process that hastened what Marx termed the 'primitive accumulation' of capital, whose end process was necessarily the creation of the world system as we know it today. As such, no analysis of European capitalism is possible without the explicit recognition of this powerful lever that forklifted European capital out of its late feudal moorings and gave it its fateful, world-encompassing trajectory, one that is all too visible in the present.[1] Indeed, it is this leapfrog advantage that was to be denied the latecomers to the original club of capitalist societies (Germany, Italy, Russia, and Japan, initially, and most of the third world countries, later), setting up at least one basis for later intraimperialist rivalry, as much as the now routine—even ritualized—struggles between the 'North' and the 'South' of the capitalist world.

In radical simplification, colonialism[2] was driven by commercial capital backed by state power (or factions thereof); it was, therefore, primarily the artifact of merchant capital, driven by a slew of commercial motives, the simplest of which was *alienation through trade*—i.e., buying cheap and selling dear in captive markets. The state that supported these efforts, whether absolutist, feudal, or protocapitalist in organization and objectives, did so for revenues, an extension of domain (both political and military), and as the response of statecraft inevitably driven to its actions by interstate rivalry. The fact that these motives were often separable is what makes it impossible to derive all of colonial policy as driven simply by the determinants of commercial policy. Sometimes *raisons d'état* won the day over strictly commercial needs, other times vice versa. Any attempt, therefore, to set up a methodologically necessary hierarchy between state and capital is doomed to empirical refutation, for each has a domain that may occasionally prevail over the other. One can only understand specific outcomes in terms of *context*.

The sheer scale of European incursions into non-European spaces was spectacular. In 1714, after the Peace of Utrecht confirmed British supremacy in Europe, the colonial possessions of Europe amounted to about ten percent of the earth's land surface, including about two percent of world population; by 1914, the commencement of World War I, this had grown to 56 percent of the earth's land area and 34 percent of world population. South and Central America were principally occupied by Spain and Portugal between 1492 and 1810; Asia was overrun between 1800 and 1947; and Africa was secured between 1880 and 1914. The booties so amassed were titanic: between 1600 and 1800, the New World supplied Spain with 22,000 tons of silver and 185 tons of gold; while the period 1750–1800 saw Portugal swallow 800 tons of gold mined in Brazil. Africa yielded even more gross value in terms of live cargo: the Atlantic slave trade carried some 9.6 million Africans to the Americas. India's prostrate peasants, rack rented by British occupation, yielded Britain of 100 million pounds sterling (valued at nineteenth-century prices) in tribute, in the short space of fifty years of English misrule; the Dutch took back about 60 million (pounds sterling) in a hundred years of 'trading' with the Spice Islands, from the mid-seventeenth to the mid-18th century. China's forced opium trade yielded Britain a net profit of one million pounds annually, and so on. How can one, without serious disquiet, set a monetary sum on such horrific pillage? Yet capitalist accounting makes such calculations entirely feasible; in stark money terms, this net transfer of values from colony to metropolis has been estimated at approximately some 850 million pounds sterling, or about 25 thousand million pounds, at 1982 prices (exceeding the entire estimable value of the world industrial plant in 1800).[3] The economic, social, and human damage so inflicted upon the hapless non-European societies, on the other hand, is surely quite inestimable.[4]

Motivations and needs apart, the two major consequences of colonial policies, amongst a host of others, were the establishment of a world market, without which a titanic growth of capital was inconceivable (a fact perfectly clear to Smith, but often ignored by Euro-Marxists), and the wholesale transfer of values from the colony to the 'mother' country (in the form of raw materials, consumption goods, bullion, etc.). In a case like England, it meant that, aside from domestic surpluses, colonialism *financed* the so-called Industrial Revolution, providing the economic justification for a revolution in technologies, and giving the system the rationale and the spur for uninterrupted growth. In an equally important sense, the growth of wealth and power in the hands of the limited beneficiary strata increased social differentiation within the mother country and hastened domestic class struggles, thereby accelerating the forces that were to finally separate the late feudal producer from her means of production, and, still later, to divest landed aristocrats of their monopoly of state power, thereby capping the entire process of the 'primitive accumulation of capital' (as Marx had termed it). In this important sense, *Europe's misadventures in its overseas dominions had the fortuitous effect of advancing its domestic capitalist constructions*, initially in the domains of trade and commerce, and eventually in industry. While it is certainly true that capitalist pecuniary impulses (allied with absolutism's inherent military-expansionist, i.e., *imperial*, leanings), though nurtured within the womb of still surviving feudal society, gave us colonialism, it is equally true that the host-house success of the capitalist revolution in Europe (and, within Europe, England) owed everything to its subject colonies. Indeed, colonial plunder, the slave trade, and plantation super-profits (sugar, cotton, etc.), helped finance the capitalist advancement of the white colonies of Europe and the Americas, as well.

While the question of European capital's debt to the Americas, Asia, and Africa is clear and obvious, more complex is the set of consequences unleashed upon the colonies, whose social and cultural modalities were to be completely uprooted and transformed by the nature of this catastrophic external intrusion. The dialectic of interaction produced transformation at both ends, as was inevitable, even if the respective forms of transformation remained quite distinct and separable. Most important, from a world historical perspective, was the creation of the *'third world'* itself, with all its accompanying nuances of dissolution, decay, and dependence, as attends the term indelibly now in the western vocabulary. Obviously, colonialism was not a uniform process, given the range of social formations of predator and prey alike, nor could its effects be expected to be uniform. On the one hand, the various occupying powers were composed of different class equilibria, and driven by varying ecopolitical needs (as evident, e.g., in the difference between Portugal and England in terms of growth of productive forces, class balances between aristocracy and bourgeois, nature and composition of the state apparati, etc.). On the other, for the 'host' receiving societies, it mattered, in the first instance, *when*, in their social evolution, they were incorporated into the world market, *how* this annexation was achieved, and *who* the occupying power was. However, equally important to such societies were their own *internal dialectic* of forces and relations of production, and the nature of political struggles, at the time they were overrun by European hordes.

Even so, in broad outline, the *colonial modes of exploitation*, irrespective of occupying power, were reasonably consistent. Where outright seizure and confiscation of land, labor, and social wealth were not the rule, long-term investments tended principally to be in extractive and primary industries, such as minerals, metals, and raw produce. Mining and plantation agriculture[5] were the 'productive' activities requiring the mobilization of native labor at any terms suitable to the occupying power. But far from being 'progressive' in their implications for emancipation from traditional forms of exploitation, as often comfortably supposed by millenarian Marxists and conservatives alike, it is arguable that European capital was simply more retrograde in its labor policies than not, reinventing servile forms as and when needed, ready to mete out the most barbarous cruelty in order to guarantee proletarian discipline. Techniques to force labor ranged from the atrocities of the Belgians in the Congo (who freely amputated limbs as a ready form of achieving labor discipline), to the civilized savagery of the British in Bengal, even as the starry-eyed storytellers of the Enlightenment, such as John Stuart Mill, reassured themselves in Europe with lullabies announcing the inauguration of the modern epoch of human rights, liberty, and progress.

The degradation of labor was only one side of the story. On the other went the despoliation of peasant agriculture, crafts, and simple industry. The push toward cash crop production and plantation economies, catering to export, implied the destruction of food crops domestically; and the stranglehold of rentiers, landlords, tax collectors, and money lenders, spelled the parcelization of land, chronic land hunger, and a purely secondary, dependent, agriculture (outside of cash crops) vulnerable to the whims of nature, the local exploiters, and the inexorable tributary demands of the colonial state. Ancient, self-sufficient agrarian civilizations were thereby transformed, within decades of colonial rule, into food importing 'nations,' with traditional granaries like Bengal[6] becoming bywords for famine, rural poverty, and squalor.

With local initiatives in industry being rendered defunct by imperial policy (cheap imports from Europe), the possibility of a diversified economic system, thriving on backward and forward linkages between agriculture and industry, was to be thwarted producing a permanent, artificial rift between organically linked phenomena. The resulting agrarian crisis in the countryside, in the context of predatory urban expansion, produced the now-familiar, near-archetypical, picture of a starving peasant hinterland lying abreast of a thriving industrial metropole as, e.g., Mexico City, or virtually any other prosperous third world metropolis, leeching off a subordinate, agrarian economy. With productive outlets either monopolized or choked off by European capital (or the state), domestic surpluses were channelled into unproductive modes of investment such as trade, petty finance, usurious moneylending, or to other *comprador* forms of activity subordinate to metropolitan capital. The economy would, henceforth, grow in this severely *disarticulated* form, with uneven productivities scattered across disconnected sectors, with a familiar, ubiquitous, core/periphery division appearing nationally, regionally, and even within districts. The key to the economic instability of the colony was chronic, seemingly incurable, *agrarian crisis*: the European impact here being comparable to a landmass being hit with asteroids that leave a permanent, indelible mark of their destruction behind for centuries to behold. The situation of India, atypical only in regard to its scale and size, where colonial policy forced the retardation of domestic agriculture and industry, setting it back by a century, must be seen as highly corroborative of this general colonial thrust. The differential paths traveled by India and Japan from the eighteenth century on (when the British blight afflicted the former) illustrate the consequences of colonialism for the capitalist development of the periphery quite vividly and, indeed more to the point, conclusively.[7]

On the cultural side were equally telling effects, *dependency* being even more pronounced in this sphere than in economic relations. The primary outcome here was to render local elites permanently *comprador* in their intellectual orientations, a dupe of spurious universalisms drawn from European history, which belied their own warped existence within the lap of colonial iniquities. *The tragedy here is that Europe managed to pass off its own parochialism as modernism, its vested interests as progressivism, and its private agenda as liberationism.* The well-known inferiority complex of capitalist (and some kinds of socialist) elites, *vis-à-vis* the west, in the third world, is a good indicator of the extent to which Europe was able to drive a wedge between these elites and their own civilizational genius to the point, ultimately, of their being swept away, as in Iran, by the wrath of the more insular peasantry, which, however integrated into the circuits of world capital, never succumbed to the treacherous seductions of European ideologies.

Perhaps the most debilitating and, unfortunately, lasting cultural bequest of colonialism was *racism*, with Europeans quite convinced, after four centuries of world-mastery, of their own inherent superiority over all other races, an ideology more completely imbued in Anglo-Saxon culture than in any other European social formation, while a dominant strain in all of Europe. The corresponding devaluation of the cultural heritage of non-European societies, particularly those aspects which stood at odds with capitalism and patriarchy, not least amongst non-European elites, is something that a prostrate third world is only gradually getting over, though in forms of reaction which may not always approximate the intense fury of the Ayatollahs. Amongst the most striking manifestation of this denial of legitimacy to *nativist* traditions of social accomplishment, was the outright denial of any independent Black African civilizational genius to the point where history was creatively deformed to read that Cleopatra was white; and having a suitably pale, caucasoid, race (the 'Hamites,' speaking a mythical language called 'Hamitic') grant us the wonders of ancient Egypt, and indeed all of Africa's great civilizations, as Professor C. G. Seligman[8] would have had us believe not so very long ago. Thus, could the great Hegel, lecturing in Jena in 1830, armed only with an impressive ignorance, speak of Africans as being peoples at the threshold of civilization, at the very infancy of (hu)mankind, indeed as being "no historical part of the world". But, contrary to racist constructions, Egyptian civilization was a gift of the Nubian Nile; as such, *Black Africa is the mother of European civilization*, through its impact on the Greeks, who learned as much of their justly fabled wisdom in Alexandria (itself on the crossroads of ideas from India and China) as they were to contribute independently on their own account.[9]

Classic colonialism, therefore, gave us all of the dubious gifts of the modern world order, setting the stage for cataclysmic reckonings to come in a world driven on to the treadmill of endless toil for the many, in favor of the endless gain of the few (without customary and conventional restraints upon the extent and degree of such a transformation, as was the rule in precapitalist societies): such was the force of European greed that was to be foisted upon the weak, the vulnerable, and the defenseless. Indeed, by the turn of the nineteenth century, it appeared as though Europe was determined to create a world in its own unsightly capitalist image at whatever cost in terms of cultures uprooted, ecologies ravaged, and societies torched.

VARIATIONS ON A THEME: IMPERIALISM

However, even as Europe indulged its worst impulses in its captive colonies, the internal social dynamics of European societies were themselves in ferment, and the old partnership between commerce and aristocracy now found itself threatened by the rise of new social forces, small (and large) industrial entrepreneurs, and the working classes. Commercial capital was challenged by industrial capital; aristocrat, by a novel, albeit brief, alliance between capitalists and workers. While steady economic differentiation, the concomitant of the concentration and centralization of capital, had bred these social tensions spontaneously, so to speak, by and large the area of resolution of these struggles was to be within the sphere of the state. In England, home of the classic capitalist revolution, manufacturers (with working-class support) successfully entered Parliament in 1832, and were thereupon able to turn economic policy around decisively in their favor.[10] The monopolists of trade now had to give way to the monopolists of industry, while the monopolists of land found their political power slowly eroded by the owners of fluid, movable capital.

While England successfully installed a manufacturer-led government, with a privileged industrial sector, it in turn found itself being defied by the late capitalist evolvers, Germany and America, both in the market for goods, sources of raw materials, and in the scramble for colonial possessions and protectorates. While still the biggest empire on earth, Britain saw industrial supremacy, in terms of cutting-edge technologies, pass to these newcomers, even as a new divide was being established in the economic sphere. Growing productivity, with a virtually shackled working class, meant rising surpluses; and with domestic markets saturated at acceptable profit rates, *vents for surplus* became the new holy grail. As such, the era of *Imperialism* proclaimed a new market adjacent to the old one of commodity exports: the export of capital. Between Waterloo and about the 1870s, for instance (but mostly between 1850–1873), Britain had managed to export a net capital surplus of almost 1000 million pounds sterling (about half of which was in government securities; the corresponding wealth, and power, of the new 'rentier' class of coupon clippers, with financial interests abroad, can well be imagined); the age of portfolio and direct foreign investment was off and running—inaugurating new crises in world capitalism, with protected colonial linkages becoming vital prizes as European powers sought to divide up the world into just so many parcels of direct rule. In terms of the so-called 'Monroe Doctrine' set forth in the early decades of the nineteenth century, the United States, already geared to viewing the entire continent as its own backyard, replied to European challenges by declaring South America, just embarked on the moment of decolonization, off-limits to the traditional bleeders of the New World. In that one declaration, the United States had already laid claim to high imperialist membership, moving quickly from a retrograde slave society to one with advanced capitalist ambitions (to be realized, beyond expectation, in the century to come). Between 1803 and 1853, this fledgling imperialist power was to annex over 2 million square miles of territory (equivalent to its own initial size) from the declining French and Spanish colonial powers, from conquered Native Americans, and from Latin America (to be complemented later by the acquisition of Alaska, the occupation of the Philippines, the annexation of Hawaii, etc.).[11]

The dominance of trusts and cartels by the end of the nineteenth century (Marxists, in fact, tend to see the last third of the century as marking the advent of the 'monopoly' stage of capitalism) was clear enough in the case of metropolitan, first world, capital. These new combines throttled weaker enterprises (using means akin to those employed by Standard Oil in driving its competitors under in the United States, in the age of the so-called 'robber barons'), by means legal and extra-legal: by blocking raw materials supplies, or labor supplies; by cutting off deliveries, closing trade outlets, blocking credit, and organizing trade boycotts; and, ultimately, by using state policy to keep a small business sector (much as the farm sector) a hostage to big business requirements. Strengthened by technological advances in transport, communications, and productive processes, the size of viable industrial units continually advanced, rendering older individual proprietorships obsolete and/or dysfunctional. The régime of *monopoly capital*, despite its superior control over the production process, exhibited all of the unflattering tendencies only weakly evident in nineteenth century capitalism: excess capacity and underutilization; deliberate sluggishness in application of new technologies and planned obsolescence; a rising gap between price and cost, secular stagnation, and permanent inflation; an abnormal increase in the size of the reserve army (to the point of defining and accepting a so-called '*natural*' rate of unemployment) of the unemployed and unemployable; ossification of the overall industrial structure; restriction of output, waste, escalation of selling costs, and so on. In terms of class structure, the new epoch was characterized by a virtual expropriation of all precapitalist vestiges coupled with a mushrooming growth of the new middle classes in professional, technical, and service occupations. Of course all this arose from within the womb of the old order, representing only exaggerated forms of tendencies inherent in capitalism itself. Lest we bewail a paradise lost, it must be borne in mind that capitalism was no less ugly and invidious in the nineteenth century, for being only more competitive, Capitalism was both born and baptized in violence and imperial ambition; monopoly capital simply displayed these ineradicable birthmarks in full maturity.

Lenin,[12] as with Hobson, Bukharin, and Hilferding before him, saw these tendencies as the new movers of the capitalist world, and felt it important enough to categorize them as constituting a new stage of capitalism—*monopoly capital or imperialism*—to which the older 'laws' of capitalism presumably did not apply. The factors outlining this new epoch were obvious to the careful observer, at least in the advanced sectors of Eurocapitalist regimes: a growing concentration of capital, the merging (liaison) of industrial with finance capital, the export of capital as a new market, the formation of transnational monopolies, and the territorial division of the world into European outposts. In key terms, Lenin was pointing to the *parasitism* of this phase of capitalism (rentiers—coupon clippers—dominating industrialists, and presumed to be in favor of immediate, as opposed to deferred, returns) that spelled some sort of an internal limit (hence the notion of the 'highest' stage of capitalism) to the dynamic expansion process conjectured to be the norm for progressive, competitive capitalism. Monopolies were believed to be technology suppressors, retarding productive capacity with the absence of any real competition, other than outright imperial rivalry, implying that the self-adjusting mechanisms fueling capitalist growth no longer applied. Hence, capitalism could now be theorized as having at last become a conservative, obsolete mode of social production, regressive and reactionary in the main. This seemed to bear out the Marxian idea that radical changes in modes of production are *internally* generated, the seeds of dissolution being present in their very womb. At any rate, all of the traditional ills of capitalism appeared to be sharpened in the new epoch: from market anarchy and periodic destruction of social values in industrial crises, to even more ravaging wars over division of markets. Worse, from a revolutionary point of view, workers, now participating in the spoils of imperial conquest, were becoming *reformist* (a major political development *à la* the Second International), and more or less peaceably adjusted to capitalist control.

Building largely on the work of others, Lenin had fashioned a theory that tried to explain much of the observable phenomena extant in turn of century capitalism (though with Germany as the 'model' advanced capitalist nation in mind), particularly the first imperial conflagration of 1914–17 that European (capitalist) historians try to pass off as a 'world war.' Truth is, of course, that capitalists of many hues, together with their mercenary machinery of state, dragged the rest of the world into their predacious struggles for supremacy. That millions of ordinary people, men, women, and children, died in the process as 'collateral' victims posed, of course, no hindrance to the aims of these high priests of guns and greed. At any rate, Lenin's characterization, unless viewed schematically, was an extraordinarily potent way of capturing, in essence, the *macro* movement of Euro-American capital. Its highlights were the accurate description of the nature of intraimperialist struggles, the parasitism and decadence of the new era, and the gradual political defeat and assimilation of the working classes into the hegemony of the ruling *corporatism* of the imperial bourgeoisie. In essence, Lenin was trying to conceptualize a new *stage* in the development of capitalism; and imperialism stood, simply, for the *monopoly* stage of that process.

Lenin did borrow many of his ideas from his contemporaries; aside from Hobson,[13] his obvious debt was to Hilferding[14] (*Finance Capital*, published in 1910, though penned earlier) and Bukharin[15] (*Imperialism and World Economy*, written in 1915, but published in 1927) whose work predated his own. It is quite true that, if Hobson is scaled in with Bukharin and Hilferding, almost all the ideas contained in Lenin's work originated with others. But of course, Lenin gave the ideas the full force of his historical reputation, and so his name is deservedly the lasting one in this debate. This is far from unusual; one has only to look at the number of economists from the nineteenth century on who anticipated Keynes's ideas, without being immortalized in history like him, to understand that this is, sometimes, simply the way with history.

Characteristically, of course, Lenin's theory was overcome, if only in parts, by *praxis*: by the end of World War I, the Soviet Union broke away from the capitalist orbit in which it had been a quasi-satellite of French, German, and English capital. As Lenin would see it, the system had snapped at its *weakest link*, leaving open the possibility of a chain sequence of slave revolts in the periphery. Of course, colonies had overthrown colonizers before, as with the United States and the independent states of Latin America, but that was in the régime of commercial capital and colonialism; now it was imperialism that was being subject to challenges under a regime of transnational capital. The breakaway of the USSR both hastened capitalist unity and forced intracapitalist warfare, since the *lebensraum* for the latecomers (Japan, Germany, and Italy) was now short one-sixth of the earth's land surface. Only after the Second Imperial war did European capital sew up its breaches and present a united-front—North Atlantic Treaty Organization—against both socialism and national liberation struggles alike. At any rate, the direct territorial rule option of imperialism was, eventually, to be ever so slowly relaxed, effecting an important change in one direction; while, in another, with the growth of self-financing—Trans National Corporations—the subordination of industry by finance was to be far less the norm internationally than it had been in Germany at the time Hilferding and Lenin were writing.

The inter-War period is therefore the critical period in which the movement toward a *new world order* on the part of the capitalist world, and the reaction to it on the part of socialist and third world struggles, took grave and definite form, the one taking cue from the other, and vice versa. Conclusion of hostilities after the Second Imperial War produced the paradoxical situation of a capitalist world united as never before under the planned aegis of the proliferation of Bretton Woods institutions—even while facing a reasonably, if not similarly, powerful socialist third-world alliance led by the Soviet Union and newly emergent China (one of the many *singularities* of that conflagration, the other being the existence of an uneasy Eastern Europe under *de facto* Soviet domination). Thereby, almost incidentally, the baton of leadership of the capitalist world had passed from ailing British to lusting American hands. Old style imperialism was bound to suffer a sea change as so many variables shuffled off their old values, most particularly in the untenability of annexation and direct rule of its colonies, given the rise of Soviet power and national liberation struggles alike. As such, Bretton Woods and the Marshall Plan were to serve as the key new capitalist policy initiatives intended to surmount the very real *uncertainty* of the new times.

THE INTERWAR INTERREGNUM

The breakaway of the USSR, the waning of British power, and the rise of fascism, mark some of the major transitions inaugurated with the end of the First Imperial War.[16] In many senses, the groundwork for the Second World War was laid precisely by these events and processes, and at about the same time. The growth of National Socialism in Germany was not merely due to the onerous reparations imposed upon Germany by the Allied Powers, and the ensuing economic crisis, as liberal history routinely doles out, but also due to the clear-minded realization on the part of German Reaction that henceforth socialism would be the new devil to tame. Hitler's single-minded determination to destroy the USSR was a vanguard 'rationalist' capitalist maneuver, and one far more important politically, and even in terms of human costs (but only in *quantitative* measure), than his quite contrasting, febrile, and wholly insane genocide of the Jews and Gypsies, a resolve that, in present times, was emulated in the doggedness of Ronald Reagan *vis-à-vis* the destruction of the *Evil Empire*, though conceived a full half century previously. Fascism therefore represented the full European capitalist response to the rise of socialism and working-class politics. Today, of course, it is the United States, not Europe, that has taken on the mission of 'thinking ahead' on such issues as the global containment of anticapitalist forces. In fact, as early as 1920, the United States, under the leadership of Woodrow Wilson, had attempted to establish the League of Nations as a sort of a capitalist Holy Alliance under imperialist leadership, but the executive branch was then to be stymied by a recalcitrant Congress. However, 1945 enabled this forward-thinking resolve to finally prevail, and the United Nations rose, like a phoenix, out of the ashes of the League of Nations, even as the United States left its agrarian isolationists, a hangover from its frontier past, forever behind.

At any rate, while the political changes of this period were dramatic, including the irresistible gathering of forces of self-government on the part of the colonial world (Egypt, India, Iraq, Philippines, China, etc.), the center stage in this period was really occupied by the growing instability in the capitalist world, culminating in the so-called 'Great Depression' of the thirties. Britain and the United States, as vanguard capitalist entities, suffered the full fury of the economic slippage, something that made the young English conservative, John Maynard Keynes, look to the Soviet Union to see for himself how the other side was managing things. Very much like Hitler, Keynes was alive to the clash between world systems, and took the unemployment of his time more seriously than his fellow conservatives on either side of the Atlantic. Assuming, correctly, that ideology was good nutrition during prosperity though bad medicine during hard times, he called for the abandonment of the well consecrated myths of the virtues of the free market in favor of decisive state action to step in wherever (and whenever) the private sector showed signs of weakness. Of course, much later, Reaganites and Thatcherites would go one step better and reclaim the old ideology, even while contradicting it in carefully devised class policies of selected intervention. In this way, they could, in effect, have their cake and eat it too in a hoary ploy of class rule—of saying one thing, and doing quite another.

Of course, in practical terms it was preparations for war that pulled capitalism out of its self-imposed Slough of Despond, rather than any attention to Keynesian prescriptions. If anything, both Adolph and Joseph, in their own ways, had shown the world the benefits of decisive state action in the field of employment and resource mobilization, and the impact of this on the imagination of the rulers no spate of journal articles could ever have achieved. No doubt, Roosevelt himself, in adopting the New Deal, was more influenced, in the first instance, by urgent domestic political necessities (given almost a quarter of the workforce rendered unemployed) and, secondarily, by the practical example afforded by Germany and Russia, than by the effete political encouragement offered by Keynes (whom he did not particularly care for).

As Europeans prepared to set new standards for barbarism and mass destruction, the rest of the colonized peoples, under its tyrant heel, found the space and time to push through their own national/social agendas, sometimes led by their bourgeoisies and sometimes led by populist alliances. These struggles, temporarily unchecked by imperialism, were to lead to major events such as the independence of India, and the Chinese Revolution, amongst a host of similar phenomena in the colonized world (the Arabs rose in revolt in Egypt, in 1919; in 1930, Brazil posted a revolution; in 1935, the Philippines achieved self-government, and so on). In Latin America, this was a time for domestic (capitalist) economic growth catering to local markets, and a widening and deepening of local capital, as opposed to their traditional 'comprador' orientations. Indeed, it is during this period that the most important early phase of autonomous industrialization occurred in Brazil, Mexico, Chile, and Argentina, owing to the relaxation of trade and investment ties to metropolitan capital. Africa, too, rose out of its colonial slumbers, as major intellectual and social movements such as *Pan Africanism* (whose first Congress was held in Manchester, in 1945), gathered momentum, in east, west, and South Africa (where the African National Congress had already been in existence since 1912), foreshadowing the long struggle to formally decolonize the tragic continent through which the Europeans had run through much like the four horsemen of the Apocalypse.

In the conventional wisdom of radical political economy, it is common to see the end of this epoch as inaugurating the era of the birth of *Fordism*,[17] or consumption-led growth (involving mass production made possible by Taylorist managerial tools, as much as production techniques), which is seen as coming to an end only in the present, post-Reagan era. Aside from Henry Ford's modest contribution to the practice of this idea, *wage-led* growth was the order of the day for several reasons. For one thing, all Keynesian economics was premised upon that idea (the importance of domestic effective demand), being, as it was, the intended antidote for the depression; for another, the fierce inter-imperial struggles made extraverted, *investment-led*, growth far more risky; and, finally, rearguard working-class struggles (unionization, etc.) actually made any other option simply unworkable. 'Fordism,' therefore, was much less a 'choice,' and, rather, more a creature of circumstances; this was so in the same sense in which the mass production of cars was dictated by the available economies of scale (i.e., Ford had no option but to take that route, if amassing profits was the goal). So mass consumption results because it pays to mass produce in capitalist economics (it is not as if Henry Ford was taking a dangerously risky gamble by cutting unit costs). Indeed, even in today's so-called *post-Fordist* era, capitalism still rests upon the primary base of mass consumption, despite the current supply-side attack on wages and job security. It couldn't be otherwise; thus, in effect, we still remain within the 'Fordist' problematic. Stated differently, capital employed a mass production/consumption strategy not because of a passionate commitment to raising standards of consumption for the masses, but because it expected, thereby, to raise profitability. The United States led the way in this regard simply because it had the largest, uniform, *domestic* market in the capitalist world within which such strategies could be readily (i.e., profitably) implemented; indeed, it is this internal scale economy advantage that the United States has always enjoyed over all other comers in the capitalist game.

At any rate, the interwar period saw a tremendous extension of the concentration of capital, monopoly, and combinations, that Lenin had viewed with such concern. In the premier capitalist economy, the United States, price rigidities (except in the more competitive sphere of agriculture, where prices fell catastrophically), excess capacity, and chronic underinvestment, followed predictable patterns contingent upon the oligopolization of the economy—even as the unproductive burdens of advertising, sales, and marketing gimmickry, grew proportionately. Despite these regressive phenomena, productivity actually grew, even as scales of output were leveled to keep profit rates acceptably high; and, in the United States at least, the real wage did not significantly decline (partly accounted for by the cheap cost of food), for those fortunate enough to be employed.

These phenomena apart, the signal keys to this period were, firstly, the fact that the rates of growth and investment, in the Anglo-American world, were now permanently tied to the direction of government policy, capital looking to the state to underwrite its investment plans in the form of irrevocable guarantees. *One might thus say that, long before the idea of a minimum wage became acceptable, capitalists had successfully pushed for a minimum rate of profit to be afforded by state policy.* The road leading to the normalization of routine state bailouts of failed corporate efforts, but at taxpayer expense, had been effectively constructed. Secondly, at least in the Anglo-American sphere of influence, the capitalist class internalized a fearful pessimism about the future that was to profoundly color their business and attendant political practices for ever after. The rationale for this was, of course, plain to see: within decades of each other, the political unity of capitalism had been rudely disrupted by the sudden severance of Bolshevik

Russia, while its economic base was nearly crippled by the Great Depression. These twin blows were to give to the normal caution of entrepreneurs an abnormal fear (most pronounced in the United States) of a dark and dangerous world. In this regard, without such considerations, it is impossible to understand the outright paranoia displayed by the United States *vis-à-vis* the remotest possible 'threat' to its interests: who else, one might ask, would listen so assiduously to toilets flushing in Kiev for so long?

The other implication of these developments was also correctly foreseen by Lenin: that capitalism would 'henceforth' be a profoundly conservative political force (of course this was true even during the earlier era of colonialism, with little, if any 'progress' visited upon the colonies), allied with the most retrograde reactionaries, its 'heroic' epoch having ended once it had achieved political and economic hegemony within its social frontiers. That is to say, considerations of order now reigned paramount over other issues. And, of course, the cold war machinations of imperialism bear out this thesis to the letter; and, anomalous as this must sound to generations of Euro-Marxists proclaiming the 'progressive' nature of capital,[18] it is clear that, throughout this period, imperialism was itself an obstacle to successful (national) capitalist development in the periphery. Indeed, the zones where capitalism was to thrive with western financial blessing (Taiwan, Singapore, Hong Kong, etc.) were just so on account of fortuitous location alone— because these countries were seen as major offsets to communist influence in the area. And one has only to see the composition of the so-called non-aligned countries to understand the extent to which imperialism disdainfully alienated its eagerly emulous, fellow-capitalist, rulers in the third world.

The sheer stupidity of Hitler, in invading the USSR (when he actually did), and the equal blindness of Japan in attacking Pearl Harbor, ensured that the ambitions of the latecomers to the capitalist table would now, albeit temporarily, be put to rest. Indeed, it is an irony of history that military defeat and wholesale destruction would, in each case of these two latecomers, become the basis for a sustained accumulation process that would, at a later date, ensure a more successful economic challenge to the traditional structures of imperialism. However, the intraimperial struggles following upon the heels of a capitalist depression did ensure that the iron grips on the colonized nations would henceforth, perforce, be relaxed. In this manner, the Second Great Conflagration made way for the decolonization struggles to follow, including the independence of India and China, with the steadfast support of the USSR for national liberation virtually assuring the irreversibility of that process. As such, the seeds of the modernist world order, and the *agendas* of the main contenders, were securely planted in the period under question.

The three ascendant, modernist, agendas may now be clarified, if only in outline. Firstly, the (ultimately successful) international capitalist agenda, resolved to sew up its breeches and regain its pre-First War hegemony; secondly, the newly empowered socialist assembly of nations pledged to resist that agenda, while building their own autarchic domains, to the best of their meager capacities; and, finally, the excolonial world caught up in a furious—if often futile—resolve to throw the European out and secure its own ecopolitical space within (and, less often, *without*) international capitalism. Post war (*macro*) history is simply a playing out of these separate, but related agendas, their particular denouement, and consummation—*not amongst themselves, but set against the rising tide of some very novel, though still largely incipient, forms of antimaterialist revolt*—being the subject matter of this book.

NOTES

1. For an avowedly partisan account of this process, see Andre Gunder Frank (1978).
2. A vast literature exists on this subject; I, personally, like Jairus Banaji's rendering in, "For a Theory of Colonial Modes of Production," in Rajani Kanth (1994), pp. 177–188. Marx and Engels's own ideas are compiled in K. Marx and F. Engels (1972).
3. Data are drawn from Ben Crow *et al.* (1983).
4. Lest this be thought of as the legacy only of the bad old days of colonialism, see Pierre Jalee (1968) for ongoing depredations throughout the period of the 'long boom' after World War II.
5. For contemporary continuations of colonial style plantation cultures, see Rene Loewenson (1992).
6. See Ramakrishna Mukherjee (1974) for a careful account of the subcontinental practices of the old (British) East India Company.
7. For an excellent rendering of these processes, see J. M. Blaut (1993).
8. C. G. Seligman (1929).
9. See Basil Davidson (1987); also, the classic work of Martin Bernal (1987). For a more general treatment of this notion of the 'peoples without history,' see E. R. Wolf (1982).
10. See Rajani Kanth (1986) for explanatory detail.
11. The decline of European and the rise of American imperialism is documented, albeit in oddball fashion, on a putatively 'geometric' scale in Giovanni Arrighi (1983).
12. V. I. Lenin (1939).
13. J. A. Hobson (1902).
14. R. Hilferding (1970).
15. Nicolai Bukharin (1972).
16. Maurice Dobb (1963) provides a useful, if traditional, Marxist account of this period; see also Paul Sweezy (1942).
17. By far, the fullest account of 'Fordism' is to be found in Alain Lipietz (1987).
18. On the proclivities of what I have termed 'EuroMarxism,' see Rajani Kanth (1992), pp. 199–210.

2

THE EMERGENT IMPERIUM: OF CONFLICTING CORPORATISMS

If classic Eurocolonialism represented the early modernist invasions of all nonmodernist domains, domestically and abroad, the early twentieth century was to find modernism battling with its own progeny (both legitimate and illegitimate), with the ensuing test of wills involving two quite distinct moments. In the one struggle, the socialist variant of the modernist impulse was to be a resolute, near-implacable foe; in the other, resurgent, and insurgent, modernists in the colonial world were to raise the modernist flag in defiance of European mastery, asking for their fair share of the widely propagated paradigm. Of course, the ensuing tussles would approximate, and far overtake, the rabid fury of the Crusades (to say nothing of its firepower), the combatants thinking nothing of nearly bringing the planet to the brink of a fiery, cataclysmic extinction. At any rate, at unspeakably unsurpassable cost, this century has now yielded to the modernists almost its very soul, as the (capitalist) European now strides the planet with giant, seven-league, boots engulfing any, and all, alternate social formations that stand in his way. Modern imperialism, then, is just the story of capitalism unbound; of modernism rampantly run riot; of greed run, calamitously amok.

THE IMPERIAL AGENDA

Failure to understand capitalism as incorporating, at any given juncture, an *Agenda*, set by entirely fallible human constituents, aside from the variegated, derivative, structural impulses flowing from its given ensemble of social relations (mode of production, social formation, etc.), has resulted in some outrageously reductionist analyses in the radical-Marxian camp, reflecting in all inanity the similarly 'economistic' studies on the part of liberal-conservative, mainstream, writers. In this mode of scientific 'objectivism,' all is derived from the economic logic of capitalist growth itself, whether from the dubious Kondratief type of crypto-mysticism, implying long waves of half a century, or the even more schematic markers provided by emphasis on so-called 'industrial/technical' revolutions at the upper end, and to wholly conjunctural events such as oil price increases at the lower end, of the intellectual scale. In such renderings, the phenomena of capitalism are seen as evolving *sui generis*, raising images of a blind sow that litters frequently, if unexpectedly, conceiving offspring that can be mutant in shape and form. Interestingly enough, mechanistic, deterministic, and positivist, as such constricted visions tend to be, they yet manage to provide post factum 'explanations' that often are no more absurd than neoclassical fantasies about capitalist growth, evolution, and change.

On the other hand, one might make a parallel mistake of seeing capitalism in purely voluntaristic terms of going anywhere, anyplace, anytime, as it wishes, without any moorings whatsoever. Some brands of spontaneity in Marxism, as in Harry Cleaver's work,[1] have indeed argued as though the unmediated 'class struggle' produces all events of significance (with the working class as their active, efficient cause). Again, skewed as this is, there is bound to be some set of events and processes that such an approach might, upon occasion, illustrate (reality being usually quite generous to interpreters). Of course, this 'workerist' posturing is purely *reactive*: that is, it is defined in opposition to traditional reductionist objectivism that subsumes workers into a homogenized 'force of history.' However, by locating subjectivism solely within the working class (forgetting, amazingly, the other *eminence grise* that looms ever ominously over the working class), this view undermines itself quite thoroughly.

How then, does an agenda perspective, as proffered here, override such difficulties? In this view, in every epoch of capital, one can generally identify a ruling vision of a capitalist solution to capitalist problems, either potentially or actually (at the level of expectations). At a lower level of abstraction, the governing class—to govern—has (indeed, *must* have) an agenda, but one that is both realized and thwarted, contextually (that is, in *practice*), by both expected and unexpected economic, social, and political circumstances. *The test of the efficacy of a governing agenda is the extent to which it can both initiate and respond to such phenomena so as to govern them, at the margin, so to speak, rather than be governed by them.* As such, efficacy is always, and only, a matter of degree. The formulation of such an agenda is up to the intellectual vanguard within the politically governing class, whether individualist or corporatist in its composition. In every conjucture of capitalism, in the European history we know of, there has been such an agenda;

and, in some periods, political economists themselves have provided the critical guidance to policy. In the period of capitalist ascendancy, in the early nineteenth century, for instance. David Ricardo provided such vision to manufacturers in England; in the period of capitalist decline in the first third of our own century, J. M Keynes, similarly, offered a program of capitalist salvation. Since Keynes, however, in the era of assured U.S. domination, the new governors have found it possible to dispense with the intellectual counsel(s) of economists (except as *ex post facto* validations) almost altogether, relying on their own, highly pragmatic, business 'horse-sense,' so to speak. At any rate, to understand this agenda is to know how to work both within and without the system. Nominally speaking, the short-run agendas in capitalist societies are set by the political parties in office, but the long-run agenda is by no means a nominal affair: *it refers to the (changing) policy requirements given by the innate logic of the capitalist mode, as understood by its corporate rulers.*[2]

Broadly speaking, the Agenda defines the expectations of the system's governors, their choice of techniques, and their degrees of freedom in their willingness to go the distance in enforcing their directives. At least in modern capitalist regimes, particularly the United States, such ruling agendas are astonishingly open and accessible, subject to debate and discussion (as referred to, U.S. capitalist absolutism has always lacked even a pretence of sublimation; unnecessary subtlety, after all, has never been a distinguishing American trait); all the more wonder when political economists ignore such revealing mandates in their economistic analyses, where only the impersonal forces of production, fetishized in the manner of mainstream 'economics,' are the preferred foci of analyses. The error of this *technicist* perspective is plain to see: it is the qualitative relations of production that provoke specific *policy stances*, which in turn work both as brake and accelerator with respect to these forces, a knowledge of which helps both in understanding the logic of a specific régime of accumulation and in developing strategies to withstand it. Stated simply, the Agenda (always on *open* system of general objectives, rather than a closed one of narrow aims) is set by the masters of the governing relations of production, in the full flower of both their wisdom and their ignorance, and on the tightrope of the class (and any other, relevant, political) balance.

In the postwar first world, the Imperial Agenda (in various degrees of coherence), for the years to come, was primarily set by Anglo-American planners in the context of Bretton Woods; *imperialism, as defined here, referring simply to the sum total of the strategies employed by capital(s) in its quest for absolute control of all aspects of production, realization, and accumulation.* As such, at least as far as capitalist expectations go, it is by no means an entirely novel epoch—the novelty being only in the institutional

The Emergent Imperium

environment designed by capital after World War II. An examination of this set of expectations, the critical vortex from which 'appropriate' rules and rotes are sprung, helps uncover the rationale undergirding the evolution of what might be termed the NATO phase of capitalist imperialism.[3]

The Agenda perspective restores the critical parameters of *intentionality* and activism to the analysis of capitalism, too often seen as passively racked only by impersonal forces such as Kondratief cycles, technological revolutions, and so on. It speaks also to the obvious fact that the monster is not just a great, big, lumbering body that moves, *sui generis*, buffeted by ineffable 'laws of motion,' but is possessed of a head as well that often gives directions, takes a turn, and charts a path. It thereby points to the importance of specific *policy initiatives*, and choices, made by a governing class, human agents that can often decisively turn the tide of economic, and other, 'substructural' forces. For instance, a given capitalist nation may or may not enter a particular war, or may enter it sooner or later, or may ally with one or other nation, and so on, all these choices making a fundamental impact on its own long-run economic fortunes (thereby opening up the possibility, as often as not, of a *political* determination of economic variables). Indeed, by way of example, one can think of the decisions made by Hitler & Co., not the wisest from the point of view of their own survival, which basically helped the Allies destroy the Third Reich quite decisively. Stated succinctly, knowledge of Hitler's agenda is vital to understand the real trajectory of Nazi Germany. No economic determinism, working blindly and impersonally through the Third Reich, ensured its obliteration. To study capitalism concretely, i.e., *historically*, is to study capitalist policy in all its scope and variation, aside from the modalities of the operative socioeconomc exigency. Any given, particularist, capitalist social formation must be studied *politically*, as well; impersonal generalities, of the economic kind (usually espoused in orthodox Marxian analyses), only work at the level of the whole, as the *outcome* of all the various tussles between agendas. *Politics is as ontologically real, and respectable, as economics, being more than just a mediated form of the latter*. Finally, agendas are not just chimerical ephemera generated by overworked sociological imaginations: they are precisely known to us through the events and outcomes they generate. As such, they are—and can be—continuously tested in, through, and against, reality.

Marxists have often made the distinction, in levels of politicization, between a 'class-in-itself' (objectively constituted, but subjectively fragmented) and a 'class-for-itself' (armed with subjective self-awareness). The analogy is singularly adaptive to postwar capitalism: arguably, imperialism, after World War II, was subjectively more aware of itself, as an organic entity, with special needs, than at any other time in the history of capitalism. This awareness, incipient since the Russian Revolution, had been (as in the case of class consciousness) shaped in, by, and through, *struggle*; small wonder that imperialism launched the cold war so soon after the conclusion of hostilities at the end of World War II. It was ready, in 1945, to recapture, recover, and reclaim the world, that it had done so much, more than any other mode of production, to forcibly link together in the form of dependent market ties. It is for this reason that it is meaningful to speak of an Imperial Agenda, in the sense of a concerted, considered plan, after World War II than, say, in the nineteenth century where—lacking powerful enemies—it was content to lurch on, willy-nilly, under various, disparate, 'national' auspices.

Of course, this articulate self-consciousness did not commence with World War II; in that respect, the Russian Revolution and the depression were the great educational shocks to the complacency of the capitalist *ancièn régime*. It was Keynes, in this regard, who acted as the Lenin, so to speak, of the bourgeoisie, drawing from those two bitter lessons important deductions as to the roles and responsibilities of the enlightened bourgeois in the dangerous new world of capitalist uncertainties and socialist advancement. More than others in his time, Keynes tried to arouse capitalist policy makers from their dogmatic slumbers, to draw up a plan to salvage capitalism, and keep its enemies (economic and political) in check. And if Keynes was the supreme twentieth-century capitalist planner of the period between the wars, he was also the driving force that tried, in and through Bretton Woods, to organize the framework for an integrated, planned, world economy, in perpetuity, under imperial tutelage. While his specific proposals did not carry at Bretton Woods, his message did, as the United States moved quickly, seizing advantage, to craft a world order under its own secure suzerainty. In that sense, Bretton Woods, indubitably, was the mother of all capitalist agendas.

BRETTON WOODS

Bretton Woods, although the brainchild of *Pax Britannica*, *à la* Keynes, was ultimately to be controlled and underwritten by the less celebrated, but more willful, agents of *Pax Americana*. While no different from traditional capitalist agendas, in *form* (i.e., to control as much of social space as possible), it was radically different in *content*. For the first time, national capitalist planning was to be superceded by *international* capitalist planning. Mostly, this was due to the fact that global reach was consistent with the newly emergent national agenda of the United States, stripped now of any isolationist pretences. In part, this was the obvious stratagem given the destruction of almost all the major non-U.S. capitalist economies (and hence their governing agendas). Partly, also, it was owing—in remembrance of the 'mistakes' of World War I—to a canny, liberal resolve (which Keynes did much to foster) to substitute reconstruction for reparations. Lastly, it was the institutional response to the newly formalized communist 'threat.'

All these complex motivations aside, the agenda itself was remarkably clear and open. The United States declared itself prepared to support the reconstruction efforts of the capitalist world—so long as stipulated monetary and trade rules and regulations were respected, within her overall leadership and suzerainty. This reconstruction, in other words, was to be within the ambit of an *integration* of the metropolitan capitalist world, first economically, then politically, and ultimately, militarily (within pacts, subpacts, and so on), all within the accommodation of the premier imperial power (as such, NATO was the fit complement to the institutional offerings of Bretton Woods). The high ambition of this agenda was quite breathtaking: the first world was being freshly cemented, brick by brick, in the context of a *new imperialism*. *Pax Americana* differed from *Pax Britannica* in the sense that Britain had always planned only in its own immediate corporate interest; however, the United States was now planning for the capitalist world in its entirety,[4] albeit in its own, enlightened, long-run interest (never a free trade advocate, the United States was always a 'free enterprise' power, the difference in emphasis being quite significant). This recalls, forcefully, the old Kautskian idea of *Ultra-imperialism* that invited such ridicule from Lenin and others in the early, still parochial years of this century. *Pax Americana* actually afforded a close approximation, but for purely contingent-conjunctural reasons, of such an eventuality. Imagine the World Bank, the UN, General Agreement on Tariffs and Trade (GATT), the International Monetary Fund (IMF), the Organization for Economic Cooperation and Development (OECD), and NATO (not to mention U.S. organized subspecies like the Organization of American States (OAS), the Alliance for Progress, and the erstwhile Southeast Asian Treaty Organization (SEATO)), working more or less in tandem, and you have the closest thing to an imperial world government the world has ever seen. In point of fact, buttressed by a host of other 'multilateral' institutions too numerous to name, such a loose coordination is, today, indeed, the order of the day; perhaps even more so, given the collapse of the socialist bloc.

In this regard, no account is complete that does not mention the special role that the IMF and the World Bank[5] have played (despite their frequent, but friendly, rivalry as fellow bureaucracies, sometimes along the lines of the old good cop/bad cop routine) in tightening the imperialist noose around the third world.[6] At Bretton Woods, the U.S.-inspired White plan (named after the leader of the U.S. delegation) prevailed over Keynes (who was seeking a system based on a relative *equipoise* between debtor and creditor capitalist entities, as opposed to the unilateral *dictatorship* of the creditors that the United States wanted) on almost all scores: (a) in imposing a quota system in the IMF, breaching the one country/one vote principle as applied in the United Nations; (b) in tying access to World Bank aid solely through membership in the IMF, and its disciplinary constraints; (c) in shifting the burden of adjustment on to balance of payment deficit countries alone; and (d) in establishing IMF-World Bank headquarters in Washington, rather than in New York as with the other UN agencies, in keeping with the desire for close U.S. administrative overview of these critical functions in international finance.

The so-called 'conditionality' imposed by the 'monetarist' IMF has invariably taken the form of 'opening up' third-world economies to first-world penetration by insisting upon one or all of the following policy imperatives: the elimination of controls over exports and imports, free exchange rates, devaluation of currencies, wage-price controls, balanced budgets, lifting of welfare subsidies, and so on. The 'structuralist' World Bank, for its part, has buttressed this effort by serving as a blatant conduit for the movement of private capital to the third world, ensuring, in its tout-like role on behalf of western capital, the creation of optimal conditions for a favorable private investment climate. Under the mantle of the philosophy of monetary and fiscal 'soundness,' these two institutions served, in effect, as proxies for the newly defunct colonial administrations, filling that void admirably. Country after country in the third world (and also Eastern Europe at the present time), held to ransom by these twin despotisms throughout the postwar period, was to find in these entities a far more powerful, and implacable, marauder than the departing and defeated colonial powers.

Given that the post-World War II phase of imperialism was a managed affair from the start, it is easy to see the extent to which *étatisme* was its dominant reality even as laissez-faire (or 'free enterprise,' in U.S. parlance) was its dominant ideology. Post-World War II imperialism was *militaristic* from the start, with the United States seeking to consolidate, and reinforce, its military might as secured during the build up of World War II. United States' (and NATO) militarism was the submerged part of the Bretton Woods iceberg, but one that could, and did, surface, whenever, and wherever, required. As the chief *gendarme* of the capitalist world, the United States managed to make the military sector the lead sector of the economy—succeeding, between 1947 and 1971, the key period of postwar expansion, in squandering a thumping 1.7 trillion dollars (enough to buy back the combined Gross National Products (GNPs) of 1969 and 1971) in that bottomless pit. In the same period, military allocations averaged at about 13.1 percent of the GNP, with military budgets accounting for almost 23 percent of all employment in the United States, directly or indirectly. Of course, this was a comedown in relation to the fact that, between 1939 and 1944, military spending had guzzled down some 50 percent of the gross output of the capitalist world, even as profit rates soared—as if, in that nightmare of near-total destruction, capital had discovered the heady elixir of life. Of course, the wealth of funds gobbled up by the military in the Reagan years, in conjunction with the Strategic Defense Initiative (SDI) effort, puts to shame all of the previous figures, making the master architect of this barbaric build up, Ronald Reagan, easily, the greatest systematic vandal in history.

Naturally, after the war, major corporations sought and found, in this sector, a state-supplied cornucopia (profit rates usually averaging over 20 percent) almost beyond the normal expectations of unbridled greed (after all, traditional cost-benefit analyses in this area could only be cynical, meaningless, or both). As Luxemburg had noted, in all prescience, a full half a century earlier, militarism is the one sector whose expansion, unlike all other sectors, is 'primarily determined by capital itself.'[7] The U.S. posture did differ, fundamentally, from all other capitalist countries for being the most *desublimated*; as the one first world entity with no precapitalist history—the ultimate source of anticapitalist values—of its own, it could pursue the capitalist agenda, both domestically and internationally, with no qualms, reservations, or hesitations, as characterize regimes whose politics involve some measure of accommodation to anticapitalist movements, interests, and forces. The United States boasted of *absolute capitalism* from the start of its short history, (and so could move, as Oscar Wilde joked, from barbarism to decadence, bypassing the stage of civilization unimpededly): which is why it could be the first and only state in history to cold-bloodedly drop a nuclear device on fellow humankind without so much as a second thought (the fact that Japan and Germany might have done the very same thing, had the means existed in time, does not by even a whit alter the fundamental infamy of that horrific act).

While militarism was the dominant form, in terms of the volume of state expenditures ('military Keynesianism,' in radical parlance), this phase also involved many important realms of direct state activity, some bearing continuity to the past, some more novel in scope, but all defining a state that served both as a hector and protector of *capitalist* interests to an extent virtually unknown in the nineteenth century (wherein the noncapitalist classes had a much stronger veto power). The imperial state is continually engaged—in a régime of permanent crisis, so to speak—in 'interventions' in all of the inescapable mini-crises associated with routine capitalist phenomena: overcapitalization, excess liquidity, cantering inflations, secular stagnation, shrinking markets, sagging profits, intermonopolist and intraimperial competition, etc., all manifestations of the inherent anarchy of production, chronic sectoral imbalances, and uneven development characteristic of the reign of production for profit. So important is this domain that politics, in a case like the United States, is less driven by any traditional notion of class struggle than it is the budgetary, pork barrel, struggle between differentially endowed corporate interests ('labor' being only one such, weak, corporate entity in the process) in a situation of *permanent fiscal crisis* (the latter understood as a political crisis of maintaining the legitimacy of any given budget in the face of competing demands of major constituencies of the corporate order). It is in this near-totalitarian extension of the mandate of the state that some of the novelty of post-World War II imperialism resides.

INTRA-IMPERIAL CONFLICTS: THE SUB-AGENDAS

However, even hegemonic Agendas have their weak links, their lesions, and their tensions. These arise primarily from ancillary sub-Agendas that operate contiguously, but sometimes contradictorily, to the principal agenda. Secondarily, these arise from what might be called the *hegemonic overreach* inherent in the postures of a hegemonic leader—to wish to be, concurrently, the world leader in production, trade, finance, and military deterrence. The sub-agendas in question refer to the whole slew of microconstellations of ecopolitical interests that lay dormant or submerged within the world order of first world imperialism as constituted at Bretton Woods, and beyond. These poles exist at various levels, national and supranational, across all possible fissure points of the system, subsisting latently until specific exigencies provoke their mutually antinomical eruption. Such poles of contest/division include NATO European Community (EC) Europe versus the United States;[8] the United States versus Japan; rivalry between Germany, France, and the United Kingdom; the United States *vis-à-vis* Germany, and so on. Depending upon level, and scale, of measurement used, one comes up with varied such paired antagonisms (at both the international, and extranational, moments). Looking at the matter purely economically, the largest such undeclared antagonism operating within the system is probably defined by the trilateral rivalry (although with Asian capitals, including China, on the rise, a *quadrilateral* economic tussle is in the cards in the immediate present) between the United States, Germany (a proxy for Europe, which is largely its neocolony), and Japan, within whose borders and/or zones of influence most of capitalist production, trade, and finance continue to take place.

The apparent breakdown of (one set of) Bretton Woods arrangements in the early seventies is usually treated as a watershed transformation in capitalist international economic relations, but its reality is not something particularly awe inspiring. Briefly, the so-called demise of the (old) system, usually set between 15 August 1971—when the United States suspended convertibility of the dollar for gold and other reserve assets—and 19 March 1973 (when the major imperial countries renounced their commitment to maintain the quotation of their currencies within the 2.25 percent band *vis-à-vis* the dollar, as set at Bretton Woods),[9] involved primarily a shake-up of the lethargy of the hegemonic leader of the band, the United States, now faced with having to yield in some of the domains of hegemony already identified (notably in trade and finance). The game of catch-up played successfully by Germany and Japan only restored, in a sense, prewar parities between the major imperial powers in terms of their economic power. In consequence, United States hegemony was by no means annulled, only abrogated, and that only in certain spheres. By itself, this was hardly a calamity except for the American ego; it is important to remember that the imperial agenda was not transformed thereby—rather, one game plan was replaced by another, and a (more) closed system by a more open one. Of course this involved both a power shift and a power loss, but only in the named domains, no major calamity within a capitalist system based on a zero-sum logic of redistribution (i.e., this gives no warrant for a socialist celebration of the 'failure' of capitalism). Also, floating exchange rates, it must by now be clear, turned out to be neither more nor less effective in abating the instability of capitalism than fixed exchange rates, the latter having been originally designed to prevent a trade-war type of a downward spiral of competitive devaluations. The system has learned to accommodate these changes; so there was always plenty of life, so to speak, in the old horse, even after the weakening of the old ground rules of Bretton Woods. By tolerating, in all complacency, levels of unemployment unheard of in the Bretton Woods period of in-step competition with the Eastern bloc, capitalism assured for the propertied classes, and their hangers-on, even higher levels of prosperity than before. In effect, the faltering edifice steadied itself, in expectable fashion, by shifting all bills (of reconstitution) on to the workers, the unemployed (unemployment in the OECD countries, in 1982, approximated about 30 million, and is averaging a steady 35 million in the nineties, which is the equivalent of the entire labor force of an average European capitalist economy), welfare recipients, the poor, and so on.

Indeed, what the United States lost, Germany (Europe) and Japan (in spite of a discriminatory surtax of 10 percent slapped on imports from Japan by Nixon) gained, much to their advantage, namely in their share of world trade (in 1987, the U.S. trade deficit was a spectacular $160 billion, while Japan's trade *surplus* stood at $96 billion, with Germany's at $65 billion). Low inflation, and low unemployment, enabled them to sustain higher rates of growth, and productivity increases, within a more or less accepted social contract (by 1980, Japanese productivity had overtaken that of the United States, with U.S. deficits starting to average above $100 billion annually). In the United States, an unaccustomed belt tightening induced a major rightward shift in ideology exemplified in Reagan's transformation of U.S. politics toward a repudiation of all social contracts, and in the spectacular military build up (seeking to build on the best in the face of relative failure on other economic fronts) that underpinned this resolve. The long-term advantages of world leadership (including, but not restricted to, *seigneurage*) being mitigated, the United States would now be forced to live more within its domestic budget constraints (as in the case of Europe) than was its wont from the fifties on, where the world largely yielded it real resources in exchange for its nominal debt, and its various stocks of capital and consumer goods. What this has meant in practice is that the United States finds more political discontent within its borders than it traditionally assumed existed outside of them, a crisis of sluggish (but not catastrophic) growth that often, topically, threatens to undermine the confidence of U.S. administrations. Stated simply, the U.S. economy needs to run just to stand still on a track in which there are now many able and athletic joggers. Domestic strife within the U.S. polity (more Americans today are dissatisfied with the way things are than at any other recorded period of recent U.S. history) is not a healthy sign in a world leader; hegemony can hardly be exercised overseas if it falters within one's own borders. It is interesting to recall that some such domestic opposition was also associated with the final phase of Britain's decline as a hegemonic leader in the twenties and thirties. The obvious mainstream alternatives to the *status quo* remain the traditional ones: of social democracy, adjusted for lower expectations of growth, in favor of redistribution (as in erstwhile Labor-led Britain), or of military expansion, jingoism, and a rightward skew to society and polity. Given the U.S. political system, and its penchant for taking the middle line in any showdown between extremes, the prevailing choice might well be a grotesque combination of both options, in various degrees, depending on which party controls Capitol Hill.

At any rate, the 'crisis' of capitalism that is supposed to have undermined the order of Bretton Woods, seventies onwards, was always something of an exaggeration.[10] The system survived, indeed even prospered, in uniquely capitalist terms (i.e., regardless of unemployment, quality of life, human rights, and so on), today more hegemonic in the world than ever before. Despite some economic weaknesses, notably in trade and finance, and the new unflattering status as a prime debtor nation, the United States remains still the prime architect of the system, *primus inter pares* in some domains, undisputed master in others. International trade has expanded along with the creation, or consolidation, of new free trade zones, such as the EC, European Free Trade Association (EFTA), North American Free Trade Agreement (NAFTA), and so on. In effect, the suspension of dollar convertibility, and fixed exchange rates pegged to the dollar, have boded no great evils. Organization of Petroleum Exporting Countries (OPEC) price increases— the supposed *coup de grâce* to western economies—are now only a matter of archival interest; worker's revolts and job actions, supposedly the factor undermining U.S. productivity, have been radically tamed; and radical third-worldism survives on, but as exception rather than the rule. In short, all the traditional set of factors listed as explanations for the great western debacle (the collapse of so-called Fordism) are now merely also-rans. Imperialism survived them all, in its natural shrewdness, so to speak, intact, the reshuffling of power roles internal to it remaining the sole object of curiosity. No doubt the class struggle voluntarists amongst us will still see in this forced reshuffling a great victory for the active, insurgent, working class, but it would have to be a dwindling minority view within an even more rapidly shrinking minority perspective.

More importantly, it perhaps bears pointing out that the term 'crisis' is oftentimes a misnomer when applied to capitalist processes for its implicit suggestion of unresolvable problems. Capitalist crises are actually the crucial restructurative devices that, when visible, demonstrate not the existence of capitalist problems (which are always *inherent*), but rather the working out of their 'solutions,' albeit from the vantage point of capital. It is quite curious that deliberate strategies on the part of capital to recover its anticipated profits and keep workers on a tight leash—as with erstwhile *stagflation*—is viewed by economists, even radicals, as constituting the crisis itself. This major epistemic error arises from a conflation, in the economists' perspective, between growth, *per se*, and profitable growth. The former is the dream of the economist (since growth is seen tantamount to 'welfare'); the latter—*profitable growth*—is the obvious preoccupation of capital. Stated simply, there are conjunctures where slow growth, in output and employment, is perfectly consistent with high profit rates (indeed, this is the trend given by the oligopolistic orientation of industrial structures), so long as stagflation recovered nominal profit rates, aside from conferring the added bonus of generating an insecure reserve army of the unemployed, it would have more than achieved its objective. Viewed thus, stagflation was not itself the crisis (except, obviously, for the popular classes that stood to lose from its exactions), but the *physic* of capital to offset it. The point is simple: what is a crisis for capital may not be a calamity for the real producers, and vice versa. It's a pity that these home truths are often outside the province of the academic scribblers.

Further comment is necessary on this 'stagflation' (price rise in a context of high or rising unemployment levels) that increasingly became the norm in the seventies in the imperial world. Given the onset of a period of declining profits (between 1948 and 1980, the rate of profit fell by over 65 percent, with both pretax and posttax profits peaking in 1966) and sluggish investment, inflation simply represented the struggle on the part of capital to maintain nominal income (keeping the nominal rates of profit high), a strategy that favors the revenue needs of the state as well, bypassing the more unpopular means of a tax hike. As such, what might be termed 'markup-led growth' was not a new stratagem, in the epoch in question, but a standard tool of oligopoly from the Depression on. Indeed, in general, anticipated, or what may be termed, *induced inflation* is a procapital strategy that has never inspired capitalist diffidence (despite its often regressive impact on income distribution which can, sometimes, rebound in the form of realization problems). This maneuvering helps to economize on investment by running up household debt repayable in devalued money, on the other hand, such financing can boomerang when it pushes the price of capital goods to a self-limiting point (with nominal depreciation allowances being unable to cover new purchases), thus precipitating an investment crisis (the problem being, of course, that capital is both buyer and seller of capital goods). However, this limit is not wholly insuperable given the potential for manipulation of interest rates, availability of credit, and the price of wage goods, so as to ensure favorable investment conditions (as such, a falling wage does not always pose a realization crisis in the short run, because consumer credit can, and does, make up the difference). As opposed to induced inflation, unanticipated inflation is a problem for capital insofar as it magnifies the uncertainty of the investment function.

At any rate, the problem for capital is not so much inflation as *productivity* (since gains in the latter can offset any incidental ills in the former). Indeed, throughout the postwar period, U.S. productivity growth experienced no dramatic slowdown; on the other hand, real wages, which had grown by about 2 percent between 1948 and 1966, slumped to a zero growth rate between 1967–1980, with unemployment, that had averaged about 4 percent in the same period, climbing to roughly 10 percent by 1980. By 1982, production had indeed plunged by about 10 percent in the United States (and other imperialist countries), but this was due more to the sudden deployment of monetarist, high interest policies pursued by the Fed (in the United States) than any other endogenous mechanism of the times. This raised the value of the dollar, reduced the competitiveness of U.S. capital, led to widespread bankruptcies (and mergers) within the United States, raised production costs, and set off a recessionary spiral (raising the spectre of 1929), which eventually dragged the third world under as well, triggering the 'debt crisis'—the accumulation of the debt being a Ponzi scheme of capital all along—as Mexico suspended its payments in August of 1982. Of course, by then, the monetarist onslaught had been curbed, with monetarism in full retreat from the summer of 1982, the Fed loosening up internally, and the IMF loosening up internationally, to help bail out a stricken system (the third-world debt being viewed, typically, as a 'liquidity' problem rather than a solvency problem). From there to the stock market crash of 1987 was but a short sail on the shoals of capitalist confusion. Viewed thus, it becomes clear that errors in policy can be wholly independent sources of trouble and travail in a capitalist economy. It also underscores the point that abstract economic modeling is powerless, almost invariably, for its self-imposed inability to understand capitalist evolution within a policy agenda perhaps best defined as *pragmatism*, implying endless experimentation on the part of the governors of the system to find the ultimate anodyne (in economic policy, this has taken the many forms of Keynesianism, supply-side economics, monetarism, rational expectations *et al.*, depending on circumstances).

The Debt Crisis?

For a while, in the late seventies and eighties, it looked as if the so-called debt crisis[11] would push the dreary fact of stagflation in the Western economies right out of the news. Suddenly, the media had discovered, in all simulated dismay, the old Ponzi[12] scheme of foreign loans (in a repetitive sequence of rollovers, write-offs, and bailouts), in effect throughout the postwar period, of 'lending in perpetuity,' so to speak, to finance a permanent export surplus *vis-à-vis* the ex-colonial world. Repayment in the form of goods was of course unacceptable, for it would compete with domestic production; indeed, this had been a U.S. dilemma *vis-à-vis* the Marshall Plan in Europe, as well (something resolved by treating the funds as grants rather than loans). And, in context of the third world, as early as the fifties and the sixties, the strains in this process had already become clear, as country after country came to the so-called 'Paris Club' to secure reschedulements of its debt service obligations. As such, all parties in the lending business were aware of the virtual impossibility (indeed, the *undesirability*) of capital repayment, settling for regular interest payments instead (financed, of course, by fresh injections of capital).

With the Nixon discardment of the gold parity in 1971, and the devaluations of the dollar that followed, money supply exploded in the imperialist countries, with commodity prices booming; the Eurodollar explosion (coupled *later* with OPEC surpluses, after 1973) now flushed the reserves of excess liquidity, which had to find a vent. Bank lending, accordingly, rocketed in the era 1971–1973, and then again between 1976–1978, both waves actually preceding the two oil shocks of the seventies. At any rate, the salient points of the consequent debt crisis should be clear. Firstly, unlike the Marshall Plan, the transfer of funds to the third world took the form of loans (rather than grants), repayable at least in theory. On the supply side, the rationale couldn't be clearer: imperialism had a permanent capital surplus—a surplus not in relation to the needs of its citizens, naturally, but in relation to profitable investment channels domestically. Transferring it to the third world in the form of 'aid' helped finance metropolitan exports, but also helped keep a tight rein on the now-subject third world economy and polity, enhancing the latter's near-chronic dependency on imperialism. Stated simply, foreign lending to the third world, in its political aspect, was only debt-peonage in contemporary form, which is why the funds were disbursed as loans rather than grants. Outright usury was a fitting adjunct to the varied mechanisms of fiscal and financial fraud that helped European capital strip the peasant and artisan of their means of production in the process of proletarianization that attended the capitalist conquest of traditional modes of subsistence. The resulting damage, given the extortionist debt service demands, was to cripple the debtor countries as the debt squads led by the IMF and the World Bank capitalized on their economic distress, forcing through their neocolonial 'structural adjustment,' and 'stabilization,' policy packages, so as to better integrate these peripheral economies within the requirements of first world capital.

Quite typically, however, the debt crisis was originally systematically mishandled, in a series of measures (reminiscent of the Ponzi game), beginning with the IMF Plan (1982–1985), which formed a cartel of creditors and called for still more, indeed *forced*, private lending on the part of banks; then followed the (Treasury Secretary) Baker Plan of 1985, pressing for more private loans, but alongside an authorized expansion of a joint IMF-World Bank lending pool. It was only with the (new Treasury Secretary) Brady Plan, 1989, late in the game, that the idea of a *write-off*, i.e., debt reduction, entered into the policy making consensus (although, the competing plan of Senator Bradley had also called for a modest reduction of the interest rate, and an annual scale-down of the debt itself, by 3 percent), as the crisis accentuated, with banks asked to take some losses, alongside the paradoxical, and neutralizing, offer of a government bailout. The net result was too little, too late, from the point of view of third world debtor countries, whose ruling classes had to muddle through the crisis with their finances even more precarious than at the start of the roller-coaster ride, as they tried, through astute public finance, to pass the costs of debt service onto their captive, subject, populations. Today, the old debts trade at a discount, somewhere between 30 to 60 percent of par, with Ponzi style access to capital markets once again restored. So the debt crisis is over for now, even as the basis is laid for the next round of a critical breakdown of international finance. Alice in Wonderland—or, better still, *Malice in Blunderland*!—would have understood it all perfectly; insanity, after all, is capitalism as usual.[13]

SUMMING UP

To review the Imperial Agenda again. The objective of Bretton Woods was to construct a (modernist) world safe and sound for capitalist investment, trade and finance, within a framework of *integration* and coordination. The agenda was successful on all grounds except the last; the imperial order survives today on the basis of a *confederated autonomy* rather than close-knit integration, in a tripolar first world of Japan (as the prominent tip of the iceberg, an emergent, much wider Pacific Rim growth zone), the United States, and Germany (today partially submerged behind the veil of the EC), each with important spheres of autonomy in politics, foreign affairs, trade, and production. The dispersion of power is within a system—imperialism— rather than outside of it. This allows for numerous sub-agendas that work at exacerbating conflicts within imperialism both internal to the EC (pitting, say, Britain, France, and Germany against each other), and external to it, such as the competition of Japan and the United States. Taken at large, owing to extraneous factors (the disappearance of the Soviet 'threat'), these sub-agendas do pose a more serious challenge to imperial unity now than at any time since Bretton Woods. Possible German and Japanese rearmament to come can, and probably will, give to these economic rivalries a keen military edge that might well balance the present nuclear threat held over the vanquished of World War II by the nuclear monopoly of Britain, France and the United States. Despite the inevitability of such ongoing intraimperial tensions, it is clear that we now live in the era of *capitalist absolutism*, thereby vindicating the promise of the hoary plans for world mastery so carefully laid at Bretton Woods. In this regard, the United States has much reason to be pleased as it approaches the turn of a century that it has so effectively dominated.

Trilateralism or not, this has been (and still is, in some regards), from many vantage points, an *American* century with the United States imposing its indelibly decisive stamp (not always by force) on patterns of production, consumption, and living, generally on the rest of the world. Neither Europe nor Japan can overlook the extent of American subsidies that helped raise them to their feet; it was motivated generosity, but it was a form of generosity all the same. While the EU and Japan seem to be playing successful catch-up, in many respects, in a very fundamental sense the United States stands alone and apart from its growing range of competitors. It is still, in the late twentieth century, by far the purest bourgeois republic there is on the face of the earth, carrying its special brand of irrationally rational (i.e., capitalist) rationality to its extreme limits. In the commercialization of social life it has simply no peers, and probably never will for lacking, at its very inception, the historically given, structural forces of an anticapitalist nature (except, in potential, women and minorities; the working class, by and large, is just as thoroughly bourgeois as capitalists and managers). These distinctive traits easily show up in any comparison between the United States, Europe, and Japan; to this day the United States is the only *consumerist* form of capitalist society; both Europe and Japan, by historical inclination, being *productivist* in orientations.

While this is only a difference in emphasis, it does carry enormous social and economic implications. Japan, for instance, with all its productive might, is a society of largely discontented consumers (high costs of consumable goods combined with a relative stringency in the terms of consumer credit). In Germany the genius of its engineering and technological talent is invested primarily in making superior machinery. Regarding producer goods, (to take but a trivial example) anyone who has tried a German hamburger in a typical German eatery will understand why McDonald's would win hands down in any contest that does not address the real issue of good nutrition.

Productivism carries an entire paraphernalia of ancillary tendencies from elitism and protectionism to the sacrifice of consumer interest so as to protect producer interests, and so on. It is its rank, but ever so accessible, consumerism that makes the United States *attractive* (regardless of the quality of the aesthetic involved) to the poor and the underprivileged of the world who have experienced, invidiously, the abuse of privileged and discriminatory market practices in their own national contexts. Finally, the world hegemony of the U.S. entertainment industry and the vital ideological underpinning of its consumerism, speaks to its inherent, sparkling magnetism albeit within the modernist wasteland. Others may craft, manufacture, and engineer; in *marketing*, the United States remains unrivaled. Only the United States has matured a social system where life itself has come to be viewed as a species of vapid *entertainment*. However self-destructively, amorally, and cynically, the United States has shown the way, to a demoralized world, to alienation as a delirious state of 'fun.' Though both points of origin and destination are indissolubly marked by the ways of Mammon, one has only to fly between Heathrow and JFK to understand the difference between abasing gloom and meretricious glitter.

The recent consolidation of the EC[14] has only rendered open and obvious the latent Trilateralism of the world order since World War II; although nominally aimed against Japanese incursions, the EC represents the openly stated desire of European capital(s) to duplicate the uniformity and size of the United States, both economically and militarily. Ultimately, however, unlike the United States and Japan, Europe remains divided far more radically into tribes, ethnicities, and reactive-nationalisms (the horror of Bosnia being, in effect, only the thin end of the wedge in this regard), that history has rendered quite insuperable. As such, no amount of capitalist unity at the top can consolidate the deep rooted fissures within society and polity. The aggressive drive for a European Union underscores only Europe's inherent, divided, fragility, cultures being far more enduring entities than economies and polities. It is culture, not economics or politics that will ultimately frustrate the high ambitions of the European Union.

In the context of north-south relations, generally, some, like Andre Gunder Frank,[15] have argued that the basis of the dominance of metropolitan capital *vis-à-vis* the satellites has been shifting over the years: from commercial monopoly, in the early period, to a general industrial monopoly, in the later; then, still later, to a monopoly specifically in capital goods; and today, apparently, in cutting edge technologies. While this is trivially true as a descriptive process, it has no independent causal significance, since it begs the question as to how the metropolis is able to corner such processes, thereby returning us to the historical facts of early colonial leads and lags. As for the technology argument, it is true, of course, that Europe prevailed over the world by virtue of its technical advantage, particularly in modes of warfare (an advantage that it has unrelentingly maintained to this day); but the technology was in place given the overriding *motivation* of conquest. The Chinese, for instance, sailed to Africa in medieval times but showed no inclination for occupation and conquest. Motivations have to do with systemic factors which engender 'necessities'; noncapitalist empires do not scavenge the world seeking markets, at least in the first instance.

In purely technicist terms, however, some modifications of industrial structures do appear manifest in the first world, which, far from charting a new epoch of capital, simply illustrate the working out of forces immanent to it. The present (technological?) pecking order in the first world appears to be as follows: within the small band of the ruling triumvirate of capital (namely the United States, Japan, and Germany), direct investments are concentrated primarily in high-tech manufacturers (electronics, aerospace, atomic reactors, chemicals/biotech, armaments, etc.). This structuring, as with Alain Lipietz, might well be termed a form of *neo-Taylorism*, where elite engineers design high-tech production units, on the lines of self-contained spacecraft, requiring highly skilled maintenance, but only small components of unskilled labor. A second cadre, composed today, perhaps, of Switzerland, Sweden, and the Netherlands, retain small, if secure holds, but in only *some* of those sectors. A third constellation, Britain, France, Italy, and Canada, are without a wholly secure monopoly base in any of the lead sectors, and therefore stand on shaky, if not sinking ground, still largely tied to traditional industrial processes. Finally, the bottom tier: Spain, Greece, Ireland, Turkey, etc., with only low wages as their claim to a (vanishing) industrial promise. The Newly Industrializing Countries (NICs), itching for a toehold in this club are, of course, South Korea and Taiwan, for now; China—and possibly—India, Brazil, and Mexico, in the not so near future, in various stages of industrial/technical maturity.

The *trilateralism* (with a *quadrilateralism*, constituted by the conjugation of China and Pacific Rim economic power, round the corner) in effect today is worthy of note, given the disparate power and range of each of the constituents. The United States is by far the strongest of the three (at least for now) if only because it has, within its borders, one of the largest, most uniform, free markets in the world (now to be strengthened even more by

NAFTA), aside from the benefits of being the hegemonic power (and the only superpower), and the one least saddled with an anticapitalist history. Of course, Germany, within the EC, has access to an even larger market, but not one that is entirely free of political and cultural impediments given the hoary facts of European history. Only Japan, despite its careful cultivation of Australia, South and East Asia, as its own preserves, seems out on a limb, almost embarrassingly dependent on free trade sentiments/practices in the United States and Europe to nurture its long-term ambitions (aside from the critical fuel dependency it shares with Germany). So far, trilateralism has been a stalemated affair, with cautious brinkmanship on all sides; given that this has been so for over a decade, it is probably safe to suggest that it will remain so unless and until the parameters tumble—if and when the incipient, but unavoidable, Eurasian challenge (i.e., Russia and China together with the Pacific Rim) takes definite form. It is not inconceivable that the limited outcome of such struggles will be a new, but slow axial polarization between Washington-Peking-Tokyo, at one remove, and Paris-Bonn-Moscow, at another. The one decided residual of such an alliance would be the further marginalization of the third world, and possibly even of Southern and Eastern Europe, in the context of these metropolitan struggles for domination.

At another remove, both the so-called NICs and the non-NICs in the capitalist third world present transition problems that remain a sundry thorn in the flesh to imperial calculations, but not of an order that cannot be subdued by the landing of French or English paratroopers, now, of course, under the UN fig leaf of multilateral respectability.[16] Bretton Woods saw the third world in exclusively colonial terms: that is, as *non-subjects* in a world they were busy redesigning. No Marshall Plan was offered for Africa or Asia; instead, the World Bank-IMF combination of old style carrot-and-stick policies, backed up by the Central Intelligence Agency (CIA) or the Marines, was seen as enough to contain their ambitions and expectations. Fundamentally, this was not an inaccurate calculation; as even more today than in the interwar, or even postwar period, finance ministers of the third world are directly accountable to the financial masters of imperialism. As such, despite difficult, even unexpected, problems posed by the sub-agendas in this part of the world (Vietnam being the most flagrant example), the first world policy makers continued to view them as entirely superable. Where precious resources were concerned, such as oil or copper, for instance, the U.S.-NATO alliance could be counted on to coordinate quick search-and-destroy policies (either unilaterally or multilaterally) from the overthrow of Allendé and Arbenz, to the humbling of Gaddafy and Saddam Hussein. The more successful NICs, of course, simply joined the club (Taiwan and South Korea), or at least qualified for associate membership, therefore jumping out of the net of problem zones; the unsuccessful ones could accept IMF style law-and-order disciplines—or face the consequences.

THE 'SOCIALIST' AGENDA

In one word, the socialist agenda, from the formation of the USSR on, in the twenties, was, quite simply, *survival*. All socialist policies, reactionary or radical, can be seen as variants of this primary life-and-death obsession. Imperialism could and did thrive on calculated aggression; socialism had to subsist on eternal vigilance. Small wonder that the despotic state function was soon to supercede all other 'socialist' functions in this cagey world of nervous self-defense. The fortress mentality was no voluntary choice of a power hungry bureaucracy; it was an irrationally rational response to the imperialist threat which, far from receding with the years, actually grew to yet more menacing proportions, ending with the spectacular Reagan scenario of Star Wars, ready to risk an amount equivalent to the entire Gross Domestic Product (GDP) of the United States in a desperate bid to end the arms race and secure unilateral victory. As such, it was imperialism that principally defined the historical distortions of socialism, enabling the success therein of the vilest forms of bureaucratic despotisms, suppressing any genuine aspirations for socialist values, goals, and aspirations. The Reaganite boast of spending the Soviet Union into the stone age was no idle threat; it was simply maleficent, misanthropic, capitalist logic. As such, the grim parodies of socialism that existed, for a while, were wholly produced and directed by imperialism, to serve as butts for ridicule first, then annihilation afterwards.

Despite the innate doom of this negative logic, the socialist regimes, from the comic to the tragic and the absurd, tried valiantly to appropriate for themselves some semblance, however truncated and deformed, of the socialist vision, of which the most spectacular example was the Soviet Union. A despotism that, even at its worst Stalinist period, nonetheless served more of the underclasses (of the world) than their ruling elites, the Soviet Union firmly showed the world the possibility of nonimperial, if not *nonviolent*, economic growth (the savagery of enforced growth being inflicted upon its own citizenry—particularly those elements constituting its 'nonmodernist' sectors, as e.g., the peasantry—than on colonial possessions and peoples without). The Soviet empire was always a *political*, rather than an economic one; a center that bled itself for its periphery, as paradoxically, Soviet colonies in Eastern Europe enjoyed higher standards of living than Soviet citizens, owing to generous Soviet subsidies, a situation unprecedented in any other known forms of empire in the history of the world. Similarly, the subsidies to Cuba and the fraternal assistance to a host of third world entities, from the ANC to the Palestinians, remain extraordinary examples of

Soviet generosity, a ragged trousered philanthropy of sorts, given the meagre per capita real income of Soviet citizenry (if not its bureaucratic rulers). Indeed, it is quite obvious that the Soviet establishment subsidized the weaker entities in the world quite often at the cost of the welfare of its own citizenry. The direct political capital payback from this assistance was quite negligible, in fact disappointingly so. And yet, the fact remains that this generosity stemmed, ultimately, from the security needs of the Soviet state.

For seventy years, the USSR (while a despotism internally) exerted incalculable moral and political pressure on imperialism, checking its more abominable intentions, *forcing an agenda of social democracy upon metropolitan capitals*, even as it assisted in defending national liberation struggles, in the third world (*somewhat marred by its focus on national fraternity rather than class support*), and the critical perimeters of fellow socialist entities. *It is imperative to note that no other major power of its kind has ever played an equivalent role in history*, allying itself, as it did, with the poor, the weak, and the defenseless, the world over (in the face of the contempt of the ruling classes of the world). As such, millions of disempowered peasants and workers, not least in the imperialist countries, owed the reformist ethos of their national (capitalist) politics (marginal as it was) to the great communist menace. The fall of the USSR, accordingly, spells only extended travails for their kind, already in evidence in the rollbacks in welfare statism, and the return to regressive labor policies, most dramatically evident in the United States. In this regard, the revanchism of the Right is only just begun.

The implications of the very existence of the Soviet Union were catastrophic to imperialism. A major chunk of the world was now denied privileged access to imperial capital; more so, when the example and the assistance of the USSR would render even more such entities plausible in the future. *As such, the cold war was another adjunct of Bretton Woods, as important for policy as the World Bank and the IMF*. Socialism, from its very inception, therefore had to prepare to fight World War III (in the case of the USSR even before World War II had ended) at every level imaginable. Aside from the military encirclement of United States and NATO bases ringing the Eastern bloc, and the barrage of western propaganda endlessly beamed at it, a virtual economic/technological blockade was also installed with Cocom (run from the basement of the U.S. Embassy in Paris) coordinating an effective export blockade, even as the United States orchestrated a ban on imports of a wide range of goods from the Warsaw Pact countries. Given these methods of deliberate strangulation, it is hardly surprising that these economies were to be turned into entrenched army camps, and military enclaves, in various degrees. The enforced military expenditures of the USSR enhanced its self-image, internationally, at the same time that it impoverished its citizens, and sowed the seeds of dissension and dissatisfaction. The lag in consumption goods, given military priorities, meant a concession and a defeat on one important plane in the ideological war against capitalism: quite clearly, to Soviet citizenry, socialism could not give them more, let alone better, commodities. And, regrettably, an expansion of commodities is exactly what the Soviet planners kept promising the Soviet people.

When socialism is willfully reduced to bigger and better pots of goulash, it is small wonder that the aesthetic and communitarian sides to the socialist vision get ignored. The very materialism of Soviet-Marxism thereby undermined its functioning; but this was not only a Soviet error. The great Marx himself perpetuated that form of reductionist thinking no less than Adam Smith. Indeed, to beat the capitalist at her own game was to prove undoable, and the final travesty was to follow readily; if you can't beat them it is then 'rational' to simply call the fight off and join them. Today Russia tries to do just that and finds—to its rather naive chagrin—doors not exactly wide open. In one of history's more dramatic ironies, the long-lived colony of Western Europe, modern Russia, stands poised to relapse into that rank again, its erstwhile 'superpower' glamour and glory notwithstanding.[17]

Sympathetic economists, like Nove,[18] have seen the problems of Soviet socialism not as problems of socialism *per se* but as problems of *growth*, as a mature economy shifted gears from an earlier period of *extensive* growth (as with Stalinism, maintaining high production levels, but at unjustifiably high costs across the scale: social, material, human, and natural) to one of *intensive* growth (with scarce resources in short supply propelling the need for efficiency), the USSR being able to manage the one phase but not the other. In capitalist accounting terms they are quite right, but then it amounts to suggesting that the Soviets failed at a fairly pedestrian capitalist game; quite true, of course, at one level, but begging the question as to why socialism (the Great Experiment of the twentieth century) was caught playing a capitalist game to begin with.[19] It is in raising this question that all the weaknesses of Soviet-style socialist economies become apparent; and they do not pertain to physical or technical variables but to qualitative ones in the domain of the philosophical and moral underpinnings of the socialist project (e.g., is socialist consumption, in terms of composition, the same as a capitalist one, except wishing to be quantitatively bigger? But this is how it did appear; any wonder that those who could, in the USSR, found the opportunity of defecting to the west a more attractive, and reliable, way of instantly achieving this 'socialist' goal?), situated squarely not just in the sphere of relations of production, but also in the sphere of social—human—relations at large.

In the case of China, the other great (but just as surely failed) socialist experiment, the great Mao tried his best to avoid Soviet mistakes[20] just as surely as he benefited from the Soviet presence. Serious efforts were made not to fetishize the productive forces, and pure economic growth *per se*, but the effort, noteworthy in itself to promote socialist values, was perhaps just as surely doomed. The very same imperialist threat required production and productivity; besides, a semistarved peasantry lately awoken from semifeudal deprivations could not perhaps, in the first instance, be preached to about the virtues of community spirit, etc. (this was the crux of the issue: top-down, near authoritarian, party *diktats* from above replaced the ample potential for *self-organization* of the peasantry, the latter made impossible by the very existence of the Maoist superstate), by a distal, authoritarian, and bureaucratized central government, at least not without first quenching their desperation for the basics of existence—something not possible without expanding the productive base of the country. So, apparently unavoidable, 'practical imperatives' ran at odds with higher order values, especially since these latter came in the form of alien, party, cajolings. An orthodox Marxist would be prompted to say that Mao had tried, mistakenly, to socialize poverty rather than wealth, but this would only be a cynical half truth. And, certainly, the popular abandonment of socialism in China[21] was not due to this species of Maoist 'error.' Maoism, even at its benign best, was a nationalist, *étatiste*, dictatorship that was as intolerant of domestic opposition to party plans as was Stalinism (and only lately have we come to appreciate the horrific magnitude of this intolerance).

It is interesting that socialist China and the USSR were to fall out rather quickly, whereas state capitalist India and the USSR were to remain on fraternal terms throughout the relevant period. This would suggest that it was not so much matters internal ('socialist') as external parameters of policy that divided the Chinese from their first friends in the world community: that being the issue of how to approach imperialism. Very pragmatically, the Soviets had adopted the course of *peaceful coexistence* (of course, Stalin had offered a similar olive branch to Nazi Germany, as well), whereas Maoist China preferred, at least in rhetoric, a more revolutionary approach toward international relations. Indeed, rhetoric apart, it is not clear that Maoist China supported more, or even better supported, progressive forces in the world than the USSR. In fact, with blind anti-Sovietism as its guiding policy, China was to woo the most reactionary despotisms imaginable (including support for military-fascist Chilé right after the deposal of Allendé), and even showing a readiness to wage war, on trivial pretexts, with a weaker 'socialist' neighbor: Vietnam. So the reality was that Maoist China wished to create a *tripolar world* that gave it some primacy, in keeping with its historical sense of dignity, as opposed to a *bipolar* world in which it was relegated as a bit player to the sidelines. To this incipient nationalist crusade, the regime that replaced Mao remained completely faithful. Chinese foreign policy therefore illustrated, quite simply, the mechanics of geopolitics unencumbered by any definable ideology while being Maoist, i.e., agrarian oriented, quasi-egalitarian, and communalist, in its domestic orientations. Today, of course, China is state capitalist in its domestic affairs as well, with a virtual abandonment of any egalitarian (if not étatiste practices) precepts. If survival relates to the original *socialist* agenda, then China failed just as much as the USSR, in the same mold of auto-subversion.

In another regard, Cuba was a third 'model,' so to speak, in the socialist lineup. The advantage of scale gave Cuban socialism a credibility obviously denied to the giants. The romance of the revolution, the charisma of Che and Fidel, and its quite credible record in welfare indices in relation to the Latin American despotisms, made it an attractive beacon for third-world radicalism; attractive, in fact, to the point of obscuring its many enduring structural weaknesses, especially its inherited economic *monoculture*: sugar. Incredibly high Soviet subsidies kept this experiment artificially alive for over two decades; and that itself is an awesome, if coldly objective, measure of the weakness of its socialist economy. Once again, imperial machinations were to keep up mortal economic pressure on Cuba, most effective in the U.S. ban on trade. It was inevitable that a sudden withdrawal of Soviet assistance would throw the regime against the wall, unable to sustain its daily economic life with the dazzle of rhetoric alone. While more genuinely popular than many socialist (and capitalist) regimes, the stark deprivations of the Cuban people is an illustration of the double hazard common to all socialist entities: unenlightened domestic policies combined with the crushing burden of imperialist machinations. If the mighty Soviets were to crumble so effortlessly, it is hardly plausible to suppose that diminutive Cuba can withstand the pressures for too much longer, most especially after the departure of Fidel.

In all three 'models'—quite an inappropriate term since these were concrete, historically situated experiences rather than laboratory controlled 'cases'— the specific 'socialism' arrived at was, necessarily, makeshift, experimental, and improvisational. *Contrary to orthodoxy, classical Marxism offers absolutely no guidelines on how to organize and operate a socialist economy, except on whose behalf it is supposed to be organized and operated.*[22] However, this is not a Marxian 'weakness,' as is often supposed, but perhaps rather a realist constraint. It is quite absurd to lay down blueprints that can be universally and permanently applicable to all societies (although, occasionally, Marxian schematism has tended in that direction). Essentially, then, socialism boils down to a matter of the political will of the ruling party, subject to the exigencies of the social milieu, historical period, and the cultural endowment of the society in question. The so-called economics of socialism has always been a trial-and-error, hit-and-miss affair, i.e., a matter of *pragmatics* (though always presented as though 'general principles' were at issue—just as with 'vulgar,' neoclassical ideology, its philosophical mirror image). Herein, the high debates between the so-called 'law of value' and the planning principle (debates carried on well into the sixties)[23] stood, roughly, only for market versus nonmarket allocation. Theory, in the politics of socialism, was no less a mask for policy.

Of course such considerations did not prevent many regimes from consciously trying to 'imitate' these alleged 'models'—always with mixed consequences, and always short of anything like a success story; for after all, socialist 'miracles,' if they ever existed, are even rarer than capitalist ones. So, while 'models' are always spurious, for being abstract and schematic, it is nonetheless true that many negative, instructive lessons (to be discussed at length in a later section) were immanent in the experience of socialist societies (but with few approaching the outright rabidity of the Khmer Rouge). They are simple lessons, in the main, but lessons that are bound to be on the minds of all those who might wish to embark again upon that hazardous road of social experiment.

In terms of purely conventional ecopolitical criteria, the record of the USSR and China, while not exactly enviable, was not entirely a sorry one. After all, given the paucity of per capita resources, it was no mean achievement to be even ten years behind the cutting edge of international (capitalist) industrial technologies as with the USSR. Nor was it a shabby record, as with Maoist China, to build up the average level of health and nutrition from near-zero to world standards (indeed bettering the latter in many cases)—whose unmistakable inheritance is evident today in the young Chinese athletes who are stunning the world with their remarkable performances. Nor is it negligible that socialist Cuba would stand at the helm of capitalist Latin America across any reasonable scale of social welfare criteria (that excludes the metric of income and the matrix of liberty). Indeed, to exaggerate the point, the fact that the USSR, first, and China, second, rose to superpower status (not just militarily), where it is not a question of sheer size and scale, was not entirely unrelated to the solid agrarian-industrial-technological base laid securely under the now defunct 'socialist' auspices. It is also trivially true, but more by way of exception, that even in terms of purely bourgeois criteria (per capita GDP, e.g.), at least one 'socialist' regime, the German Democratic Republic, overtook important entities of NATO capitalism, in the eighties: Italy and Britain. But these are, as pointed out, conventional criteria, in both their strengths and their limitations.

As mentioned, the socialist agenda was, internationally, a defensive one, but internally it functioned pretty much as a normal (but authoritarian) welfare state might: trying to reconcile social equity with economic growth, with the particular emphasis, and balance, depending upon both the international situation and the vagaries of the faction that happened to be governing at a particular point of time. Lacking a party system, factionalism *within* the party substituted for different platforms; with frequent purges being the functional equivalent of voting a party out of office. Being welfare states, such regimes always operated on margins of scarcity; with some measure of social needs having to be met, budgets were always constrained (unlike capitalist systems, where budgets can show highly artificial 'surpluses' with large scale unemployment, poverty, crime, homelessness, etc.). As such, permanent scarcity is the hallmark of any society that embarks on a national program of access and equity for the masses. Indeed, this helps define erstwhile socialist societies quite succinctly: they were regimes based on a relatively unchanging combination of *permanent insecurity* (the external constraint) and permanent *scarcity* (the internal constraint). While imperialism contributed the one constraint, the very goals of these regimes kept afloat the second. It is easy to see how Yeltsin's right-wing Russia shakes off both constraints: kowtowing to imperialism annuls the external constraint, while dismantling the welfare state eases the budget constraint. Of course, the 'free-market' capitalist ideologue (even in ex-socialist form, as with Janos Kornai)[24] praises both these retrograde steps as the essential signs of economic and political progress. Fundamentally, then, it would be correct to say that the Socialist Agenda, in its own terms, failed (although China and a few other countries survive on as quasi-collectivist, *étatiste*, entities) by simply failing to survive as per their own objectives.

The fundamental questions about these 'socialist' experiments still remain the *qualitative* ones, involving interrogations about the reification of growth as against equity, and within the frame of growth, the emphasis on crash industrialization (as the means of raising aggregate values) as compared to, say, a more pacific agrarian strategy; on the high valuation of investment *vis-à-vis* consumption, on security against liberty, and so on. The simple answer here is that these policy 'choices', made somewhat exclusively by the ruling strata, were as much derived from the security requirements of the state, given the international climate, as they were the fully theorized options within a standard, materialist, Marxist mode of analysis, even more 'productivist' in its inherent logic than capitalism itself. It seems quite extraordinary that the 'pig principle'—more *is better*—routinely satirized in even undergraduate critiques of neoclassical, capitalist, economic theorizing was taken over, *tout ensèmble*, into the serious calculations of Marxist policies. Of course, a little reflection makes clear that the epistemic of 'more is better' thrives particularly in a climate of generalized scarcity, more so when the scarcity is hierarchically, and differentially, distributed. But the antidote to a paradigm of scarcity is not necessarily a philosophy extolling unlimited growth, based—as it had to be—on unremitting labor for the many. One option would have been to distribute scarcity more equitably; another would have been the complementary encouragement of the idea that, perhaps, less is better, weighing positive social relations higher than indices of material production and consumption. Neither route was pursued, however, in the USSR; instead, somewhat suicidally, the regime promised more and delivered less even as some had, obviously, more than others. Only within so fetishized a mind-set is it possible to fathom the near-incredible fact that minor industrial crimes against productive property in a 'socialist' society like the USSR were, quite often, in a rabid rejection of even simple humanism, judged to be *capital* crimes. Clearly, the socialist resolve here was not a pacification of human existence, in all its emancipatory potential, but the repressive consolidation and reverence/worship of strict industry and diligence, and disciplinary/military values, more befitting a regime of slave drivers than a society of 'associated producers.' Given these hideous deformities, the wonder is not that the system caved in when it did, but why it endured as long as it did.

World War III, to determine which variant of modernism was to seize the world, in effect, was fought for some forty years and finally won by the capitalist west. While only a cold war for Europeans, it proved to be an era of hot wars (about 127 major wars between 1945 and 1989) for the many proxy warriors who perished in the third world, directly as a consequence of east-west rivalry (about 22 million, from just 1960 to 1990, which is about three times the total casualties of World War I). Ironically, it is the populace of the 'losers' (Eastern Europe and Russia) that won important new freedoms. Thereby, the peoples of the 'winners' (NATO countries) have won absolutely nothing, in consequence, except the dubious benefits of living under a new absolutist capitalism with even fewer checks to its pretensions.

Indeed the defeat of the socialist challenge will imply a rollback of social democracy and civil rights in the capitalist world, especially in nations of weak working class politicizations, as in the United States, tendencies that are already incipient in the latter country. Not only was the USSR the implicit shield of partial autonomy for much of the third world, it was also the manifest goad to social democracy in the west. The fragmented Eastern bloc faces challenges not unlike those suffered by the third world, despite the technical superiority of their extant modes of production. In Russia, the period of 'market Stalinism'—under state anchorage—is rapidly giving way to a near-anarchist, Mafia-style, robber baron capitalism, given the rapid delegitimation of traditional bureaucracies. With very little of the promised economic aid materializing from the west, Eastern Europe and Russia can hope only for one or other of three alternatives, *in the short run*: (a) the rise of a regressive, right-leaning, crypto-military dictatorship, as an interim arrangement to buy time; (b) a neocolonial, enclave economy with widespread iniquities, unemployment, and demoralization; or (c) a slide back to Stalinism, but perhaps with a more Gorbachevian 'human face.' Eastern Europe, given its marginally better economic basis, is probably going to be in Trac II; Russia, and its erstwhile republics, possibly will find their short-run moorings in Tracs I and III.

THE THIRD WORLD: A DUAL AGENDA

While the first and second worlds had fairly determinate agendas to pursue, in the third (ex-colonial) world, given the very existence of the other two world systems, the agenda was split, irreconcilably, between the procapitalist tendency and the anticapitalist tendency (though the latter did not, generally, encompass an *antimodernist* tendency, as characterized a good bit of the Gandhian *oeuvre*). In fact, even the capitalist tendency was fractured between those who gained from a *neocolonial* stance, and those who stood to benefit from a more nationalistic, *postcolonial*, path. As such, it was the third world that was always home to the predominance of the *political* moment as these tendencies fought each other, sometimes to the finish, aided and abetted by forces from the first and second worlds. So, while both the first and second worlds were pledged to variants of *economism*, it was only in the third world that genuine struggles over the nature of the good society took precedence over the obvious desire to elevate living standards. The average third worlder was overdetermined, so to speak, *politically* (hence deemed unstable by corporate measures of stability evolved in systems marked by the virtual, and not surprising, disappearance of such questions from the body politic). The politics, generally, was of an inexorably *redemptive* nature—a far cry from the venal 'spoils system,' as prevails in the United States (where a politician is simply an as-yet-unapprehended scofflaw), and similar systems based on the 'who gets what' philosophy. In other words, third worldist struggles, within a modernist paradigm, were usually fought less over relative shares of the pie, than over the nature of ingredients going into it.

This situation of high politicization was far from self-inspired; it owed its existence to the virtually incomplete, hybrid nature of the socioeconomic transformation inflicted upon it by the European colonial powers. Given that the European colonial resolve was only to create, and drain, the surplus as cheaply and as speedily as possible, the nature of institutional transformations it effected were just as often retrograde, and reactionary, as progressive, if not actually more so, and more often. In one illustrative case, that of India, the British left behind, as their pet creations, a pauperized peasantry, chronically destitute landless tenants, a thwarted, skeletal industrial structure, a backward, semi-starved agriculture whose modern sectors were skewed to export promotion of cash crops, and a whole range of parasitic operators from extortionist moneylenders to matchingly rapacious tax collecting landlords.

In both India and Egypt, in fact, a few decades of colonial rule were sufficient to transform self-sufficient agrarian economies, dating back to antiquity, into chronic food importing nations with hunger as the predominant condition for the multitude. Aside from the host of problems attending a successful transition to capitalism in an agrarian context—by and large the problematic of *national agendas* in many third world entities—the quality of difficulty in the ex-colonies may be appreciated in reference to just one fact: unlike the European experience, no 'empty' world exists without to be colonized as the new agrarian revolutions expel the masses from the countryside. In effect, Bangladesh is not well set to conquer Britain as a dumping site for its 'surplus' rural population. This implies that, in the case of the third world, such a revolution is to be sustained in the face of a vast majority of the rural populace continuing to subsist in the rural hinterland, a situation without precedent in the first world. Third world capitalism cannot hope, therefore, to repeat the depredations of the first; in the capitalist race, the early risers bag all such dubious 'advantages.'[25]

At any rate, this situation of near bankruptcy of economic modernisms allowed for many competing agendas to surface in the excolonial world: subagents of the imperial nation, connected perhaps to plantations or mining, seeing their economic future linked to neocolonial connections with the mother country; budding national industrialists, seeing their futures as better served by a protectionist government pledged to development of the domestic market; and agencies of peasants and workers, and later women, seeing their interest as remaining unserved by either of these strategies for capitalist accumulation. As such, the postcolonial period, largely coinciding with the postwar period, was to witness a mighty tussle between these forces. The so-called nonaligned movement was, by and large, dominated by countries whose agendas resembled the national-economic one of an internal development of capitalism under government protection. In Central America, the neocolonial variants prevailed; in the rest of Latin America, there was a fair mix of both these strategies, much as in Africa and Asia. To some extent, advantages of size, diversity, and degree of social development (such as a politically unionized labor force), encouraged the tilt to national capitalist agendas, though not always so. Smaller entities, with subordinated labor movements, like Singapore, found the neocolonial route of the *entrepôt* economy more congenial. In each case, though, it was the nature of the economic inheritance from colonialism, the class balance, degree of democracy, and the politicization of the class struggle, that determined which strategy was either 'opted' for by the ruling class, or arrived at by some process of class compromise.

The national path toward autonomous capitalist development, as an international movement in the ex-colonial world, is perhaps best reflected in the third world resolve to be economically and politically independent, as announced first at the Bandung Conference of April 1955 (held in Bandung, Indonesia), attended by twenty-nine African and Asian nations, and then again, slightly later, affirmed in the Non-Alignment Initiative taken by Nasser, Nehru, and Tito (meeting in Brioni in June 1956; first summit in Belgrade, in 1961). The strategy, preeminently national and capitalist, as was to be subsequently worked out, involved the prioritization, extension, and development of the *domestic* market in favor of production of the means of production and/or the production of mass consumption goods. For such a plan to be workable, it was clear that many strategic variables in the economy would have to be securely within domestic control, variables such as: access to local markets, industrial wages and prices, agrarian productivities, financial machinery, and relevant technologies. These would have to be weighed against the colonial legacy of variegated dependency/weaknesses in many areas such as: chronic agrarian crisis, food shortages, military weakness, mounting foreign debt, technological dependency, penetration by transnational capital, and so on. Clearly, the balance between the effort made and the effort needed to surmount obvious obstacles was a critical one; and, in varying degrees of success, or failure, a handful of countries did dare to run the gauntlet of import substitution: India, Brazil, Algeria, Mexico, South Korea, etc. Indeed, the last gasp of this old national capitalist strategy in the third world was their domination of the 6th Special General Meeting of the U.N. in 1974 where, against the favorable background of rising raw material prices, an extensive catalog of demands to restructure the world economy in favor of extended access to 'developing' nations, called the New International Economic Order, won majority support—only to fade away, ever so swiftly, as the world crisis deepened.

On the other hand, the export promoting *neocolonial* path, such as that taken by Pakistan, Saudi Arabia, Kenya, Zaire, and much of Central America, implied a closer integration within the circuits of world capital, financial markets, and trading blocs, with trade seen as the engine of growth on classic, comparative cost, principles. In general, growth here was faster, albeit more superficial, with the strong *extraversion* leading to the composition of production heavily skewed in favor of luxury consumer goods, primary produce and/or minerals, etc., intended for export. Authoritarianism, and/or outright dictatorship, built upon the backs of popular resistance (as with much of Latin and Central America) was the political counterpart of this 'extraversion.' In many contexts, there was a seesaw battle between advocates of the two different paths (as in Jamaica, where Manley and Seaga battled it out at the hustings, time and again); of course, in other cases, as in Chilé during the Allendé regime, issues cascaded beyond simple electoral politics.

Of course, the nature of the outcome of these struggles was far from predetermined by the colonial legacy alone. Here, the continuing imperial interventions, led by the rapacious United States,[26] ensured that movements that strayed too far from course were either scuttled *en route* to power, overturned after gaining power, or held at dagger point forever after. As such, not only did Europe (and its braggart offspring, the United States) prepare the soil for turmoil in the third world, but it also tried to ensure that the turmoil would redound to the benefit of itself. To undermine and destabilize anticapitalist regimes was, of course, another rational offshoot of the Bretton Woods resolve (though usually not seen as connected with it). Less obvious was the more prevalent situation of imperialism continually intervening to prevent, via changes in land tenure, even a capitalist agrarian revolution from taking place. Land reform found imperialism as its enemy in most of the colonized world, with the United States' courting of landed military-fascist oligarchies of Central and South America being stereotypical in this regard. As in the case of colonialism, imperialism was ready to make peace with retrograde, even byzantine, social forces so long as its own predatory interests could be the better secured. At least in this regard, to understand the present is to understand the past.

With the cold war finally won, it is conceivable that imperialism now withdraws its objections to capitalist agrarian revolutions, so long as they take place within a controlled, moderate, compromised, reformist mold as typified with the Philippines under the impuissant regime of Aquino. This withdrawal of military sanctions is by no means the automatic inducement for either the long-suppressed, much-needed, agrarian reforms or for industrial stability afterwards, given the inherent difficulties of sustaining such near-autocentric capitalist regimes in the economic space allowed by imperialism. A national capitalism requires both a favorable external context and a favorable internal situation. In the twentieth century, such contextual happenings, in the non-European third world, are a matter of pure chance: for example, South Korea, perhaps the prime candidate for such a transition (although with China now snapping at its heels), had World War II, American planning, domestic dictatorship, and the cold war as its conjunctural allies.

How then did these third world agendas fare in the period in question? In retrospect, it is tempting to say that today virtually all third world regimes are neocolonial, i.e., *capitulationist*, in their relationship with the IMF. Indeed, when the solidly state bourgeois nation, India, is ready to kneel in front of IMF, only to beg for the right to mortgage its economic future, as with the present regime, it is hard to see how the weaker regimes could fare any better. Nonetheless, this judgment might well be an overstatement in the case of India, as tactical surrenders may often be offered as temporary gestures in the face of a long-run strategy of ultimate nondependency (given the subtlety of the Indian ruling class in leeching off both east and west throughout the era of the cold war, this is not just idle speculation). As such, it is safer to say that the line demarcating a neocolonial capitalist class from a nationally oriented capitalist class may not be so hard and fast as imagined; it is all a question of history, timing, class balance, and so on. Further, economic kowtowing may not always be accompanied by political accommodation. Indeed, if nonalignment were viewed primarily as a declaration of political independence rather than economic independence, then it is perhaps secure to suggest that the number of politically independent third world regimes has not radically diminished at the present time in spite of the general mood of abject submission.

In this regard, it is necessary and important to note the small number of ex-colonial countries, mostly Asian, that have actually crossed that critical line, or are on the verge of doing so, something which enables them to at least apply for associate membership in the club of successful 'national' capitalist economies. South Korea and Taiwan are obvious candidates, ahead of, say, Brazil and Mexico, and represent the successful localization of first world capitalist institutions in a culturally different milieu, especially the all-critical ones of finance and manufacturing, much like Japan itself. Aside from cold war special treatment, the fact is that both nations owed their subsequent trajectory to enlightened (if self-serving) *land reform*, carried out by the United States, in the one instance, and Japan, in the other. While there are many imitators, and would-be imitators (both within the Association of Southeast Asian Nations (ASEAN) and elsewhere), it remains to be seen how many more shall make, and survive, the transition. For now, at any rate, the so-called NICs, when valued in traditional economic terms, represent the exception that proves the rule of economic sloth and indigence in the rest of the third world. Oddly enough, though, the newfound economic strength of the highest ranking NICs has not been accompanied by corresponding political maturity, both South Korea and Taiwan being neocolonial in a political sense, serving as a blackleg force against progressivist currents in Asia far more than they are submissive, so to speak, in the economic sense. Whether this lag is transitional or chronic remains, of course, to be seen. It needs be remembered that all the principal 'Asian Tigers' were the earmarked beneficiaries of imperial attentions in the planned '*cordon sanitaire*' designed against Communist South-East Asia, with the containment of China (Vietnam and North Korea) being the principal reason for the special terms granted these entities (reciprocally, city-states like Hong Kong and Singapore also served, additionally, as important offshore financial havens for imperialism). The situation is a near parallel to the long-term Soviet special assistance for Cuba, except that the latter effort, though equally beneficent, was a dismal failure in its ability to create a strong, self-sustaining Cuban economy.

So what happens when sub-agendas clash, as they will and must? If in the domestic domain, it depends on the victor, the extent of the victory, and the mode of victory. Neocolonial Sadat replaced post-colonial Nasser, inaugurating a change in direction for Egypt's nonalignment as much as for its internal alignments. Something similar, but with more wholesale domestic slaughter, accompanied the counterrevolution that put Suharto in place of Sukarno in Indonesia, more akin to the internationally coordinated repression in Chilé. Occasionally, however, these paths clash internationally, dissipating their energies in UN votes, where SEATO and OAS nations functioned as lackeys of the west throughout the period of the cold war. And sometimes, like India and Pakistan, as with ignorant armies taken to field, they have repeatedly clashed by night, in all futility. On balance, it would be safe to say that, despite their clearly demarcable orientations, the two strategies are now merged. Whether this represents a success or the failure of either strategy remains to be seen. It is, after all, still the age of uncertainty *vis-à-vis* both the second and third worlds.

While the record is incomplete, a summary judgment may still be offered. The *(modernist) capitalist agendas in the third world are well on track, if not on target, the distinction between neocolonial and postcolonial capitalist paths being less important today than a wholesale rejection of alternatives to capitalist development*. This is significant inasmuch as it suggests how categories are always defined by the dialectic of history; thus with the unilateral success of imperialism, and the complementary failure of socialism, the schism between neocolonial and postcolonial paths to capitalist development becomes only a historical curiousum, of archival interest alone. A choice between the paths was made permissible by the existence of the USSR: its evaporation, all too quickly, attended the dismemberment of its patron. Stated differently, economic nationalism and political independence on the part of the colonial world was as much a domestically inspired and sustained policy as it was a posture made possible by the material condition of the aid and friendship of the USSR. Post-USSR, we, in the third world, are almost all neocolonial now (the new consciousness of a singular European identity, on both sides of the Urals, returning Europe to its pre-1917 state of mind, has particular implications for non-European societies. Perhaps an analogy might suffice: capitalism came to maturity within the womb of feudal society because of the inherently *fragmented* power structures of feudalism; it might not have succeeded had feudal suzerainty been absolutist. Something similar is indicated in the ex-colonial world: its ability to sustain its own impulses was never so strong as when its European masters were busy feuding among themselves; now that the latter are increasingly presenting, more or less, a united front [as evident in the Gulf War] autonomy is that much more difficult to attain).

Along with the world defeat of socialism, the *anti-capitalist* agendas in this sphere, agendas primarily built around peasant and workers' organizations, sometimes affiliated to a socialist-communist party, are either in obvious decline, or in indeterminate *stasis*. If one groups alongside these those regimes that tried to reject a neocolonial capitalist path in favor of some form of radical antiimperialism, the list, in various degrees of credibility, is longer than their combined effectiveness: Nicaragua, Mozambique, Angola, Zimbabwe, Grenada, Libya, Algeria, Ghana, North Korea, Ethiopia, Somalia, South Yemen, Vietnam, Laos, Guinea, Burkina Faso, Benin, Madagascar, Congo, Seychelles, Uganda, Mali, Cape Verde, Tanzania, Guinea-Bissau, Afghanistan, Cambodia—a mere handful of rag-poor, dire hopefuls. Some on this list, with once serious Marxist inclinations, such as Ethiopia, Somalia, Grenada, Nicaragua, Afghanistan, Cambodia, and South Yemen, are already off the map; and the trajectory of the others remains unclear, just as much to their own governments as to outside observers. It is hard to view this tenuous cluster of nations as contributing any enthusiasm to others to follow suit and copy their example. Only Vietnam and North Korea[27] are, perhaps, regimes of a different order than the others on the list, offering the possibility of surviving the present leadership, although a reunification of the Koreas might put an end to the latter entity also in the near future. In almost all the others, it was radical anti-imperialism that was always more important than any necessarily 'socialist' organization of society and polity other than the easier route of statism. Much like the second world, these nations had to devote resources as much to merely survive against imperial machinations, as to build for a future in some variant of the socialist (étatiste) vision. Clearly, these pallid attempts—constituting a sort of a quasi-agenda—were to fail quite as decidedly as world socialism at large.

However, this unqualified negative judgment does not apply to a host of novel and unique forms of *antimodernist* revolt that are actually on the ascendant, not necessarily based exclusively on either peasant or workers' movements. These are the highly politicized environmental and ecologically minded movements (in India, Kenya, and Brazil, to name but a few areas), women's movements, civil rights movements, tribal/cultural struggles, and so on, which represent very different political bases, and with agendas far more challenging to capitalism than the hoary rhetoric of socialism.[28] To call them Green-inspired movements in the third world is to blunt their cutting edge, for they are far less sedentary, far more practical, and far more earnest, than any Green initiative in Europe. Quite unlike the socialist movement, these struggles make full use of their own, indigenous, cultural tools, representations, and practices to make their point; and as such, they are far less alien to local wisdom and mores and sensibilities, than, say, the texts of Marx and Engels as transposed in a Zulu village. The importance to the third world of the emergence of such indigeneously based political visions is hard to exaggerate.

Viewed uncritically, this might seem a regression to parochialism, and 'nativism,'[29] as opposed to the putative proletarian 'internationalism' touted by socialism, but this would be to seriously misread rhetoric for reality. Peasant womens' demands, like those of the famous Chipko struggles in India, are no less universal for being couched, quite appropriately, in the cultural idiom of the peoples of the foothills of the Himalayas. As an obverse, in contrast, one can easily visualize a dialogue on the merits of a Calcutta subway system being couched in the overblown rhetoric drawn, say, from Marx's *Critique of the Gotha Programme*, only because an urbanite, Marxian, movement is spearheading the struggle (for, or against, the project, as the case may be) in Bengal. Both are local issues, whether building a subway or felling timber in the Himalayas: yet one constituency uses its own language, forged through its own experience of struggle; the other prefers to refer to rarefied, European, texts. The alienation, in each instance, I will let the reader judge for herself; obviously, Eurocentrism—and its inherent sin of an abstract universalism—has been the bane of mainstream and Marxist alike, amongst the elites of the third world, for far too long.

These new anticapitalist, antiétatiste (therefore, rejectionist *vis-à-vis* state socialism as well) movements are the solid heirs to the failure of international socialism, and would represent the lambent silver lining to the otherwise dismal cloud of defeat and derision. Being incipient, in the main, their hour in the sun is not yet come; but feminists, ecologists, and cultural autonomists are likely to carry the masses (but not *en masse*) to *new* political movements, much as socialism was able to do in the past. Their agenda is on the ascendant, much as the latter's is on the decline. Although with few direct connections to similar such movements in the first world, it is clear that this is not just a *third worldist* struggle: it is, rather, a universal struggle for *self-determination*,[30] still finding its feet cautiously in the slippery sands of all total capitalist successes. Should these movements succeed in capturing the imagination of peoples, much as socialism did once upon a time, the capitalist victories of the nineties will seem but a pyrrhic victory, only a prelude to a gentle cataclysm of rejection to come.

Thus far, as a heuristic, we have discussed the agendas of the three worlds independently; now to look at the interactive domain, in which such stark outlines get murkier. Indeed, there is a profound asymmetry that binds the worlds together in radically different ways. The ex-colonial world, historically, has always been an adjunct of the first; as such, it has had to operate within a space largely defined and confined by the first. That is to say, only the socialist world had the semblance of 'freedom' from the other two (partly by choice, partly by circumstance) in both economic and political terms; the first and the third were always locked in a mortal embrace of asymmetrical dependency. Of course, many areas of the third world were dependent upon the Socialist world as well, but this was a voluntarist, political/military, dependency. No third world economy was ever structurally enmeshed in the economies of the socialist world as they almost all are within the calculations of the first. This is an important point, because it explains how and why it was always possible for a third world entity to bid farewell to the second world, regardless of assistance received, virtually overnight, without fear of reprisal (think of Sadat's Egypt, for instance). However, for a third world entity *vis-à-vis* the first world, no such severance was easily possible without mighty retaliation (think of Allendé's Chilé; Walker's Grenada, etc.). Quite simply then, the Soviets approached the third world as friends (a friendship that was often neither understood, nor appreciated, by the very people upon whom it was bestowed. In the Middle East, for instance, the Soviets were always referred to, derisively, as 'Americans without dollars'), regardless of their strategic importance, whereas the capitalist world has always approached its periphery in the unmistakable form of masters and conquerors.

This interlock between the first and third worlds is what is credibly captured in all 'world-systems' analyses (as in the work of Andre Gunder Frank, Samir Amin, etc.), but the economic reductionism there has always failed to appreciate the logics of autonomy and semi-autonomy still politically feasible within the latter so long as the USSR stood guard at the flank as the ultimate, if not always effective, deterrent to imperial aggression. Whether Allendé's Chilé, Mossadegh's Iran, Nasser's Egypt, or Manley's Ghana, the third world has always been replete with (failed) attempts to chart an independent (usually state) capitalist path in diverse geopolitical contexts. This underscores the important point that, contrary to the tenets of economic determinism, *determined political will can often overcome structural socio-economic weaknesses*, although whether it can survive them remains open to test. Indeed, the east-west struggle, i.e., the cold war, necessarily spilled over to the third world, to the latter's everlasting detriment. The ousting and/or martyrdom of many third world economic nationalists (Arbenz, Nkrumah, Sukarno, Lumumba, Allendé, etc.) owed its wretched vindictiveness entirely to this shadow play between the two powers. Every effort made by progressive forces in Asia and Africa had to be fought, inch by inch, against the solid resistance of U.S. power to any change, other than one in a military-fascist direction. As such, it is miraculous that the decolonization that actually occurred in, say the African continent, was possible at all. In this, as in other instances, the moral and material debt owed by the west to the peoples of the south is simply immeasurable.

One issue that needs be addressed, a point of contention in both mainstream and radical analysis, is whether the first world 'needs' the third as a matter of dire economic necessity. In historical terms, it would perhaps be reasonable to accept that the very fact of colonialism ensures recognition that Eurocapitalism (in the past) found obvious use for the colonies. But what now? One way to approach the issue is to look, structurally, at the specific crises of capitalism, and then see if the conditions in the third world can serve at all to stave off or offset them. As defined in this work, the crises of capitalism are, almost inevitably, in the spheres of *production*, *realization*, and *accumulation*. From the production vantage point, low wages and cheap raw materials are an obvious lure (particularly when some resources are the bounty of geographical quirks). So long as the indices here are favorable (and not offset by negative markers like instability, high tariffs, transportation costs, overvalued exchange rates, and so on), transnational capitalist interest in the ex-colonial world may be taken as given. In the realization domain, as a market for goods, the potential in the third world is probably greater than its actuality (given the eventual competition of budding industrial giants, like India and China, still in the offing), without gainsaying the obvious fact of its current role as an important sector of the intraimperialist market for consumption goods. In the accumulation realm, direct foreign investment is possibly a better candidate for third world locations given their many suitabilities (low levels of wages and/or government regulation, etc.). All in all, it is clear that, to the extent capitalism demands cheapening of production costs and an extension of the market for goods (and capital), the third world periphery, organized within a tight IMF-World Bank regime, recommends itself. To state matters succinctly, there is no economic necessity, *in general*, that ties the first world to the third; but there is, as has always been, *capitalist* economic necessity (in terms of dry data, the record is one of flux: in the fifties, 40 percent of international trade was intraimperialist trade; by the seventies, this had risen to 61 percent; and by the late nineties, this had fallen off, again, to about 47 percent. Of course, aggregate figures conceal more than decomposed data, indicating specific patterns of 'dependency' in both directions of the north-south divide), given by its inexorable greed for expansion.[31] And, as the third world grows more capitalist, the dependency will, quite naturally, be more and more reciprocal, if asymmetrical as well.

In sum, the procapitalist Agenda in the third world is on track; the traditional forms of anticapitalist resistance are in decline, and the more novel forms of resistance, based on freshly rediscovered local customs and traditions, is fitfully awake and on the rise. So, the record is a mixed one with continued uncertainties, hesitations, and indeterminacies. One thing, however, is quite clear: with the collapse of socialist utopianism, the only genuine countervailing force today, in the realm of ideas, with the potential power to roll back capitalism (but not in one fell stroke, as dreamed of in the socialist tradition), is the legacy of *precapitalist* social norms. Ancient wisdoms, expressed in philosophy, and embodied in 'other' cultures, are the only refractory set of social ideas that have the inherent strength to resist the hegemonic litany of greed and guns, demoralization, and dictatorship: they cannot fail, because they do not understand, or accept, the rational, materialist notion of 'failure.' In this respect, in all irony, the early, 'reactive,' emotive critique of industrial civilization first posed by the so-called romantics (Carlyle, Ruskin, etc.)—poets, dreamers, and visionaries lamenting the execrable onset of the scrofulous neuroses of 'modernism'—and ridiculed soundly by the political economists of the time (mainstream and Marxian) seems far more robust, and credible, today than the vacuously high analytics of the 'scientific' socialists. 'History'—the favored, if bowdlerized, refuge of the modernist—certainly has not proved their premonitions wrong.

To examine the indicators of human welfare, as in standard economic analysis, at the abstract levels of 'worlds,' 'states,' or 'nations' (as is the vogue in, say, reports by the U.N., World Bank, etc., *and also in much of the foregoing analysis in this very book*), or to relations between these entities, is to renege on a realist understanding of the problems and preoccupations of everyday people that usually do not stand at the apex of either corporate or statist machinery. As such, 'international political economy,' even of a radical bent, can only be, at best, an irrelevant scrutiny of aggregate variables (usually under the control of domestic and/or foreign elites) of interest only to the architects of corporatist strategies be they economic, political, or military. Living at the grassroots level, the lot of the vast majority, is of course undoubtedly affected by the machinations of macro-planners, but it cannot (indeed, perhaps *must* not) be transformed by initiatives from the top stemming as they routinely do from the interested calculations of but another corps of vested interests. Moreover, purely 'economic' indicators, regardless, of the level of unit of analysis, far from exhaust the catalogs of well-being, as casually assumed by many variants of modernist economics. As such, it is irresistible not to note the obituary to political economy emerging from these considerations: that political economy, radical or otherwise, has elided, by virtue of its methodological bias of aggregation and its materialist focus on production and consumption, the wider panoply of issues that constitute the basis of an edifying life on the part of ordinary people. It is only a peripheral failing, then, that it would, ipso facto, also miss out on the real calculus of their commonplace aspirations. *The truth is inescapable: that economics, the patron science of modernism, has almost nothing (useful) to say on the subject of emancipation.* Stated differently, to reclaim the rights of self-determination involves stepping, in the first instance, outside the circuits of capital and the state, in both practice and ideology, as an important auxiliary of self-tutoring; alternatives to modernism cannot be mediated by the institutional artifacts of the latter without suffering subversion and/or co-optation. Reform, from above (liberal or radical), is usually another stratagem to securely entwine, and entrap, any and all secessionist impulses. Under such circumstances, to bypass the encompassing *logos* of Leviathan, in everyday living, wherever and whenever possible, would seem the more effective means of resistance.

Clearly, whether in capitalist or nominally socialist forms, the age of corporatist monoliths is upon us, the world over, like a pox today, set ready to devour every square inch of unincorporated social, economic, and political space that may be wrested, inveigled, or otherwise appropriated from the direct users. From the latter's point of view, the fact of the expropriation is really all that matters; their disempowerment is just as total whether the confiscation takes place nominally under the auspices of an all-conquering market or an all-conquering state. In this regard, from the vantage point of the dispossessed, the three worlds have always amounted to much the same, in effects; it is only the modernists that have been restlessly divided into various, competing, and mutually conflicting, segments of it. The victims of modernism have always, therefore, lived in but *One* world of stark, naked, deprivation. As lone, downtrodden, but solid, repositories of patience and sanity, it is their time that is nigh; from out of the long night of their banishment and exile will come the premonitory inklings of a restoration and redemption of the inherent, ineffable, dignity of the age-old, common heritage of humankind. The new world order of corporatism will one day (when not destroyed by its internal logics of conflict and contradiction), surely and securely, come to grief on their simple, but virtually irrepressible, resistance.

NOTES

1. Harry Cleaver (1979).
2. Agencies like the Trilateral Commission, and other corporate think tanks generally, are the self-conscious agents of this process of drafting and debating such Agendas behind closed doors and away from democratic, and even simply public, scrutiny. There is definitely a sense in which the ruling and the governing class(es) do not coincide.
3. The most comprehensive student of imperialism in modern times is, undoubtedly, Noam Chomsky. See particularly his newest work, *World Orders Old and New* (1994), which mirrors much of my own analysis. For an academic perspective on Marxian theories of Imperialism, see Anthony Brewer (1980); for select problems within imperialism, see Roger Owen and Bob Sutcliffe (1972), which still remains an outstanding detailing, despite the passage of time.
4. For this, important, 'Government of the World' idea, see section so titled in Chomsky, *Ibid.*, pp. 120–129.

5. For patient exposes of the operational logic of the IMF and the World Bank, see Cheryl Payer (1975; 1982).
6. In the burgeoning literature here, it is worth glancing at Elmar Altvater *et al.* (1991), and D. Ghai (1991).
7. Rosa Luxemburg (1968), p. 466.
8. An early, but creditable, attempt to theorize this growing tension is available in Ernest Mandel (1970).
9. See Ricardo Parboni (1981).
10. See Alain Lipietz (1985; 1987), for descriptions of this period. Also, Ernest Mandel, *Ibid.*
11. Three useful, though differing, accounts of the debt crisis may be found in Cheryl Payer, *op. cit.* (1991), Peter Korner *et al.* (1986), and Sue Branford and Bernardo Kucinsky (1988).
12. Named after Charles Ponzi, a con man in the post-World War II era in the United States, and signifying any plan where early investors (in a fraudulent scheme) are paid off by the subscriptions of later investors—until the bubble bursts, that is.
13. For an archetypical, mainstream, approach to the debt crisis, in the smug tones of a wholly a *posteriori* wisdom, see Rudiger Dornbusch (1993).
14. The groundswell of conventional literature, rarely rising above inspired descriptivism, in this area needs be noted. See L. Thurow (1992), also D. Burstein (1991) for popular summations; P. M. Lutzeler (1994, ed.) and H. J. Michelman and P. Soldatos (1994, ed.), for more academic perspectives.
15. Andre Gunder Frank (1967).
16. See Stuart Corbridge (1986) for the 'problem' of capitalism and 'underdevelopment'; a more convincing work in this area is Samir Amin (1990b).
17. Of course, such humiliations, as are to be expected at the hands of the west, might well move it back to a milder version of state socialism a second time.
18. See Alec Nove (1986).
19. A classic, if idealist, posing of such questions, can be found in Rudolf Bahro (1976).
20. See, for an explicit critique, Mao Tsetung (1977).
21. On this theme, see William Hinton (1990).
22. Marx's best efforts here are in the justly famous *Critique of the Gotha Programme* (K. Marx, 1971). Engels, on the other hand, did provide a schematic account of at least the transitional phase, but approximating only what today would be termed simple (but radical) social democracy. See, K. Marx and F. Engels (1964), pp. 67–83, edited by Leo Huberman and Paul Sweezy.
23. For an inspired defense of the idea of socialist planning, but which makes nonsense of much of his earliest orthodoxy, see the brilliant essay by Ernest Mandel (1989).
24. Janos Kornai (1980; 1985).
25. See Paul Baran (1957), and Samir Amin (1990b), for more on these themes.
26. For an update, here, see D. Broad and L. Foster (1992, eds.).
27. An attempt to theorize third world socialisms is to be found in Gordon White *et al.* (1983).
28. See, for instance, Vandana Shiva (1989), C. Mendes (1989), and S. Hecht and A. Cockburn (1989), for a full accounting of such struggles.
29. Surprisingly, in the work of Edward Said (1985), who did so much to expose the charade of 'Orientalism,' this is a derogatory term. We remain, apparently,

Eurocentric even during the very moment of a critique of it. Even the work of Aijaz Ahmad (1992), despite its superb critique of Said's book, remains bound to it on this score, given the author's Marxist orthodoxy.
30. See my short note on the subject in Rajani Kanth (1994), pp. 255–259.
31. J. A. Schumpeter tried to argue, valiantly, that all imperialist impulses were just 'cultural lags' from an earlier, and naughty, feudal, epoch; an astonishingly counterfactual argument given that he personally lived through the times when United Fruit owned and operated most of Central America—of course, it would hardly be credible to credit the United States (the host nation of United Fruit) with some disagreeable, 'precapitalist' mentality expressed in this naked imperialism. See J. A. Schumpeter (1976).

3

A Critique of Political Economy: On Elisions in Materialism

The crisis of the seventies, that marked the dissolution of some of the modalities of the postwar imperialist order, and the inception of tendencies that today are alleged to constitute the so-called 'new world order,' was to become a theme for extensive theorizing in political economy. As remarked earlier, political economy—the very embodiment of a materialist ethos—is the crown jewel of the ideological temper of modernism in all its variants (mainstream or radical); as such, a perusal of its radical wing(s), claiming to offer emancipatory alternatives, is instructive, illustrating, as it does, its fundamental incapacity, indeed impotence, to move beyond the modernist paradigm even at its rejectionist best. If the economic moment is the very heart of modernism, to employ (a materialist) 'economics' itself as an argument of resistance is quite otiose, for trapping the critique on the very terrain, and terms, of what is being criticized. *No counter-'economics' can, thereby, ever shake the foundations of modernism* (as the socialists have learned, after decades of terrible toils), for the kingdom of greed is quite irresistible; the definitive critique of the order that oppresses us all must aim, instead, at the very basis of its warped outlook on life. *The conclusive, all-exhaustive, antithesis of modernism is culture* (in any form; modernism, the empire of greed, has no culture, not even an anticulture, which is why it can fit into Taiwan just as easily as Timbuktu); the revolution, thereby, has to be fundamentally cultural in strategy, scope, and significance.

Modernism is ideologically, and intellectually, critically powerless to respond to a cultural critique; it is radically ignorant of this domain—it has, put flatly, nothing to say in this area. Of course, when at bay, shelving the realm of discourse, the modernist can always turn to the old standbys of arms and artillery, but he has no real arguments to offer (the military response being the hallmark of modernist persuasions). Unfortunately for him, in the long run, guns without arguments fail to fire almost altogether (as with the USSR under Gorbachev); the point could not be clearer—in a true cultural revolution, untainted by materialist demands, modernism collapses swiftly, and silently, of its own innate, bankrupt weightlessness (it is this great truth that Gandhi discovered, in his own valiant struggles). As such, the coming eclipse of modernism is written indelibly in our own spiritual resolution(s) to expunge it.

At any rate, the various schools of critical political economy have little to tender by way of any serious cultural alternatives to the regime of capital—they share far too much of the latter's world-view. Eurocentric and economistic, in the main, such renderings are usually devoted to a delineation of first world 'economic' problems, with only marginal attention paid to the fortunes of the second and third (these being considered only insofar as they impinged on the fortunes of the former). Though the exposition offered here is perhaps somewhat schematic and symptomatic, and the sample roster of schools documented is far from being exhaustive, an accounting of the representative visions that have dominated discourse in this area for the past decade or two is quite useful, if only to understand the many lesions inherent in western radical traditions of political economy. The key object of this discussion is to underscore the inherent weaknesses of a 'materialist,' aggregative analysis that quite often focuses on sets of factors ('variables,' such as 'state,' 'nation,' etc.) no different from conservative economics, except for a vague aura, where at all visible, of partisanship of the underprivileged.

At another remove, analysis of these materialist diagnostics, no matter how rudimentary, confirms the intuition that mere *explanatory* schemes, no matter how rich in content, do not advance the cause of human well-being even a whit. Indeed, the academy-based critical 'observers,' in the modernist frame (aside from being as divided amongst themselves, epistemically speaking, as the ontology they analyze), even at their radical best, exist securely far apart from the real movers and the shakers who remain shrouded in the spiteful anonymity eternally visited upon ordinary people. Even within the general sterility of academic discourse on such matters, it is clear that unless the organic, ontological connections between theory and policy, and economy and society, are firmly grasped, political economy becomes crippled by its own academic, disciplinary, biases surrendering therefore to the very epistemic separatism—the bane of capitalist conceptions of the social order—that serves to conceal the real, explanatory, and causal mechanisms within the totality of capitalist ontology.

The spectacular failure of radical political economy in this sphere, as a case in point, was its complete inability to apprehend either the collapse of socialism, or its implications for the unexpected resurgence, and reinforcement, of capitalist influence worldwide.[1] Traditional Marxists, for instance, could now only stare aghast at each other, in silent surmise, as to why the supposedly 'late' capitalism had just become that much more belated of a sudden, and without warning. However, it is doubtful if, even in that fertile state of intellectual shock, they can still comprehend the salient fact that the grand elisions of materialism are far greater than its many, demotic, half-truths. At any rate, this truly ineffable fiasco of materialist dialectics demands nothing short of a complete restructuration of traditional conceptions of both human motivations and societal change stemming from the capitalist Enlightenment; anything less would be to compound utter defeat with rank capitulation.

THE 'SOCIAL STRUCTURE OF ACCUMULATION' (SSA) VIEW

Popularized by Bowles, Gordon, and Weisskopf,[2] possibly the leading radical economists in the United States, the key to this perspective lies in the self-conscious, if mechanical, linkage of economic to political concerns (agendas) in the sphere of 'advanced capitalism' (i.e., the United States). As such, U.S. economic history is divided into three distinct segments: the pre-Depression era, marked by a weak state, weak working class, and strong business interests; the post-Depression era, marked by strong players on all three fronts; and a post-1966 era of a reshuffle, ending with the re-emergence of pre-Depression-like conditions.

In this schema, 1966 is the marker for a decisive decline in the United States after-tax profit rates (and also of 'Tobin's Q,' a measure of capitalist profit expectations), accounted for, in this analysis, by the growing power of the working class domestically (as represented in the successful insurgencies of minorities, women, nonunioned workers, and so on), the competition from Germany and Japan, and the stresses and strains of U.S. imperialist adventures, notably in Vietnam. Thus, rearguard working-class power explains why U.S. capital was forced to its knees in that period. However, the reaction to it, in the form of the Thatcher-Reagan counteroffensives, is what characterizes the 'new' order. This *Amero-centric* analysis is then backed up by various econometric estimations (such as 'cost of losing your job index,' 'costs of corporate power,' and so on) that are understood by the authors as the clinchers in the argument (almost as if they write with an eye to mainstream economics readership rather than any alternative, heterodox, or popular audience).

The authors of this perspective are so busy with their regression analyses, and so on, that it is quite plausible to assume that they fail to comprehend the implications of their own analysis: that largely well-fed, if dissatisfied, workers caused the productivity slowdown, *thereby blaming workers for what was spectacularly a managerial failure on the part of well-fed, and smug, corporate barons* (who, in just one case—a major sector—automobiles, didn't see the Japanese coming anymore than at Pearl Harbor).

In point of fact, the fairly widely attributed productivity slowdown of the time is not at all as dramatic as usually assumed. Also, given the fact that real wage growth was virtually nil between 1967 and 1980, while unemployment grew at 3.5 percent, the idea of U.S. workers upstaging capital from a position of strength seems quite improbable. Further, their proffered solution of a soulful capitalism, where workers and managers cooperate to share profits and wages, keeping capitalist production (i.e., *alienated* production) high, and its associated tensions and waste low, without any credible discussion of how such regimes are to be secured and defended within the realm of capitalism—aside from the question of how we get from here to there—is simply John Stuart Mill in modern, if econometric, guise (i.e., capitalist production, but with a suitably 'socialist' distribution, aesthetics, and so forth).

To see the growth of 'productivity' as a necessary goal, and 'democracy' as the critical value to achieve it, is, of course, to go no further than rather antiquated liberal wisdom. In this light, the fact that they actually make heavy weather of the idea that accumulation is not just an 'economic' process (hence the somewhat ponderous *Social Structure of Accumulation* (SSA) notion, incorporating state and class relations, nationally and internationally) is to retreat only as far as the world of classical economics (of the nineteenth century) in terms of the *fons et origo* of this putatively freshly minted wisdom. *To retain capitalist social relations and still achieve 'a decent society' is, of course, an old fantasy of social democracy.* The irony is that they have to work that hard just to get as far as that old marker. As radicals, it can be presumed to be their business to go to the root of the matter; but Bowles, *et al.*, either accept, or leave standing, so many parameters of the capitalist state and society, in their ideal system, that they appear unable, or unwilling, to move beyond those markers.

It is true, of course, looking at the matter in larger terms, that proletarian internationalism has proved a spectacularly spurious hope; but to rest content with nationalism (wherein analysis is confined to reviving a putatively ailing United States) as a substitute is hardly to take a step forward. The steadfast *economism* of the SSA stance thus leads only to the harmless, if improbable, utopia of a wisely managed capitalism where the lion and the lamb, predator and prey, capitalist and worker, sit down to feed contentedly from the same trough. However, the primary quest, which is apparently the design of a more efficient production function than the mainstream economists can construct, could hardly have yielded anything more than such beatific, if largely irrelevant, visions.

At another remove, despite the emphasis on the importance of policy and politics in the accumulation game, the tendency herein to view them only as *exogenous* parameters rather than as driving forces lends the analysis little else than a spurious realism, where economic forces still operate autonomously, free from the constraints (and boosters) of political agendas, which are seen only as reactive agents. Imperialism is, thereby, not theorized independently; and the role of the third world within the first is largely relegated to the sidelines. But, as pointed out, in the era of imperialism, the policy agenda and political intrusions, generally, are a decisively active (and inevitably reactive) force, trying their best to impose order on the anarchy of the process of capitalist accumulation.

As such, the SSA analysis loses track of much of the original forest for a lot of tall trees, reproducing the micro-orientations of neoclassicism, in mirror image, quite completely. Indeed, if the overblown notion of the SSA (known to us only *post factum*, of course), were to be replaced by a study of what I have termed the 'Agenda', then the clue to the corporate strategies of a given period/phase is perhaps much more readily ascertained. At any rate, having correctly identified the importance of policy (politics, state, class-struggle, etc.) variables, the authors of the SSA perspective seem to have no systematic theory at all as to how the various subsystems of capitalism might be organically, linked. The failure is entirely a *disciplinary* one (meaning a heuristic error of '*economics*') of reneging on an obviously required understanding of a broader *social theory* of capitalism, over and above the banalities of a technicist 'economics' still wedded to bourgeois conceptions of production and consumption as the keys to the good life.

WORKERS AS DRIVING FORCE

A somewhat related view, largely the handiwork of Harry Cleaver[3] and Peter Bell[4] (in the United States), and a doughty band of (autonomist) Italian Marxists, this analysis envisions workers not as victims, but as masters of their own destiny. Thus workers are, so to speak, preempowered in ideology (if not in practice). In this version, which approximates the Bowles *et al.* analysis, at least as concerns the onset of the crisis for imperialism, it is third worldist revolts (Vietnam, Cuba, etc.), and student-worker minority-women's protests worldwide (including the United States), that made the system virtually ungovernable in terms of rising inflation, a growing productivity crisis, and chronic budgetary deficits. Hence the breakdown of Keynesianism, and the suspension of Bretton Woods agreements between 1971–1973, the third worldist debt crisis (seen as a transfer of values from U.S. workers to Arab sheiks, who funnel it into the vaults of U.S. banks, who then loan it to third world dictators), and the consequent shallows the capitalist world has lived in since the seventies.

Suppose we concede to the argument that it is workers—in a global context, from Solidarity in Poland, to the Vietcong in Vietnam, and student-worker militancy in the United States—that brought the system down as the active precipitant agents; the fact is that the system came down *right upon them* (just as true in the case of Solidarity as of U.S. student/worker/civil rights movements). Today, the U.S. working-class, not to mention its cognates in the third world, is weaker economically, social security wise, and politically, than ever before since the forties. So how this can be anything other than a pyrrhic victory remains to be explained. Otherwise, the analysis amounts to saying only that when the working class wins, periodically, in struggles against capital, it also loses (and much more than what it wins).

Perhaps that is how it is; but it is hardly an occasion for neo-Marxist triumphalism. Thus, the fault line in this mode of theorizing should be clear: any attempt to empower the working class, *à la* Cleaver, needs to go beyond rhetoric and look to reality. History, regrettably, can in essence only be littered with the corpses (such as the ill-fated Allendé) of those who have underestimated the power of capital in the postwar era. It could hardly be otherwise.

Aside from the many radical oversimplifications, the plain empirical facts of the time fail to bear out the calculations of this perspective. By way of example, OPEC surpluses, which are seen as the dominant source of third world loans, represented, at best, only about 20 percent of the total funds invested in Eurodollar markets, and available for disbursement. The productivity slowdown is similarly exaggerated, since the rate of growth of the real net domestic product per worker hour (at least in the United States between 1948 and 1978) showed no signs of a dramatic collapse. Moreover, when it does slow down, it seems more reasonable to attribute it to flagging rates of profit, and the consequent decline in net investment, than to any direct labor activism.

On another, brighter, plane, to couch analyses in the frame of class dynamics in world terms, instead of state-to-state dynamics, as in conventional economic studies, might seem a step in the right direction. However, this posture is ultimately quite specious—since class struggles are primarily operative *within national contexts*. Therefore, such supranational extensions become empirically unwarranted (regardless of how much such scenarios may be desired by old-fashioned working-class internationalists). Try as it may, the Somalian working class is unable to exert pressure on Japanese capital directly. Class struggles, inevitably, come mediated through discrete, national, state entities. Also, at another remove, to obliterate, as at least one of the authors of this view (Cleaver) does, all distinctions between the relative specificities of the first, second, and third worlds, is to seriously distort and dissolve critically real *ontologies* in favor of the radical *epistème* of working-class fervor. In the end, in defiance of existing, and operational, imperatives, the analysis transmutes the three agendas into one overarching one: international capital pitted against international labor.

The *simpliste* nature of this analysis is obvious; and, given the fundamental error of conceptualization, the analysis is quite impotent, at the macro remove, in deciphering the various complementarities, and contradictions, in the political economies of metropolitan capital, erstwhile state socialism, and the third world. At a more disaggregated level, it simply cannot distinguish between, say, a national path (agenda) of capitalist development from a comprador one (vested with economic, social, and political differences that are real, even from a working-class perspective), competing routes that have arguably existed, in all coherence, in the postwar period, in the third world.

Stated succinctly, no more than the working class, capital is far from being a monolith vested with a single, unified, interest and ideology; it is, rather, a cluster of structures, sites, and practices. These various subinterests and quasi-ideologies, moreover, need to be located and understood, in their transformations and internal tensions, *historically*. In analyses which visualize workers as the driving force, class struggle is divorced from any notion of history, in a near-fetishism of relations of production that is the error obverse of the mainstream reification of the forces of production. Finally, any epistemology (radical, Marxian, credentials notwithstanding) that hopes to entirely dissolve ontology, on its own, in all socialist bravado, is simply delusory. Class struggle, in the last analysis, is not an irreducible datum but a contingent one. Besides, workers are not the only human grouping deserving of the boon, and the blessing, of emancipation; indeed, why be niggardly when doling out the largesse of liberation?

NIDL/GOP Perspectives

In this set of largely academic views,[5] compiled from many sources, constituting a fairly dominant stream within contemporary economic *heterodoxy*, it is argued that there is a new international division of labor (NIDL) between North and South, from the seventies onward, involving a shift of critical manufacturing sectors from the first to the third world, committing large scale exports of capital, and requiring the mobilization of novel forms of international finance to fund these flows. Given intraimperial competition for favorable third world sites, there is also a stepping up of fairly intense trade rivalry and competition between the major first world powers.

The ensuing internationalization of economic activity renders national government interventions futile, while also leaving workers in the first world vulnerable to low-wage third world competition. As such, the so-called NICs are seen, paradoxically perhaps, *both as part of the strategy of capital to beat down workers in the first world, and as the new giant-killers posing a threat to first world capital itself*, threatening the safe markets of the older powers.

In the only marginally different Global Organization of Production perspective, there is the additional implication of a growing escalation in the power of the TNCs, but at a severe cost to national sovereignties (and traditional national planning, Keynesian style), alongside a new industrial form of decentralized, fragmented, production processes that can now be farmed out, and scattered willy-nilly, across the globe (hence the acronym GOP, standing for the '*Global* Organization of Production'), depending on the relevant tax/tariff/wage advantages to be gained.

Are these views, shared by so many, tenable? Firstly, as tendencies a long time in the making, some of these attributes of contemporary capitalism were quite in evidence a long time ago; after all, the export of capital was a phenomenon common in Lenin's time, so it is, quite obviously, no great discovery of the present. Given the inevitable resuscitation of Germany and Japan (and Europe generally) after the devastation of World War II, it is only to be expected that intraimperial economic competition would intensify, as it clearly has, say in the arena of trade. It is also true that first world wages and employment will be affected, at least *ab initio*, by the shift to foreign locations of select industries; indeed that is exactly the latent function of capitalist schemes like NAFTA and so on, in continuation of the well-orchestrated Reagan/Thatcher crusade against domestic labor (although any negative employment effects could just as easily be offset by the newer grade of high-tech information/service industries that are taking their place, as, say, in the case of the United States). It is also quite reasonable to assume that finance capital would find ways and means to evade government regulations, given the structurally inherent lack of national limits to its operations.

Fundamentally, therefore, taken together, the NIDL/GOP constructions embody some obviously current truths. However, where they go awry is in implying that these tendencies actually constitute a 'new world order,' or a new stage of world capitalism. Indeed, much of this could just as easily be read as a return to old conditions: either pre-World War II, or even pre-World War I (particularly in the case of the NIC share of world trade and production), or a simple extension of past trends. Nor is it at all reasonable to assume that the combined power of South Korea, Taiwan, Singapore, and Hong Kong is enough to shift existing economic parameters of capitalism dramatically, a scenario much more credible if mainland China were to be included amongst the NICs (however, it is usually not).

Also, while it is true that the Pacific Rim is a major new area of capitalist growth, it is not true that it presently poses any serious challenge (that cannot be met) to the might of the traditional Euro-Amero-Japanese first world. The NICs increased their share of industrial production a piddling 3 percent between the sixties and the eighties, hardly a disequilibrating movement; worse, the tempo of Asian NIC growth slowed down radically in the eighties. Finally, despite modest gains, the third world share at large in the eighties was no higher than it had been in the forties. Far from any deindustrialization of the west, as in many cry-wolf accounts, peripheral capitalism is simply approximating—'catching-up' with—industrial structures in metropolitan centers.

The fact that trade dependence has increased both in intraimperial terms, and within metropolis/satellite chains, is suggestive only of the success of the strategy of integration of the capitalist economies implicit in the Bretton Woods agenda. As far as the Asian NICs go, quite obviously, Hong Kong will soon revert to China; and it is likely that Taiwan will also one day merge with the mainland. That leaves only Singapore, a midget city state, and South Korea (even after an expected reunion with North Korea), perhaps the only serious contender for a new Asian national capitalist miracle on the lines of Japan. Indeed, all this portends not the high drama of pouncing Asian tigers, in a menacing Bruce Lee scenario, as much as the ponderous stirrings, and the slow rise, of a new mega-Leviathan: China.

What is really interesting, but critically missing, in these alarmist perspectives of the New International Order (penned in the unmistakable tones of a dirge on the 'decline of the west') is the emphasis on the following factors. Firstly, we have the all too-real tussle for economic supremacy *amongst* the major powers (in Europe, Germany vs. all others; in general, the EC, the United States, and Japan, in a tri-polar axis of competition, soon to be made messier by the rise of China alongside the NICs of the Pacific Rim), with *Pax Americana* continuing uninterrupted in the military sphere, but subject to much challenge in the areas of trade, finance, and economic weight. Next, there is the general abandonment of traditional welfare statism in favor of a tilt to the Right, strengthened by the defeat of socialist ideology worldwide (hence the dumping of Keynesian ideology, if not always Keynesian practice). It is important to bear in mind that *it is not state intervention per se that is being jettisoned; only state intervention in favor of the 'welfare' of the nonpropertied classes.* And, lastly, there is the clear thrust to establish a world government, via the UN, over a prostrate non-NIC third world, now chafing under the heel of Euro-American imperialism, and subject to the *diktats* of the United States and its Allies (checked only by the possible resistance of Russia and China, in their own interest, to this effort).

One residual issue, an old question, still remains: why does first world capital seek to migrate to peripheral locations as often as it does?[6] The traditional answers come all the way from the period of colonialism: capital seeks low wage, low cost production sites (or at least lower wage/cost profiles), cheap raw materials, etc. But cost of production is not the only concern (when most costs, oligopoly style, may yet be passed onto consumers).

Clearly, after-tax profits are just as important. Hence, the preeminent choices for third world locations would have to be some combination of low wage/cost cum favorable tax/tariff possibilities. Obviously, dictatorships, where labor indiscipline is no concern, is another major draw, assuring both continuity of production and high rates of exploitation. This was why Eastern Europe was so attractive a site for so many U.S. producers who learned, to their delight, that in a socialist economy workers cannot, easily, go on strike (the ironies are, surely, endless). Finally, corporations migrate to play catch-up with their rivals, even if no immediate payoffs are involved.

These are simple considerations, empirically confirmable, and known to any TNC executive worth her salt. But in the divided world of political economy, these issues become grist for the mill of a quite specious partisanship. In these debates, the issue is usually polarized between *either* a low wage *or* a low tax haven, as competing causalities, only one or other issue being assigned the role of the prime lever of direct foreign investment. Why? Because, if low wages are the rationale, then the first world is still 'exploiting' the third (as it always has): this is a 'third-worldist' position unacceptable to Euro-Marxists and (most) western radicals, to whom the triumph of the west is solely a matter of western technical efficiency and the magic of domestic social relations alone.

Thus great pains are taken, in this endeavor, to invent/discover a nonwage rationale for capital migration such that the myth of the self-generation of advanced capitalism may be effectually sustained. This is the unacknowledged (unconscious?), implicit agenda of writers as diverse as David Gordon, Alice Amsden, Robert Brenner, and so on; and this is why such theorists find the Alain Lipietz analysis so repugnant, for Lipietz allows for something like a 'third-worldist' view to be sustained.[7]

Indeed, the savage rejection of dependency theory, the hallmark of Euro-Marxism of the New Left Review variety, is based precisely on this consideration: dependency theory, like Lipietz, allows, however obliquely, for the admission of the ongoing first world pillage of the third (in Lipietz there is a temporary respite, in this process, between World War II and the collapse of Fordism, where first world domestic, and/or intraimperial, economic exchanges are said to outweigh relations with the peripheral third world). Hence the odium bestowed on it for almost a generation. But, as pointed out, this is a vacuous academic debate: reality, minus clever econometric manipulation, encompasses both sets of data. Capital migrates for a host of advantages: to evade first world taxes, to browbeat first world workers, to seize low cost/low wage, low tax/tariff havens, to keep up with the other imperialist rivals on the block, to be near the source of an important raw material, to be near a lucrative market, and so on. Business, unlike radical theory, does not operate in a purist either/or ether; for when there are profits to be made, there is no time for getting the ideology right.

Alongside this issue is another matter of interpretation: is the emergent new international division of labor a continuation of secular trends?; is it part of some long, cyclical, swing of capitalism?;[8] or is it a new transformation altogether? While the interpretive latitude in answering such questions is always quite large, some things can be discounted on methodological grounds alone. The long swing, when applied to world capitalism at large, is but a statistical proposition and, as such, it is of little explanatory significance; rather it *is* the *curiosum* that must be explained. The idea that what is extant today is a radically *new* transformation of international roles, as compared with the postwar period through the sixties, is also quite unsupportable. Indeed the rise of the (primarily Asian) NICs—aside from the collapse of socialism—is the only geopolitical 'transformation' of significance within the domain of capital; and it owes its existence to so many special factors of a political nature that it is correct to say that the Asian NICs were the deliberate creations of policy.

We are, therefore, left with the proposition that, apart from the capitulation of the Socialist bloc, the changes from the sixties to the nineties are far less significant, and far more *evolutionary*, than the changes in the imperial order occasioned by World War II. In the epochal sense, the 'Great Divide' within the world of capital was 1945, after the first cut of 1917; a similar Great Divide attends the collapse of socialism in the nineties. The fact that, since the seventies, we live in a *polycentric* world of capital today, however important to the individual entities concerned, has not altered capitalist modes of functioning radically.

Stated differently, the changes have been more quantitative than qualitative. Possibly, extended quantitative transformation could still trigger a qualitative change—but we are not there yet. *Such a transformation, if at all, can only come from the open capitalist trajectory of the three Asiatic giants: Russia, China, and India. Capitalism in the twenty-first century will be, in terms of sheer economic weight, predominantly Eastern.* Indeed, a current issue of the *Economist*, valuing GDPs at purchasing power parity, puts China and India already within the fold of the five largest economies in the world, ranking third and fifth, respectively. So, the record suggests a prolonged interregnum: the old order is not yet dead; the new, on the cards, is not yet born.

But all this is still at the empyrean, largely irrelevant, level of megaentities; where, one might ask, in these analyses, are ordinary people, the subject-citizens of these great, macro orders? Where the discussion of their quality of life, of their control over their life-chances, of their autonomy, of their rights to self-determination? Regrettably, *the economists have no answers to these questions*; indeed, what is singularly striking is the fact that they are quite incapable, within their rarefied discourse, of even framing such questions.

Global Fordism

Primarily in the work of Lipietz,[9] of the so-called Regulation School, it is argued that the old *Fordist* 'intensive' accumulation path—i.e., wage/demand/consumption-led growth coupled with mass production and *Taylorist* management, the latter aimed at appropriating the 'craft' of labor for capital in exchange for a share in productivity gains—perished in the seventies, 1979 being the marker for what is termed a '180 degree' turn in policy. The residual legacy was to give way, or so it is argued, on the one hand, to a 'Post-Fordism' in the United States and the United Kingdom, characterized by a dismantlement of the welfare state, a shift to profit-led growth, and fragmentation of jobs and the working class through subcontracting, outsourcing, etc. On the other, to an extension of Fordism (the so-called American 'way of life') worldwide, specially in new, favorable locations like the NICs, where they would coexist with continuing, so-called, 'bloody Taylorist' labor discipline. This latter phenomenon is viewed as a new strategy to make up for the deficiencies of the old reliable economic steamroller that ran into the 1971–1973 maelstrom of falling profit rates, rising materials costs, and generalized worker/third worldist indiscipline.

The primary cause of the abandonment of the old model is understood as the sudden and unexpected dysfunctionality of old-style Taylorism, which allowed workers no say in the organization of the labor process, thereby provoking rank-and-file disillusionment, protest, and indiscipline, and, eventually, to productivity decline. To shore up productivity, in the face of this new modality of labor truculence, management invests heavily in costly new technologies which, in classical Marxian fashion, depress the rate of profit and hence accumulation as a whole. At any rate, in consequence, capital now deploys its productive apparati overseas, thereby inventing the NICs as a distinct economic zone, designed to sustain metropolitan profits.

This carries the implication that capitalist world trade grows faster than the domestic markets of metropolitan capital, leaving the old 'national' model of accumulation, sustained by Keynesian policies, behind, and raising new difficulties of maintaining order in international trade and finance. The net consequence, aside from the transnationalization of production, is that the south is now serving the north again, but in a new strategy, where they are *complementary* industrial producers, in some areas, and *competitive* in others, rather than being merely traditional labor and raw material suppliers as in the old epoch of colonialism (by implication, the period of 1945–1970 is seen as an era where metropolitan capital had little use for the third world, at least in economic terms). Of course, this is said to constitute a new international divisional of labor, a 'Post-Fordism,' where peripheral Fordism is the engine of growth tied to a 'primitive Taylorism.'

Clearly, then, the implication is that the impetus to old-style Fordism was the spectre of *underconsumption* (though Lipietz understands it as a crisis of over-production), even as it was the guiding stimulus to Keynesian policies. Whereas, the provocation for the new global/peripheral Fordism is said to be lagging productivity growth, rising costs, and falling profit rates. Put differently, the Great Depression was a crisis of inadequate effective demand, whereas the new morass, from the seventies, is a supply-side crisis of *profitability* (although the OPEC energy price boost did generate a short-lived demand-side crisis as well).

The problem with this analytics is that it is altogether too neat and tidy at one level, and extraordinarily facile on the other. Obviously, one sees a counterpose here between two old bugbears of Marxian political economy: Underconsumptionist theories of crisis, vs. Falling rate of Profit theories (of course, the latter is seen as the politically correct one in orthodoxy). Lipietz, to his credit, offers the suggestion that capitalist crises can be propelled by different stimuli in different periods. But, on the other hand, while the causation issue may have been neatly captured here, two problems still endure. Firstly, the falling rate of profit is not a final cause, as much as a summation of all other causes: as such, it only invites further questioning. Secondly, while causes of crises are easily assignable, their 'solutions' need not be the ones actually taken historically. For example, fascism is just as easily a capitalist cure for prolonged depressions, as for prolonged crises of profitability. The fact that social democracy *à la* Fordism is 'chosen' is a matter of chance, context, contingency, and other residual causation, that need to be analyzed specifically, placed in context, and explained. Where Lipietz is ineffective is in explaining *why* Fordism was the ultimate United States response to the depression: to treat it simply as a *de facto*, common sense, political derivation from internal, domestic causes alone is to renege on more interesting levels of analysis.

There are also other problems of a simpler nature. There is no explanation in the Lipietz account as to why Taylorism, the very remarkable engine of productivity growth in the United States throughout the postwar period, suddenly ran dry in the seventies (or, alternatively, as to why Taylorism succeeded for as long as it did). Indeed, it is by no means certain that productivity collapsed quite as dramatically as routinely made out. In fact, productivity starts to flag in the late seventies well after the rate of profit slumps, and even then still remains ahead of the rate of growth of real wages and unemployment. Further, to tie profit rate declines of the period to 'rank-and-file' worker protest is improbably *simpliste*, aside from blaming the victim unwittingly (this version is indeed far better sketched by Bowles *et al.*), without any reference to a possible managerial failure on the part of a lazy, complacent U.S. corporate-industrial machine, accustomed to a 'soft,' pliant, international environment.

Besides, to view the U.S. slump solely as a 'supply side' crisis, in the light of the growing export competition from Japan and Germany, is again to confound reality with oversimplifications. From the seventies on, the United States was slipping steadily into its later role as a *debtor*, in chronic deficit on its balance of trade, and a net importing nation: between 1970 and 1978, the United States ran up a current account deficit of $30 billion; by 1988 this had reached an astounding $500 billion—equivalent to nearly half of the entire third world debt.

Further, it is also evident that the Asian NICs were a *policy* creation of the cold war, rather than an economic necessity forced by the economic crisis of the seventies. Also, while the 'organic compositions' of industry rise from the late sixties on, on account of new investments in productive capacity, U.S. capital still tried to get by on older *technologies* (as with U.S. Steel, and the auto industry), with disastrous effect, a point insufficiently noted by Lipietz. Finally, a shift to the Right, always a political option in the context of imperialism, does not in and of itself constitute Post-Fordism as a new epoch, the domestic pendulum swing of policy being something less than a brave new *strategy*. Indeed, Lipietz is on much stronger ground in his discussion, *èn passant*, of *Neo-Taylorism* as the new, emergent, industrial mode of the leaders of the capitalist pack.

At any rate, given these deficiencies, Lipietz's analysis, for all its interesting subtleties, survives only as a descriptive account of the history of contemporary capitalism. Of course, the description does seem to mirror ongoing realities efficiently, but it fails, in almost all cases, to explain them, except in terms so panoramic that they blur the lines of argument. Also, to suggest that Global Fordism is a new era of capitalism, in some qualitative sense, is to mistake purely quantitative changes for qualitative ones. The failure here, again, is to grasp real policy agendas, as opposed to topically changing economic events/processes, effectively, within a political vision of the whole.

Finally, to see capitalist accumulation, from 1948 to the late sixties, as a 'golden age,' as Lipietz does, is to show up the extraordinary capitulation to capitalist accounting ideologies, common to the Marxian tradition, of looking at one side of the ledger alone (and incompletely, even at that). To see the era that began with the Korean war and ended with the holocaust in Vietnam, to say nothing about all of the other degradations, social and ecological, as a sort of a Camelot unchained, is surely a gross surrender to the values of capital. Even the innovative Marxian is quite unaware of his blind, near total, participation in the ideology of capital and the dreams of its ruling orders.

At the level of the 'system' (the favored modernist entity), the crisis of the seventies was, quite simply, a crisis of *competitiveness*, located in the domain of international trade; orthodox Marxists find this truth to be quite unpalatable, with their insistence that all major markers in capitalist transition originate in *production*. But, as pointed out, capitalism is crisis prone across all its differential moments of existence. To squeeze this trait into a straitjacket of politically necessary (and 'correct') explanation has been a Marxian vice for over a century, although Lenin was blissfully free of any such determinisms in his analysis (content to make up his own 'theory' when the situation demanded it). The crisis of the seventies was a crisis of *Pax Americana*: it was triggered by a *realization* crisis that precipitated a compression of profits, economic space, and growth, first in the United States, and then, through its desperate reactions (devaluations, etc.), throughout the capitalist world, except in the Pacific basin.

The truth is that, since that time, a new strategy akin to Bretton Woods has neither been formulated nor agreed upon (the Reaganite revolution being only a U.S. driven tactic to restore a lost preeminence) by the major powers, even though it is obviously overdue, given the collapse of the Eastern bloc. The reason for this is as much the intraimperialist rivalry between the United Kingdom, United States, Germany, and Japan, as it is the uncertainty that they collectively face *vis-à-vis* the indeterminate policy thrusts of Russia and China, the new giants in the economic power game. As such, it is developing realities in these last mentioned nations that will display whether or not such a unified strategy will, finally, emerge early in the twenty-first century. Bretton Woods may be dead, though not its inspiration; and its replacement is not yet in sight. We are certainly on the threshold of a dangerous new epoch; but we are not there yet.

However, whether we go from here to there, or there to here, the lives of the subalterns, upon whose backs the 'system' rests, remain fundamentally unaltered, regardless of how capitals, states, and 'nations' reorganize and rearrange their largely irrelevant balances. The world order of the underprivileged, the dispossessed, and the downtrodden, the world over, has not appreciably changed since the advent of the modernist assault on their autonomies; and when it has, it has been simply to compound this tendency, and/or multiply it n-fold. It is their aspirations, rarely 'articulated' by the contemptuous elites of modernism, that will constitute the critical subject matter of the imminent history of the coming millenium, the latter being inevitably the product of their redoubtable determinations. Suffering and suppression, the grim lot of the nonmodernist, have a way of steeling the iron resolve of resistance.

A FEMINIST VIEW: THE MIES ARGUMENT

A highly original, if overly imaginative, German feminist, Maria Mies[10] has argued that there is a new drive to accumulation, a new International Division of Labor (IDL), so to speak, designed by the OECD, that is solidly built upon the backs of women. The new capitalist plan, according to Mies, is to export labor-cost intensive production to the colonies to exploit cheap labor, alongside the modernization of cash crop agriculture in the periphery, so as to produce luxury consumption goods (such as orchids, for instance) for the first world. Seeking workers ready to accept the lowest wage rates, then, is to automatically discover young women as the optimal labor force. The argument is that, as against the heroic male proletarian as the star of accumulation, as in traditional political economy—paid a full wage, and armed with benefits, unionization, and pension plans—capital has now discovered women as the ideal workers: nonunionized, meek, submissive, docile, working almost gratis—much as they do at home as nursing mothers, caring sisters, loving wives, etc. And, as such, they can be paid wages far below their 'value,' and subjected to harsh labor discipline, while meekly turning out quality products given their inherent productivity, devotion to duty, and so on.

This leads Mies to conclude that the new production sites in the third world are all *gynocentered*, i.e., female selective, in their choice of labor force: the third world being, in effect, genderized as the zone of female producers. In contrast, the flip side of the story, first world women are being beaten back into the household, forced to resume their customary role as 'breeders,' interrupted only by the short-lived feminist movement of yesteryear, short-circuited as it was by armed right-to-lifers (the scabs of the feminist movement, akin to the workers enfranchised by the so-called 'right-to-work' clauses in many U.S. states that were to offset union strength on the labor front). While third world women are the new (oppressed) producers, first world women are now the super consumers, with ugly male capital living off both species of women: the 'good', and the 'bad'—in various ways.

While it is quite effective in pointing out the gender imbalance in labor force composition in many industries in the NICs (such as textiles, electronics, etc.), the argument, like many of Mies's arguments, is a dire exaggeration. The fact that there is no role, in this NIDL, for men, either as consumers or producers, is simply astonishing. Clearly, feminist passions can be as much blinding as they can be eye-opening in political economy. Similarly, the glaring deficiency in the Mies 'model' is the absence of any explanation as to why the old IDL suddenly went off the rails in the seventies. Obviously, the general thesis of sinister, patriarchical, strategies is incapable of being stretched to accommodate that particular watershed.

On the other hand, in noting the fact that women under patriarchy are the model workers (all work, no pay, as with housework) capital would love to see emulated at large, Mies has drawn attention to an otherwise neglected dimension of current modes of capitalist labor mobilization. That workers in the first world are increasingly asked to raise productivity without corresponding wage increases, security of employment, or enhancement of benefits, only underscores the power of the Mies metaphor of housework as representing and epitomizing the new industrial model. Moreover, what feminist scholarship, like Mies's, has demonstrated is the myth of the subsistence wage (seen as a truism since the age of classical economics), by showing that male workers have always relied upon *unpaid* female housework in all the tasks associated with the reproduction of the labor force (and the family).

This important strength aside, the crucial error in Mies's formulation is in seeing gender as a sort of a mechanical, knee-jerk, replacement for both class and race, the very mirror image obverse of orthodox Marxism which dissolved, in reverse error, gender, and race in class. Obviously, merely standing patriarchy on its head is not equivalent to furthering adequate analysis; gender is only a complementary ontology to other modes of social differentiation and oppression—it simply cannot erase them altogether. Stated flatly, the grim truth is that human suffering is not solely reducible to the (manifold) agonies of women; in a modernist frame it is, almost, now, a *universal* condition.

THE DELINKING PROBLEMATIC

Amin,[11] in another version of a 'world systems' perspective (based on a critical distinction between the dominant 'center' and the dependent 'periphery'), argues that the crises of the seventies were the consequence of the slow working out of the (malfunctioning) 'law of value,' on an international scale, being overall, fundamentally, a realization crisis that expresses itself in a fall in the rate of profit. The deficiency of demand is now expressed as the deficiency of demand in the *periphery*, owing to the prevailing condition of *super-exploitation* of third world workers. Given this situation, the remedy (evocative of Keynesian solutions to the depression) can only be a massive redistribution of values to the south. Of course, this does not happen, and the crisis persists, posing a threat to international capitalist stability and, *en passant*, to U.S. hegemony within it.

Samir Amin has possibly struggled harder than any Marxist to shake off the naive Eurocentrism common to Marxist analyses. As such, his work has been roundly denounced by Euro-Marxists as being 'third worldist' (and, therefore, shot through with contradictions). Be that as it may, Amin, like Andre Gunder Frank, has incorporated the 'center-periphery' dichotomy as the critical distinction serving to categorize contemporary (and historical) capitalism. Capitalism is herein seen as inherently polarizing, both between center and periphery, and within the periphery itself; as such, Marx's 'law' of the immiseration of the proletariat is now seen as validated in the international domain (though not applicable, anymore, within the confines of metropolitan capitalism).

The huge productivity lead of the 'centers,' built up at a time when wages were held down (as during the industrial revolution) helped establish, via lower absolute costs, the basis for international specialization that is the root cause of *unequal development* (akin to the Marx-Lenin notion of 'uneven development'). Subsequently, the center permitted, or accommodated, a gradual wage increase, but not at the cost of productivity, such that high productivity continued despite the high wages. In the periphery, forcibly channeled as it was into resource based export promotion, the situation was one of similarly high productivity, but with a much lower wage rate. As such, the stage is now set for the operation of the mechanisms of 'Unequal Exchange' as per Emmanuel's[12] formulations; because labor power is immobile, but capital and goods are not, the necessity for an equalization of the profit rate (*à la* Volume One analysis) implies a requisite transfer of values from periphery to the center.

At any rate, the agenda of metropolitan capitalism in the imperialist epoch becomes, simply, the supersession of a 'revolt of the periphery'; as such, the modalities of peripheral resistance imply that the agenda of the periphery, at best, could be some form of *'delinking,'* or a severance from the logic of imperialist accumulation. In this account, it is easy to see the Bolshevik and Maoist revolutions as classic cases of the 'revolt of the periphery' against the depredations of the center. Of course, the delinking strategy can follow either of two paths: a national capitalist effort to delink, within a capitalist framework, as opposed to a socialist attempt to break away from the capitalist world system altogether.

The problem with Amin's analysis is the residual *economism* that still denigrates *Agendas* in favor of worldwide operations of the 'law of value' (this latter may well, arguably, constrain the former, but it cannot, in orthodox Marxian style, subsume it to the point of swallowing it completely). Given that such *Volume 1 analyses are quite inapplicable* in a world of monopolies, superpowers, markup/transfer pricing, and administered trade generally, the analysis can only be, at best, an intellectual curiousum. *Indeed, 'economics,' mainstream or Marxian, under the guise of 'model' building, has taken the route of argument, not by empirical evidence, but by a priori assumption* (an old tactic of thereby 'proving' anything you want, inaugurated by Thomas Robert Malthus and Ricardo).

Assume 'perfect competition,' as with neoclassical economics, and of course capitalism maximizes welfare quite innocently, while also producing the laissez-faire rabbit out of the deductive hat! Similarly, Marxians make Volume One 'assumptions' (just as unreal as the assumptions of pure competition), and Marxian *value theory* (almost) works out quite well (stretching a point or two, empirically and logically). This kind of fudging, using a bag of 'immunizing stratagems,' as the philosopher Lakatos[13] calls them, will not do:

economics is an empirical science, not a deductive one, and if the 'assumptions' are fantastically unreal, then the 'deductions' can fare no better.[14]

At any rate, much of Amin's analysis is highly questionable. Firstly, and most importantly, to view 'delinking' neither in class terms, nor in popular autonomist terms, is to link it to an inexorable '*étatism,*' which can only serve capitalist, or nominally socialist, ruling classes, having little to do with the aspirations of the common working people in either domain (the idea of '*delinking' is a highly meritorious one, but only if applied far more generally than Amin does; stated simply, we need to delink from the modernist world altogether, at any, and all, of the variegated levels of social life*). Secondly, while the debt crisis certainly showed up the acute paucity of resources in the third world, it appeared more as a consequence of the 'crisis' in the first world, than as a *stimulative* cause. Thirdly, the system—as a whole—took the debt crisis in its stride, without crumbling, with first world and third world ratepayers picking up the tab, eventually, on behalf of capital. Finally, *it is by no means certain that the major share of capitalist world trade is accounted for by third world demand, given the volume of intraimperialist trade, not to mention the vast domains of local demand extant within the domestic borders of the first world*. As such, it is truly hard to conceive of the present crisis in the first world as precipitated by a 'realization' crisis originating with the periphery.

Be that as it may, the imperial doldrums since the seventies are not merely a crisis of insufficient demand, but a vicious combination of the several crises of production, realization, and accumulation (each reacting upon the other), and all within a context of increased intercapitalist competition. In the simplest possible terms, the 'systemic' crisis (as opposed to the far more important crisis of the common [wo]man) is a crisis of *Pax Americana*, with the hegemonic leader finding, in the late sixties, the return to international economic parities as they preexisted World War II, a threat to its artificially contrived dominance. As A. G. Frank[15] has correctly pointed out, the crisis of the seventies was one of *international competitiveness*, which was itself linked to differential productivities (linked to differential advances in technique). And, seeing its relative economic position deteriorate, the United States called off the game that had guaranteed it quite supernal success for some twenty years.

Bretton Woods was, after all, a U.S.-dominated gambit from its inception; when its trusty, rusty mechanisms turned suddenly dysfunctional to its economic interests, the United States canceled its obligations unilaterally (much like it shunned the U.N. in the seventies when faced with negative votes), showing, neither for the first, nor perhaps for the last, time its real proclivities as a preeminently scofflaw nation, always ready to impose rules on others, but rarely willing to allow itself to be so governed (as in its insouciant disregard of more than one World Court ruling, to say nothing of its brutish trampling of the sovereignty of smaller, weaker nations).

Naturally, given this apostasy, the fellow imperialists had to follow suit, and opt out as well. This set the stage for the continuing uncertainties that were to prove such a major deterrent to U.S. business investments, in the seventies and eighties, but that are slowly easing up in the nineties (particularly with the careful engineering of protected markets like NAFTA, a twentieth century Monroe Doctrine, so to speak, none too subtly crafted to resist the EC and the Japanese). However, until Russia and China define their imperial ambitions clearly, a state of normalcy in world capitalism—business as usual—simply cannot be reached. Even at the best of times, capitalism is plagued with uncertainties as to investment activity; but in times like the past decade, it comes close to exhibiting a near paralysis of will.

Ernest Mandel: Marxist Orthodoxy

Possibly the most prolific Marxian political economist, other than Amin, has been (the late) Ernest Mandel, in the classical Marxian sense of combining rigorous theory with an active political *praxis*. Over the years, his self-imposed, Trotskyite blinders had gradually, and largely, been shed, though in favor of an equally dubious Kondratief style 'long-wave' orientation (the long wave in question is said to have originated in 1940 for the United States, and 1948 for Europe and Japan) that provides grand, suprahistorical, explanations for what are essentially conjunctural events.

At any rate, Mandel[16] treats the seventies crisis as a 'classic' *overproduction* crisis, combined with a 'reversal' of the long wave between 1974–1978 (the Kondratief upswing having died out in the late sixties). The long postwar boom is said to have triggered the 'third technological revolution' in the history of capitalism, thereby provoking an accentuation of the concentration of capital at the same time that workers grew strong (economically and politically) given near to full employment conditions. Accordingly, the rise in the organic composition could not be offset by raising rates of surplus value, thereby depressing the average rate of profit in conjunction with an erosion of technological profits—producing the stagflation of 1970–1971 and the 'slump-flation' of 1974–1975 (seen as the first generalized recession since World War II)—as the system tried desperately to offset the profit slump with rising nominal (markup) revenues, and inflating credit, without thought for the morrow. Indeed, the postwar period is said to be marked by this new phenomenon of nationally controlled 'credit cycles,' quasi-independent from the industrial cycles (but compensating for them).

Astonishingly, transhistorical forces (Kondratief waves) and parastructural economic laws (rising organic compositions) suffice, in Mandel, to account for all the dilemmas of the seventies. As such, the rise of trade competitiveness (Japan and Germany, Europe and the NICs, etc.), such an idelibly marked feature of the time, is seen as not at all (fundamentally) relevant to the crisis, but, if at all, as a resultant of it. All is left to the naked play of productivist 'economic forces' alone, as described in the several volumes of *Capital*: very little is granted to policy, politics, imperialism, and agendas. The practical implication, for the rational reader, can hardly be other than setting a stopwatch, and marking time, for the next Kondratief wave, like some avid surfer of the seas, to sail on to the next predestined incline in economic affairs, a fatalism that seems to both gainsay, and sustain, the original Marxian inspiration. Mandel,[17] provides perhaps the classic, if extreme, example of Marxian style economic reductionism, heroically aggregating entire economies into one big, analytical, lump of 'organic composition' putty, which is then the basis for generalizations about rates of profit internationally. His analytics is only a tribute to the reification of categories, the well traversed bane of orthodox, Marxian political economy; easy to see how the high modernist, be it even in the Marxian guise, is the willing prisoner of grand, totalizing abstractions that sweep the world much like an ill wind that blows nobody any good. Marxism, as a masculinist super science, has always spoken, with suave self-assurance, in the distal, recondite, high patois of the very elect.

THEORY AND POLICY

As noted in the foregoing, in almost all conventional, but heterodox, accounts of the capitalist world crisis, the inherent conceptual errors are mainly due to the insufficient appreciation of the distinction/overlap between economics, politics, and social factors. Even Marxist political economy, in self-perception the heroic antidote to vulgar economics, has devolved, now, into being an academically aseptic radical 'economics' on the lines of the highly heuristic (and hence abstract) Volume One analysis in *Capital*,[18] with all its attendant weaknesses, reproducing, as in a mirror image, the equally abstract renderings of neoclassicism.

It is curious that even varieties of political economy that explicitly recognize the inherent, immanent links between economics and politics (read wealth and power) in the sphere of capitalism (such as Marxism, for instance) nonetheless remain imprisoned within the fenced off academic divisions of disciplinary autarchies to the everlasting detriment of realist analysis. This is particularly characteristic of radical and Euro-Marxist academics who are defined by the discipline first ('economist,' 'political theorist', and so on) and then a particular bent within it ('Marxist,' 'radical,' 'institutionalist,' etc.) afterwards. They cannot, of course, have it both ways: either social life is the 'totality' they assert, or it isn't. Interestingly, the fragmented separatisms of the capitalist world-view, designed to subvert a unified comprehension of the whole (not just in the social sciences: the atomism carries over into other sciences as well to the point where the physician of the toenail is unqualified to understand the physiognomy of the toe) triumph ultimately even over 'radical' challengers to the extent that the latter succumbs to its organizational principles.

At any rate, of all modes of production, perhaps only capitalism—but in its unselfconscious phase—at the level of its totality, is capable of being analyzed in 'theoretical' terms. This is because, quite unlike, say, feudalism or socialism, where the economy is (more) directly controlled by identifiable agents, in a spontaneously driven capitalist economy the system works impersonally, behind our backs, so to speak, so that random economic forces lead the system up and down, willy-nilly, as classes, and individual agents, scramble to unravel the 'mystery' behind it all. However, in the current phase of conscious self-regulation (however ineffective this might be), where many of the operative variables (rate of interest, rate of markup, and so on) are planned, and/or instituted administratively, abstract theory is better shelved in favor of direct apprehension of far simpler, but more concrete, qualitative, *policy* options taken by easily identifiable, institutional agents (corporations, state agencies, etc.). In effect, contemporary capitalism functions, 'visibly,' much more like the more transparent, and 'political,' modes of production of yore.[19]

It is this set of *explicit policy tools* that amounts to what I have termed the *Agenda* (of the system). The emphasis now shifts away from mechanical forces to be guessed at, or 'modeled,' in favor of organic interventions on the part of the state, and other agencies of corporate capital, that may be directly (or indirectly) *observed. Stated differently, policy now becomes more important than theory.* It is true, of course, that intentions are one thing and outcomes are quite another; but no longer is it possible to study the latter without reference to the former, in the guise of studying 'real' economic factors alone. In the language of critical realism, subjectively inspired interventions in the capitalist economy are as ontologically important as the impersonally secured laws of supply and demand, which may now be manipulated to secure desired ends (in varying degrees of efficacy).

In the age of the IMF, the OECD, and 'managed' trade, generally, to see markets as the final allocators (as in many Marxian models, as well) is, quite simply, to court absurdity in results, revealing only the *naivete* of the economics profession, and its rather humdrum middle-class point of view, there being far more to the *organon* of capitalism than dreamed of in its pedestrian philosophy. In the age of imperialism, capitalism is quite overdetermined, both *politically* and *ideologically*.

Capitals (of the smaller kind) may still take their investment decisions individually (Michal Kalecki, in another era, was fond of saying that capitalists don't invest as a class; but, today, they do strive to guarantee a *desired investment climate*, as a class, both domestically, and overseas), and nonstrategically. However, in the case of the TNCs this is patent nonsense, given their extremely close coordination with their governments and with each other to stay on track of strategic variables and to bring them under control, by means of concerted action, wherever possible. The fact that capitals compete against one another, internally and externally, is not a sufficient condition to believe that they act as petty neoclassical maximizers, with blinders on, and with no weights to throw upon markets, governments, and policies. In the case of the United States, where even the presidency is merely the office of the prime henchman, and tout, for corporate capital, the idea of a radical divide between governing class and capital is perhaps just outright liberal-Marxian fantasy.

Of course, the United States, unlike most European states, has a unique history insofar as the state, from the beginning, was the naked creation of capital. In Europe, the state preexisted capital and had to be, across centuries of class struggles, brought under control. Indeed, in the case of Germany and Japan, wartime devastation of institutions, and their reconstruction under U.S. auspices, enabled them to be rid of many, if not all, precapitalist throwbacks, both ideologically and institutionally, leaving only a grim resolve to dedicate all efforts to capital accumulation, much on the lines of the United States. Dame Thatcher, of course, tried something similar in England, but it was a case of too little, too late.

All this makes of the Marxian notion of the 'relative autonomy' of the state—written, unconsciously, with European states in mind—a joke in the case of the United States, though being slightly more probable, within limits, in context of European formations. In general, it's a good idea to study such matters *historically, i.e., contextually, and not 'structurally,'* as per some inexorable theoretical dicta; the latter are, always, in some manner or other, idealist flights of fancy. At any rate, be these as they may, the era of imperialism is, decisively, one of politics in command.

In the argument advanced in this book, from an emancipatory perspective, transformations at the level of the 'economy' and the 'state,' planned by enlightened revolutionaries (at the level of an intellectual 'capture' of the whole), no matter how 'progressively inspired,' will always remain either coopted, or cooptable, by ruling strata (old or new). As such, ordinary people, living everyday lives, have little to gain in any such dizzy initiatives taken at the 'top.' People do not, indeed cannot, live at the moment of 'state' and 'nation' (though they are routinely ruled and robbed at those points of enforced collections); these are only the duly fenced off poaching bounds set by various, rival classes of oppressors. *The political economy (much like organized science itse-lf) that chooses to concentrate its energies at that level of distance from the common weal of ordinary peoples is, in the ultimate analysis, as irrelevant and futile (reflecting extant ontological schisms quite faithfully), not to mention self-serving, as the system itself.* Theorizing oppression, or resistance to it, may be a very diverting parlor room pastime; but it cannot reduce its real, ontic weight even one whit. In human society, oppressions are *felt*, and then acted upon by largely untutored people, the theorist always arriving (like Lenin during the Great Russian Revolution) fashionably, and safely, *late*—to record the commotion, and, if at all possible, to 'take charge' of it. All modernist, professional revolutionaries have brought up, ingloriously, only the *rear* of actual revolutions, while the people have pressed on, willy-nilly, spearheading the momentum of the process, driven only by their passions (for better or for worse). The elitist modernist intelligentsia, blissfully unself-conscious of its own colossal impotence, is still largely unaware that liberty, freedom, and self-determination are not academic issues where the ponderously learned hand down *obiter dicta* to the quiescently illiterate: it is entirely driven by the quality of personal initiatives taken by ordinary people acting in their own best perception of (self) interest. They may not care to *study* political economy; but they do dare to author and make it every day.

Scientific knowledge—rarely clear, coherent, or consistent—is *not* a precondition, necessary or sufficient, for initiatives whose mainsprings stem from other, far more robust, and fecund, founts of social energy. Emancipation is not a 'scientific,' but a moral, spiritual, and 'political' process (to turn it into a routinized regime/recipe of activities, much like its obverse embodied in the run of conservative institutes devoted to the 'study' of counterrevolution, is another great conceit of modernism). As such, political economy (mainstream or radical) is splendidly irrelevant to the common aspiration, and the gathering movement, for a generalized emancipation from the bonds of modernist constraints. As the great Diogenes is reported to have said to the all-conquering Alexander, when regally asked what favor he might desire of him, so we too can say unto the high priests of organized Science: 'Stand out of my sunshine!'

NOTES

1. It is cold comfort to say that capitalist ideologues were similarly stymied by circumstances; after all, radicals and Marxists have always claimed to know more, and better.
2. See Samuel Bowles *et al.* (1981; 1987).
3. The roots of this approach go back to Harry Cleaver (1979); see also Cleaver (1989).

A Critique of Political Economy

4. Peter Bell has moved away from the original Cleaver framework to a more inclusive agenda of ecofeminism. See P. Bell (1992).
5. For the NIDL model, see F. Frobel et al. (1980); for the GOP approach, see B. Bluestone and B. Harrison (1982). For more, on both, see Alain Lipietz, *op. cit.* (1987); also M. J. Piore and C. F. Sabel (1984). For an econometric disclaimer of these claims, see D. Gordon (1985).
6. See Roger Owen and Bob Sutcliffe, *op. cit.* (1972), for the most complete discussion of the economic imperatives of imperialism.
7. For a taste of this, see Alice Amsden (1990) where the periphery's importance for the center, past and present, is dismissed offhand.
8. For expressions of faith in these long swings, and analyses based upon them, see David Gordon, *op. cit.* (1985), and Ernest Mandel (1980).
9. Alain Lipietz, *op. cit.* (1983; 1987 and 1992), for additional analysis of post-Fordism see M. Rustin (1989).
10. Maria Mies, *op. cit.* (1986).
11. Samir Amin, *op. cit.* (1990a; 1990b).
12. A. Emmanuel (1972).
13. See I. Lakatos (1978).
14. For more on this critical issue of methodology, see R. Kanth (1991); also (1992), pp. 161–163.
15. Andre Gunder Frank (1984), p. 233.
16. Ernest Mandel (1978).
17. For a brilliant rendering of the Mandel position, but minus the Kondratief infusion, see Anwar Shaikh (1984).
18. For acknowledgment of the tension between Volume One of *Capital* and historical materialism, see Samir Amin (1977), p. 250; and (1990a), pp. 112–116.
19. Unlike many variants of post-Keynesian theory, that still retain a Kaleckian penchant for empirical 'realism,' neoclassical theory, quite anachronistically, still plays with abstract theoretical models of the economy, as though all the key variables were 'unknowns' in some abstruse maximization problem. To this extent, pure neoclassicism is an obsolete paradigm of 'rational choice,' in a real world of *integrated economic policy* between the state and large scale, quasi-monopolistic, economic agents.

4

Capitalism and Socialism: The Twin Faces of Janus

The Case Against Capitalism

The recent, near total, victory of the capitalist mode of production—in the Great Modernist wars of this century—might lead one to believe that the resistance to it that has long existed, in some shape and form since 1917, first with the USSR and then with many third world movements, was simply mistaken, misinformed, and/or misconceived. There is, in fact, little warrant for such a belief; in history, material success is no guarantee of virtue (otherwise, the Nazis would have been 'right' had they, and not others, won World War II). The strengths of capitalism, such as they are, were as perfectly apparent to Karl Marx as they were to John Stuart Mill, in the mid-nineteenth century; as such, they hardly merited the banal, and tendentious, reiteration by the Thatcher-Reagan squads of latter-day ideologues. Its insensitivities, elisions, and inherent cruelties survive on, and indeed are grown to greater proportions in our own time (though apparently unnoticed by the same Reaganite privateers). In truth, the classic *Communist Manifesto*, circa 1848, provides a balance sheet of pluses and minuses that, with few changes (e.g., a *severe deflation* of some of the alleged pluses!), one could still apply today, quite effectively, to the capitalist world. The problem with Marxism, yesterday as today, is not that it is inaccurate in its critique of capitalism, but that it is inadequate, for being only a *partial critique*, and for sharing far too many of the assumptions of the modernist, bourgeois world-view that it supposedly rejects.

It would, therefore, be quite trite to repeat the hoary arguments against capitalism, were it not for the fact that it still confidently presents itself as the best of all possible worlds. Indeed, if survival itself constitutes all-total merit in some social Darwinist sense, it is truly the most meritorious system around, for the simple reason that it is ready, willing, and apparently able to vanquish all other alternatives to it, without the slightest scruple. As such, it is the most predacious of all known modes of production, not merely ready to live out the laws of the jungle, but to own, operate, and make profit off the forest as well. In a nutshell, capitalism is arguably the most alienated and alienating (the next chapter offers a more complete definition of alienation) mode of production (and social formation) conceivable, because it *naturalizes*, unlike any other known mode, the ordinary, everyday, sociohuman interactions of production, exchange, and distribution. Small wonder that bourgeois economics presents economic laws as equivalent, in kind, to 'laws of nature' (among other things, this stems from a quite incurable 'physics envy' that the profession has always suffered from, little palliated even with the wholly gratuitous institution of a Nobel memorial prize in the subject), thereby reducing the human subjects involved in the economic life to the status of mere reactive, subatomic frequencies. In production, capital exercises dictatorship over workers; in society, it cajoles them into assuming the role of passive, mindless, consumers; in politics it renders them impotent; in culture, it renders them denuded and bereft of all but the simplest of creations (the Lincoln Center was neither designed by or for the *sans-cullotte*; indeed, therein lies the significant appropriation of 'culture,' by capital, unto itself).

Worse, it divides the propertyless into as many fissures as it can discover, across gender, race, ethnicity, and so on. Along with the degradation of the human subject that is their concomitant, the profit-motive and the cash-nexus both create, and perpetuate, the grimly selfish hells that constitute privatized, everyday life in 'advanced' capitalist societies, defining their stark deformities, their advancing pathologies, and their growing normlessness. The abiding structural violence that maintains the status quo breaks, every now and then, into real violence: at one end of the scale represented by the senselessness of a serial killer; at another, by the frequent preparations for all-out, jingoistic, imperialist wars. In short, a regime based on violence against workers, violence against women, and violence against nature, can only turn into a generalized violence toward all forms of life not ready to cooperate with the demand of capital to subsist solely by (and on) exchange value alone. But enough; for those who wish to see and feel for themselves, one has only to walk the newly liberated streets of Eastern Europe, lately broke with Stalinism, to see stark capitalist perversity in all its uncensored squalor—and *they* have only just begun (in fact, having visited recently, I can confidently say that Budapest will soon make Vegas seem like Sweden). Indeed, the worst thing that can be said against capitalism is that, more often than not, it almost makes Stalinism—but for the grace of Stalin—seem the preferable option.

In short, capitalism now, as in the past, rests on exploitation, violence, and rank amorality, not an iota of which can be cancelled off against its vulgar productivity gains. In fact, if material values were to be attached to these phenomena on *both sides of the ledger*, it soon appears that capitalist production has always rendered a more than equivalent, wantonly prodigal, destruction of values, both social and natural, in its drive to appropriate social wealth. As such, the GNP is not a measure of *goods*, but indeed a severely inadequate, grossly distorted, measure of the *bads* produced, only capitalist accounting sleights of hand suggesting that the net gain is a plus. One look at typical metropolitan United States, with its virtually unbreathable air, undrinkable water, inedible food, and unlivable cities, and one gets to measure exactly how far, and how deep, this destructive potential of capitalism has gone—all but unnoticed. As Marx foresaw a century ago, the expansion of commodity production, and its consequent market dependency, involves a diminution of life, a shrinkage of social space, and a despoliation of nature. It is a measure of the *Alice in Wonderland* epistemology we share in the economics profession that such a steady, inexorable, and quite desperate regression into self-destruction is seen, quite uniformly (sadly enough, by orthodox Marxians as well) as the inevitable by-product, if not actually the sure sign of, *progress*.

The crises of capitalism, which Marx peerlessly understood and explored, are with us now just as they were in his time. Other than monetary and financial crises, which undergird them all, in the broadest possible terms, these crises are: firstly, the crisis of *production* (i.e., getting workers to work), involving, historically, the forcible creation of the working class from peasant, tribal, and traditional societies, at a price and a pace acceptable to capital (technology determines only *potential* productivity; actual productivity is up to worker cooperation with technology). Secondly, the crisis of realization (i.e., being able to sell commodities at prices that yield an acceptable rate of profit); and, finally, the crisis of *accumulation*[1] (i.e., being able to reinvest surplus value, again and again, at profitable terms). Each crisis is renewed over and over, in Sysiphian rhythms, as the system lurches from moment to moment, pitting class against class, nation against nation, corporate entity against corporate entity, in a never ending wave of varied quantities, and qualities, of violence. Typically, looking at only the technical side of this destructive process, conservatives like J. A. Schumpeter,[2] in true economistic fashion, ignoring the all too real costs in favor of the alleged benefits, could wax eloquent as to the waves of innovation yet fashioned out of the débris of past achievements. But, as we should all know, capitalism unleashes far worse havoc than the putative 'gales of creative destruction': imperialist wars, counterrevolutions, and the lowest impulses of pillage and rapine humanly conceivable—in the economy first, but spreading, like a pox, as if by osmosis, to other societal institutions as well. Unless checked, the sum total of this spiral process can only be some form of military rule, fascism, and/or wholesale destruction of the very possibility of civilization.

This understanding of crisis as normal to the everyday functioning of capitalist society is slightly different, in emphasis, from the genre of putatively Marxian 'crisis' theories, where crisis is defined loosely as 'a widespread economic collapse', or as a major contraction of production, as understood also in traditional mainstream usage.[3] In standard Marxian analysis, for instance, such 'crises' are described as stemming from 'Underconsumption' (when the capacity to produce outstrips the capacity and/or willingness to consume), or 'Disproportionality' (when there are serious sectoral imbalances between Dept. I and Dept. II, that is capital goods, and consumer goods, respectively), and/or from the falling rate of profit due to a rising level of 'mechanization' (when the technical composition of capital, driven by the 'competition of capitals' to enhance productivity, rises).[4] However, this way of looking at things forces attention more on the various *manifestations* of what I am terming *crisis-as-usual*, than the underlying *forces* that cause these crises, and, in general, it is always better to concentrate on the *generative mechanisms* that produce phenomena than on the (resultant) phenomena themselves. In my rendering, capitalism is a system in *permanent crisis* (in social relations of production, not just in technicist terms), as capital chases its own tail in an endless chain of a *posteriori* corrections. In a larger sense, as explained in Chapter 4, it *is* the crisis in human relations, for having regressively inverted some fundamental propensities of social existence.

THE CASE AGAINST SOCIALISM

If good intentions were enough, the Soviet Union should have turned out to be a worker's paradise instead of the dull, dreary, stodgy prison that it actually was for the millions who couldn't shop at the GUM (department store), or have access to hard currency, a government car—or a chauffeur, for that matter. At the heart of its spectacular failure is a Marxian notion whose reductionism is still mind-boggling: that guaranteed goulash was both a necessary and sufficient condition for happiness. Inmates in U.S. penitentiaries usually eat better (at least, in *quantitative* measure) than most of the poor in this world, without pretending to be enjoying it. That liberty was a fair trade for security was the unstated assumption of Soviet rulers, and they were, quite simply, wrong. (Wo)man does not live by bread alone; nor indeed, by dread alone, either. It is in this extraordinary *economism*, in this stupefying materialism, that built worker's homes like rabbit hutches, that offered them jobs much like cattle are worked, that gave them political choices like Henry Ford and his Model T ('You can get any color you want, so long as it is black'), that the everlasting failure of socialism surely lies.

To strip people of control over their lives, of the freedom to choose (including the freedom to *reject* socialism), is to turn them into abject prisoners.[5] That, in effect, was what the Soviet Union turned into: a giant prison camp/workhouse whose monotony was overshadowed only by its ineffable grimness. As such, the many local gulags were surely redundant; the entire society functioned as a gulag. Indeed, this would be unendurable even if there were no failures in production and distribution, no graft and corruption, no police state. Liberty, not the dole, is the true basis of conviviality— this, the great lesson to be learned from the Soviet experiment; and all socialisms, to date, have turned their backs on this simple truth—to their great detriment. *No group of men and women, however bright and well-meaning (and powerful), has the right to inflict its vision of the just society on others.* But this is precisely what 'actually-existing' socialisms were built upon; when the peasantry in Russia opposed socialism, they were rolled over, by means both legal and extra-legal (being denied even the 'bourgeois' privilege of universal suffrage). When sailors in Kronstadt revolted against Bolshevik dictatorship, they were outgunned. When liberals, or just decent people generally, protested such excesses, they were silenced.

Sometimes, this issue is posed (particularly amongst the Left) as though it were simply a matter of 'democracy'; more democracy would imply more or better socialism, and so on. But this, too, rests on a misapprehension: democracy, as conventionally understood, *ipso facto*, allows for the possibility of despotism by the majority—in the worst case, 51 percent can decide for the 49 percent remaining. Clearly, this is absurd, as noted by many generations of critics of bourgeois notions of democracy. A prison is a prison whether run by 51 percent or one percent of the populace; the point could not be simpler or clearer—a gulag, is a gulag, is a gulag. Votes and electoral procedures do not, indeed cannot, change its content. Pushing through regimentation or autocracy, with majority sanction, does not make it any less autocratic or pernicious. As such, the issue was never merely one of democracy, as the capitalist roaders would like to pose it in the manner of Yeltsin, bringing to mind that the ancient saw democracy being the 'paradise that unscrupulous financiers dream of' (but amended to include unscrupulous politicians as well). The overwhelming rejection of socialism by average people in the eastern bloc was not over the dearth of 'democracy,' caring no more for politics than their counterparts in the west, but over something far simpler: *liberty*. Democracy pertains only to formal voting procedure; liberty has to do with something much more fundamentally human. Trite as this may sound, people wish to be free (as Chomsky has often suggested, the impulse of freedom is *innate*) of external, and invidious, controls and constraints, even when such constraints, arguably, are in their favor. Freedom, of course, is nothing other than the possibility of making autonomous choices. Even Marx's original vision of a communist utopia did not embody the notion of 'democracy'—majority rule can hardly be taken to be utopian—but pertained to be an *anarchist* prospect where the state ceases to exist as a means of coercion for either a majority or a minority.

The principle at stake, buried in a century of capitalist and socialist propaganda, is an old one: it's called *self-determination*. In greater or lesser degree, every socialist, and hence every *étatiste* regime, has abridged this fundamental right of human societies, as a matter of course. At least in capitalist societies, the delusion of freedom restrains the average citizen from open revolt against the system (if not from rioting, randomly, against fellow citizens!); in socialism, however, there was not even the soporific illusion of freedom. Surely, no greater case against socialism is even conceivable! Indeed, the critique of Marxism can now be made explicit: while correct, but incomplete, in its diagnostics of capitalism, it has proved totally impotent as a guide to a credible alternative to it (for its crass materialist *reductionism*, on par with bourgeois modes of thought); and ill specified, or under specified, utopias can obviously turn into indefectible recipes for disaster.

Stated succinctly, it was not a simple set of economic errors ('imperfect planning,' e.g.), or equally facile political blunders ('lack of democracy'), that forced the widespread disenchantment with socialism (something that was in evidence aeons before its actual demise). Rather, that the project was, all along, fundamentally misconceived, *resting on the grotesque misapprehension that happiness, welfare, and contentment, in a human society, are the simple reflexes/correlates of increased social productivity*. In this reification of the capitalist paradigm of work (meaning alienated labor), socialism turned a worthy ideal into a sorry mess of pottage; therein, its near-fatal reductionism and materialism; therein, its dire Eurocentrism, and its deadly reliance on the bourgeois Enlightenment view of 'progress.' It is this constricting mind-set that now needs to be expunged from the annals of socialist thought, much as the indescribably horrific crimes of Stalinism.

The road to hell, it is said, is paved with good intentions; it is tempting, accordingly, to exculpate the Bolshevik pioneers on the grounds of the sheer scale of moral and physical energies invested in at least trying to build a better world. But, upon serious consideration, even such a posthumous pardon seems unwarranted, given the burden of misery inflicted upon millions upon millions of human beings who were the (however unintended) helpless victims of their ferocious zealotry. It is not just that an 'experiment' failed; it is that generations of irreplaceable, innocent, lives were destroyed in its wake. Indeed, socialism failed, quite spectacularly, on almost all serious scores; it failed to reconcile the 'contradiction' between individual self-interest and the general interest; it failed to eliminate alienated labor and commodity production; it failed to level differences between town and country;

it failed to reduce the domain of an oppressive state; it failed to prevent the re-emergence of a ruling stratum effectively divorced, in its life-chances, from the real producers; it failed to lift its citizenry out from the realm of necessity into that nether realm of freedom; it failed to pacify existence, and to annul scarcity; and, finally, in all-crowning indignity, it simply failed to survive.[6]

THE MATTER OF COMPARISON

Naturally, in comparing the relative efficacies of capitalism and socialism, it is not these considerations that have occupied the attentions of the economists (mainstream or Marxian). Instead, the debates are usually ranged over per capita incomes, rates of economic growth, and tons of physical output, as though these were the sole criteria employable—and as if the average citizen, east or west, were to take heart and rejoice simply by virtue of the fact that his or her 'system' produced more megatons of coal than the other. Such abstractions, dear to the economist, are of relevance only to military planners and masters of the polity, with their own axes to grind. For all others, such dubious characterizations of *human welfare* (with which any real economics ought to be concerned) have revealed only the nature of the long, socialist, traverse over patently false terrain.

Not only is this false terrain, it is treacherous as well, since all accounting systems are ideologically laden, both self-consciously and unconsciously. In the former category of dissembling, the World Bank recently shocked a predictably gullible world by suggesting that its decades of data on mainland China were simply false; suddenly, the Chinese economy—now that they're in the IMF, and playing ball in earnest!—hitherto always dismissed as a bumbling third world entity, was the third, maybe even the second, largest in the world . . . and growing. Just as interesting—even amusing—is the fact that, at the height of Reaganite shenanigans, East Germany unexpectedly overtook the per capita GDP of Britain and Italy, to obvious capitalist chagrin: for years afterward, there was suddenly no reportage on the GDR anymore in the World Development Report. Another colossal error in estimation was the systematic overvaluation of the Soviet economic potential, for years, by a self-serving U.S. Government anxious to appropriate larger and larger 'defense' budgets. Suddenly, after the collapse of the USSR, the latter is now seen for what it is—a rag-poor nation, only a whit above a moderately successful Less Developed Country (LDC). Put simply, numbers, in the public domain, are misleading, and aggregations are treacherous; it would of course be best (or at least more correct, from a human standpoint) that the truths of economics were approached, instead, *qualitatively*. At least, then, the analytics would be self-consciously normative, and the capacity for deliberate, or accidental, mathematical fraud, accordingly, would be more or less negligible. Indeed, all economic accounting systems, such as the Keynesian national income accounts, rest upon some theory of the economy, and as such they are shot through with as many holes as implicit in the original theorizing. It is quite astonishing, therefore, to see the extent to which even supposedly radical thinkers have taken over Keynesian accounts wholesale, without the mildest critical scrutiny.[7] Economics is a *paradigmatic* science, and its 'truths,' such as they are, do not survive across paradigms.

Even were there to be no political skew to things, and no estimating errors, accidental or systemic, there is still a much larger paradigmatic issue that simply cannot be evaded: capitalist calculations, based on market criteria—*'exchange values'*—are simply powerless to estimate real values—*'use values'*—of noncapitalist modes of production and social organization. As such, all of western accounting (as in the World Bank's Annual Tables) of those third world economies with a substantial peasant/tribal economy are gross, horrific, distortions of reality (this applies to socialist economies, also, with their large sectors of nonprice allocations). Failing to spot domains of marketable commodities, entire habitats of native opulence, supporting millions for millenia, have been dismissed as rag-poor locales, desperately in need of elevation to market dependency. Indeed *real poverty* (as opposed to *relative poverty*) in the third world begins precisely when capital turns over such healthy, subsistence-oriented, communities into market-allocated, commodity-producing, wastelands. Real 'economic' welfare is always an issue of the balance between needs and resources—and there is virtually no tribal/peasant mode where, in the long run (unless subject to the whims of nature, or the more systemic capitalist/socialist style of marauding), this balance is seriously askew.

Indeed, given that in all the regimes of both capitalism and socialism, (contrived) 'needs' seem to always run desperately ahead of real resources, it is these simpler modes of social existence that have always been the original affluent societies. Of course, to speak to such issues as 'economic' welfare in the case of such organic entities, whose value system still binds material values in the lineament of nonmaterial ones, is to commit category error in the first instance, revealing our own 'advanced' inadequacies. In the process of stamping upon them our seal of exchange value, not only do we thus *epistemically* devalue simpler societies, we *ontologically* destroy their subsistence economies as well. A river, a forest, a mountainside that supports entire ecosystems, including human habitation, has no economic 'value' until the river is 'productively' dammed, the trees are 'productively' felled, and the mountainside is 'productively' strip-mined—such that a dead river, a dying forest, and a razed mountain, together with all living creatures dependent on these resources, are now faced with extinction—an extinction quite 'valuable,' of course, for someone other than themselves (profiteers, privateers, state functionaries, etc.). So it is that our *culture of death*, one which values nothing that may not be destroyed, prevails over the more pristine modalities of simple social life. It is a tribute to the human faculty of self-delusion that such execrably ruinous industrial economies could have been held up, for so long, as the very apex, the final pinnacle, of human *productive* achievement.

In general, comparisons, or perhaps contrasts, of the quantitative kind are only marginally interesting for the light they shed on individual 'performances' in either world (socialism or capitalism), being fundamentally powerless to answer any really important questions. This is because one does not ordinarily 'choose' between capitalism or socialism on the grounds of data sheets, of either promise or performance, over chosen common grounds. Individuals, it is true (given the possibility of defections), are free to choose, within limits; but societies do not have 'choices': they only have a *history*, that is both enabling and constraining. And traditions, given by history and culture, are not usually scaleable onto a metric of comparison. The only meaningful comparisons, to determine whether something, or someone, is better or worse off, are *within* a given society over a period of time, and according to their own expectations. And these always involve matters of personal judgment—not objective, recorded fact. As such, *no abstract comparison between socialism and capitalism is sustainable as an argument for either system*. And in this regard, the usual employment, by western economists, of per capita GDP, as though that measure represented per capita access, or per capita entitlements—simultaneously—in making invidious comparisons with the Socialist bloc, is an index only of their own rabid ignorance and prejudice. A less sterile exercise might be to judge a system against its own official ideology ('worker's paradise,' 'liberty and freedom,' etc.). Clearly, in such a reckoning, neither capitalism nor socialism live up, even remotely, to their dissembling promises. At least in some instances, this is perhaps just as well.

THE ROOTS OF THE MALAISE

The ills of both capitalism and socialism, regardless of who triumphed and who lost on a material scale, may be traced back to their joint provenance, philosophically, in the dialectic of the European 'Enlightenment.' Too often, the Left sees this period simply as the site of bourgeois conceptions of state and society; and just as often does it neglect to reflect on exactly how much of Marxism is infected with similar notions. Indeed, while political history has effectively seen to the ideological divarication of the work of Adam Smith from that of Karl Marx,[8] it is highly instructive to understand the shared, modernist, vision of history that linked Marx securely to his 'class-enemies' in the Scottish Enlightenment. Whether in the 'stages of history' idea, whether in the relationship between state and civil society, or whether in the coupling of progress with material advancement, Smith and Marx shared a confident historical materialism, with its inevitable correlates of both determinism and reductionism.

In Smith's case, the problem lay in his acceptance of the prevailing bourgeois notion (as with Mandeville's *Fable of the Bees*) that a definable good may yet come out of commonly accepted evil (even worse was the corollary that good intentions always result in bad consequences), one of the most powerful ideas shaping both European and American institutions. This blatant self-justification of the capitalists' role in society was taken on lightly by Smith, suggesting that selfishness is the mainspring of economic growth, and therefore, a next step in the devolution of thought, to be acquiesced to. The logic of this bourgeois conception could not be clearer: asocial behavior, when *productive*, can, and should, be condoned.

Here was the first step in that fateful reductionist logic which would 'condone' anything that promoted the accumulation of capital, since material values were the prerequisites, the *sine qua non*, of happiness. Good comes out of evil, and even more good comes of accumulation; indeed accumulation is good, in and of itself—regardless of the costs, social, ecological, etc., of this reckless drive to produce, consume, and appropriate.

Marx changed the parameters only slightly. Material production, and consumption, are still the critical yardsticks, even in the 'socialist' régime. Indeed, Marxian reductionism often argued as if the expansion of wealth were the necessary prerequisite for the expansion of freedoms, higher values, and so on (obviously converting European history into a logical, hence 'necessary,' sequence). Thus, the good society (communism) would have to rest on a sound (meaning growing), wealthy, economy. The linearity is unmistakable: we are getting better all the time. The arrow of social history flies in one direction—in the direction of *progress*, as measured by production. On these grounds, capitalism was to be worshipped, by an entire Marxian tradition, as a *necessary* step to socialism (although Marx himself, true to character, was never quite a Marxian, and had increasing doubts in his later years, as made clear in his advice to Russian Marxists to bypass the capitalist 'stage,' if possible).[9] Why necessary? Because among other things, capitalism expands the productive forces necessary to build socialism (one, apparently, takes the route of purgatory before entering heaven). So the qualitatively superior society, socialism, required a material underpinning to make it work. Here, in a nutshell, is the entire roster of rather dubious notions: *reductionism, linearity,* and *progress*—bearing close kindred to bourgeois perceptions of the same.

The costs of this material advancement, whether ecological, societal and/or cultural, were all deemed affordable, if only implicitly. India could be bled by capitalist England, in the name of progress, because Indians, after all, were the lowlives who worshipped Sabbala, the cow, and Hanumana, the monkey[10]—instead of commerce and credit, as with the canny Englishman. It was all simply part of the (unconscious) English mission to occasion a social revolution in India (thereby moving its inhabitants closer to the Great Redemption of socialism; in retrospect it would seem quite providential, then, that India escaped such an exciting fate). It is worth noting the *anthropocentrism* that Marx shared, as part of his Judeo-Christian ancestry, in his barb aimed at the Pantheism of the Hindu,[11] who sees objects of adoration and worship in all of creation, instead of viewing 'man,' as Marx did, 'as the sovereign of all creation' (to use his own words). This domineering attitude towards other species and ecosystems, peaked in the *Baconian*, i.e., *classical bourgeois*, 'scientific' posture of triumphalist despoliation that was to have such devastating consequences for the planet, as capitalism (and later, socialism) ran amok, wreaking immeasurable havoc on the fragile balances of nature.[12] In current times, the machismo expressed in Robert Solow's speech, in process of accepting his Nobel prize for bourgeois economics, without awareness of any irony, arguing that 'we' (the super species!) can do without 'nature' (natural resources), is symptomatic of that very orientation.

If this was the legacy of Smith and Marx, the fate of the world at the hands of their epigones can be readily imagined. The hallmarks of both capitalism and socialism in the twentieth century have been the ruthless destruction of cultures, peoples, and ecologies, willy-nilly, in the name of material advancement. This fetishism of productive forces, this forced creation of market dependence, this wanton destruction of autonomy, self-provisioning and self-care, is what has united Marxists, however unexpectedly, with their nominal class enemies. As such, Marxists have been quite as much a part of the very problem that they accuse capitalists of being, and rarely more convincing than the latter in their own dictatorial, authoritarian, centralist, elitist blend of policies and practices; indeed, being quite conjoined with the latter in their contempt for the ordinary mass of humanity. After all, as Lenin had eloquently put it, decades ago, the enlightened Marxist credo was, in the unmistakable title of one of his pamphlets: *"better fewer, but better"!* Few corporate capitalists, past or present, surely, would care to disagree.

At any rate, the malaise of the modern world, its deep-rooted disenchantment, is deeper and darker than any reshuffle of power structures, or rearrangements of relations of production, could possibly hope to cure. European ideologies, serving elite governing orders, have exploited the almost helpless craving for redemption, on the part of ordinary people, by promising grossly distended material heavens on earth (unlike religions that usually offered it, wisely, in the hereafter) and demanding superhuman sacrifices in return, while taking care to ensure that dreams of too radical a schemata of change would always be perceived as impossibly 'utopian.' As such, popular yearnings for emancipation have always been abused to buttress the power and privilege of cynical ruling classes, with the mass of the innocents serving only as cannon fodder in 'larger' political games staged well beyond their comprehension. Today, as modernism rages victorious, that age of credulous innocence is almost at an end; the so-called 'arc of instability,' that old bugaboo of conservatives, that conceptually marks today only a given geopolitical arena of traditionalist opposition to it, will one day invincibly encircle this planet, transcending existing geopolitical poles, quite completely.

NOTES

1. There is also the more general 'political' crisis of 'legitimation' of the entire process that is concurrent with all these crises. On this subject, see Claus Offe (1985).
2. J. A. Schumpeter (1942).
3. See, for example, A. Shaikh (1978).
4. The most readable presentation of issues here is still Paul Sweezy (1942).
5. Oddly enough, Rudolf Bahro (1978), true to his orthodox Marxism (later to give way to Greenism, and still later, to a form of born-again Christianism) of the time, does not, in his otherwise stirring critique of Stalinist societies, stress *liberty* as an issue.
6. For a prosaic account, by an insider, of the economic and political problems of socialist societies, see W. Brus (1973). For a fiery, Marxian fundamentalist denunciation of such societies, see R. Bahro (1978, *op. cit.*). For a perspective on how the Western Left received the short-lived Gorbachev era of reform, see M. Kaldor *et al.*, (1989); and for more of the same, but with extra hindsight, see M. Kaldor (1991).
7. For an attempt to construct an alternative Marxian accounts, see A. Shaikh and E. Tonak (1994).
8. A non-Eurocentric history of economic thought has not yet been written; but it would, once accomplished, show up the shared philosophical orientations of all of classical political economy. The case of Marx is also an illustration of the proposition that, too often, the passionate critic succumbs to the force of what is being criticized, however unconsciously. We need a new political economy, freed of the debris of the European Enlightenment.
9. See T. Shanin (1983), for some elaboration.
10. Marx's great (and often anthologized) diatribe against the imperfections of Indian/Hindu village society/ideology may be found in K. Marx and F. Engels (1972), pp. 40–41.
11. For a discussion of Marx *vis-à-vis* 'Orientalism,' see Bryan Turner (1978).
12. See Vandana Shiva (1989), Chap. 2, for the specifics on the nature of Baconian science.

5

AGAINST EUROCENTRISM: BREAKING WITH THE ENLIGHTENMENT

It is, of course, a simple historical fact that the European Enlightenment was the philosophical provenance of the great emancipatory projects of capitalism and socialism that have been the dubious gifts, if not the very bane, of the epoch of modernism. As such, it is quite instructive to recall the intellectual underpinnings of that critical watershed in European history,[1] that was to divide so many from so much in the checkered chronicle of human evolution. Briefly, the three ideational colonnades, on which the entire edifice of the Enlightenment rested, were (a) a triumphalist science, tied to (b) a progressivist ideology, both firmly undergirded by (c) the metaphysics of materialism. So common were these interlocked systems of ideas, to the models both of socialism and capitalism, that it would be fair to argue that both Adam Smith and Karl Marx, despite their many differences, were in implicit agreement over these fundamentals: the sanctity of science, the actuality of progress, and the inescapability of materialism.[2]

SCIENCE AS TRIUMPHALISM

The principal features of the new science[3] spawned by the Enlightenment are easy enough to note, being major currents, as well, in the mainstream of contemporary science today. The emergent scientific tradition, as epitomized perhaps in the legacy of Bacon,[4] was preeminently *Reductionist* in at least three important ways. Firstly, it reduced, by fiat, the 'knowers,' by confining the latter to a narrow, self-anointed, caste of 'experts' who alone could hold office, pronounce judgments, exercise authority, and so forth, thereby instituting a *corporatist exclusivism* to the rites, rituals, and practices of science (in fact, the real tragedy of the corporatization of science is that the common genius of ordinary human, lived *experience* [the original fount of all 'science'] has been thwarted, circumvented, and devalued in favor of the modus of esoteric, enclave production of *experiments* by an anointed, elite cadre of specialists in remote laboratories, sacralized only by distance, jargon, power, and privilege. The deliberate insulation of science and scientists in a hermetically sealed sphere of hallowed authority stands testimony to the elitist confiscation of the means of knowledge now expropriated, for their own ends, by the masters of the polity. Despite the fanfare, the glitz, and the gluttonous consumption of public funds, the fundamental contributions of Organized science hardly measure up to the momentous revolutionary discoveries of humankind such as the wheel, agriculture, and the reproduction of fire at will, the contribution of the very primitives that modern science despises in all contemptuous arrogance). We might term this, quite simply, its *Elitist tendency*. Secondly, it reduced the domain of scientific knowledge by eliminating and/or suppressing alternate, and rival, ways of knowing, i.e., by dismissing competing wisdoms (drawn from other cultures, e.g., or from ancient traditions) as 'nonscience,' thereby being imperiously subjugationist in relation to all other forms of social knowledge.[5] Perhaps we could call this its *Subjugationist tendency*. Thirdly, in its analytics, it reduced all things, as far as possible, to single components forgetting that the whole is greater than the parts, and thereby instituting the symptomatic tunnel vision, the partial perspectives, and the unwarranted divisions between closely allied subjects typical to the organization of science to this day. This might be called its *Atomistic tendency*, divisive and separatist in its essence, and customarily identified with Descartes, but fairly characteristic of the entire scientific movement of the time. The organic holism, or the 'totality', of society was, thereby, being segmented into so many mechanical parts—as a heuristic initially, and a useful ideology of disconnectedness later.

Alongside this radical Reductionism went what might be termed the *Mechanistic tendency*, where the machine model, testifying to the general fascination with that ubiquitous tool of the fledgling industrial age, was uncritically applied to all things, to nature and society, whether in Cartesian models of the mind (viewed as a sort of spectral machine), or in Lockean views of the alleged social 'contract.' Easy then, for social science to become the necessary adjunct to endlessly improvised social engineering!

These Mechanistic perceptions of the universe were coupled with the omnipresence of extraordinarily *simpliste, Linear* views of time (history), in nature and society, quite often accompanied by teleologies of necessary progression.[6] Smith and Marx's (and Hegel's) stages of history and society, and other such escalator models of social evolution, are a good example drawn from the social sciences; and, of course, that time's arrow flies in one direction only is a conviction of most mainstream western physics as opposed to more cyclical views connected with the idea of the *regenerative circularity* of time[7] extant in both non-European[8] and precapitalist modes of thinking. The vulgar notion that things are 'getting better all the time' is but one example of this progressivist imagery, subtly enshrining linear thinking as a useful ideological reflex in the popular consciousness. Given its application exclusively to the European context, whose history was 'hot' (as opposed to the 'barbarians,' whose history was not), the notion also comfortably carried the implication that the European, inevitably mounted on this rising escalator of destiny, was foredoomed to be the savior of the world.

In line with these novel conceptions was the peculiarly illiberal form of radical dualisms that, increasingly as a scientific tendency, marked the course and content of analyses. The real world, social and natural, was to be broken up into binary bits, and the bits paired off into sets of *Antinomial Dichotomies*, that have, arguably, done astonishing damage both in the stunting of popular perceptions of the universe, and in the stultification of the ensuing practices based upon such spurious divides.[9] Whether in Levi-Strauss's nature-culture divide, or in Cartesian mind-body dualisms, and individual-society partitions, or in everyone's male-female and orient-occident separations, the world was rudely split into clusters of irreconcilable oppositions, apparently carrying with them the implicit policy imperative that one side of the dyad had only to subjugate and triumph over the other to 'overcome' these vexatious oppositions: mind over body, culture over nature, men over women, occident over the orient, and so on. The intolerance of the European bourgeois, ready to refashion the world in his image, in effect, was to receive a self-sanctifying, 'scientific' blessing in such perverse analytics. Of course, the concrete, Hobbesian, near-nihilistic adversarialism of capitalist ontology was to be mirrored faithfully in the pitiless, critical scrutiny of this '*scientific*' posture soon to become generalized into the omnipresent, life-negating, everyday hostility of mass society with mutual distrust the only affective bonding between fellow human beings.

Behind—and in spite of—these quite unprecedented practices lay a posture of supreme confidence in the putative objectivity of the scientific enterprise. Not only had the real world, social and natural, been reduced to atomistic objects, inert and passive in the main, but the consequent objectivication of the universe was, *post factum*, seen as a validating complement to this pose of detached scientific objectivity. Related to this fetishism, and reification, of what might be called the new religion of *Objectivism*, was the parallel arrogance of *Absolutism*, where science presumptuously laid claim to ineluctable truths assumed to be both timelessly and universally applicable. The self-assured *Universalism* of European science had its provenance in this absolutist, self-congratulatory, conviction of infallibility. Thus Piaget, in a later era, could speak easily of invariant stages of cognitive development among children without any presentiment of the very limited milieu within which he ran his experiments; similarly, the great Freud could dignify the ailments of a decaying Austro-Hungarian empire into universal, timeless, neuroses of the human psyche. So Economics could claim, in *a priori* terms, the 'propensity to truck and barter' (as with Adam Smith), not to mention the antisocial, hedonistic individualism it presupposed, to be one of those universal, axiomatic, and self-evident truths that it had discovered through what Ricardo had once termed 'inspired introspection.'

European science was, in all careless bravado, casually legislating for the entire world, the non-European majority of which it knew, and cared, next to nothing about. The undeclared enemy of this supreme arrogance was of course, the simple, effective, indisputable (if silent) antithesis of *Relativism* which was always anathema to European science, then as much as now. Relativism, quite simply, could offer no facile pretext for conquest and domination.[10] Worse, it humbled the high pretensions of science (and scientists) quite decisively by suggesting, in all ingenuousness, that even canonical pronouncements aiming at transhistorical transcendence might just be a parochial reflex of time, place, and context (as follows from the notion of 'epistemic relativism'). For the modernist predators, aching to rationalize their dismal conquests as morally justified, this casual legitimation of other traditions, besides themselves, as epistemic equals, could only be wholly intolerable.

The arrogance of Absolutism, and the assurance of Objectivism, were to undergird the many resultant European versions of *Determinism*—another major attribute of the science of the time—in both nature and society, where mechanical laws were deemed to govern timelessly in a closed universe.[11] Thus we have Marx with his 'laws of motion' of society, and the many attempts, as with Auguste Comte and Saint Simon, to achieve a rigorous, Newtonian, finish to what were, after all, only social speculations of rather limited scope. Capitalist policy makers, for instance, have similarly proved themselves, time and again, no less rigid economic determinists than socialists, expecting nonmaterial consequences to flow quite naturally from materialist imperatives (capitalism as a secure basis for 'democracy,' and so on). And in Physics, even Einstein, despite his brilliantly nontraditional discoveries, had some trouble accepting the idea that 'God' in fact does play 'dice.' The high, anthropocentric, mind-set of infallible science could brook no affronts to its specious dignity.

Finally, the dominant scientific school was necessarily *Positivistic*,[12] in its approach to questions both of epistemology and ontology, with its concomitant protocols of a radical separation of subject and object, the privileging of the perceiver as a passive, yet accurate, sensor; the reification of empirical information to the status of final 'facts,' and the total lack of appreciation for what might be termed the *ontological depth* of reality. A cold, flat, monist, stationary, homogeneous universe, that could be molded at will, was always central to its scientific prejudices. Looking upon social facts as 'things,' it forgot that this could be true only in a universe where *things* themselves, as Sartre once argued, had suddenly ascended to the high status of being the preeminent social facts.[13]

Taken together, then, it is clear that *European science was merely an ideology that specialized in concealing its own ideology*—virile, misanthropic, mysoginist, determinist, intolerant and subjugationist, in the main. In plain truth, of course, it was only an epistemology with no special claim to any necessary cognitive superiority: it prevailed over other forms of thought (e.g., religion) only because it had state power solidly under its belt, and/or for cunningly rigging the game in its own favor. Indeed, if the organic bond of medievalism was the symbiosis between Church and State, the new, post-enlightenment power equation was to be the life-sustaining embrace between Science and the State, each battening off the other's status and power. Finally, contrary to its avowed 'positive' pretensions, this new science was never an impartial recorder and observer of a given reality; it was, rather, an active, indeed partisan, agent of transformation (as with, say Ricardian 'science' and the Corn Laws, in England,[14] in the past, and the notorious Chicago 'boys' in our own time) in favor of the various topical parries and thrusts of the ruling corporatism. Indeed, this was true as much for science under capitalism, as for science under the auspices of the now defunct Soviet state. Once petrified into an establishment, cushioned by the somnolence of wealth and power, science fell easy prey to all the grim susceptibilities of social corruption.

Materialism: The Spirit of the Age

The Enlightenment inaugurated the *Age of Capital*, and with it the worship of the technical arts, like no other epoch before it. Capital accumulation was to become the very *sine qua non* of state policy, if not quite the *summum bonum* itself. The materialist totalitarianism involved in this view of the public good, and the revolution it implied against traditional approaches to the subject, was quite breathtaking; all societies in human history have produced and consumed without reifying productionism and consumptionism as veritable ideals. Indeed, previously, even in Europe's own 'prehistory,' productivity had been but a minor branch of ethics (like economic affairs, and pricing policies, generally). Now, a distributive ethic was both derived from, and based upon, the narrowest technicist, and individualist, understanding of productivity, to be enshrined as a utilitarian decision-making rule in public policy to the everlasting defeasance of the older, more 'primitive,' notion that all subjects and citizens had a right to existence independent of any assumption of a given level, or quality of, productive effort. The domination of the (new) economic moment, in the new epoch, much as religion and politics had dominated medieval discourse, was to become quite total. Even today, the fact that, of all the social sciences, economics alone is blessed with a Nobel (Memorial) prize is a striking index of the value placed by modernism on the material sphere. This despite the fact that the scientific rigor, not to mention the real informational content, of a purely deductive 'science' like economics is, by any standard, much weaker than, say, the putatively 'soft,' but empirically far more solid, discipline of anthropology. 'Economics' is quite simply the codified, canonical, and representative ideology of the Age of Capital; hence the gratuitous bounty of all its special dispensations.

Reversing centuries of explicitly *contra* thinking, the new age of materialism announced blithely, as with Smith[15] (building on Mandeville's *Fable of the Bees*, published in 1714), that private vices, more often than not, led to public virtues, carrying the corollary that good, i.e., moral, intentions (such as, say, a 'utopian' drive for equity and justice) inescapably had 'bad' social consequences. In effect, self-interest was now enshrined as the ruling human passion, itself conceived in the narrowest possible 'material' terms; thus human behavior, 'at best,' could only be reliably, perhaps even unalterably venal, since altruistic inclinations seemed to lead only to predictable ruin. Even at the abstract level of face value, the ancient Christian ethic (which had, in a bygone era, at least juridically, constricted various forms of antisocial commercial activity, such as Usury, etc.) of generous, compassionate behavior towards fellow beings was now being derided as not just irrelevant in an incorrigibly wicked world, but indeed as positively baneful.

No statement could be clearer as to the new protocol of outright banishment of ethics from social life (simultaneously with the expungement of qualitative indicators of human welfare in favor of the new preference for quantitative measures), which was another 'great' contribution of the Enlightenment to the fabrication of the social order of modernism. To concentrate on practical outcomes is the quintessentially modernist, materialist 'realpolitik' approach of looking solely to the 'ends' effected, in any course of action, rather than the nature of the intentions or means employed. However, to be civilized is to precisely evaluate on the basis of the quality of intentionality and the morality of the means chosen; practical success, much like the preoccupation with 'efficiency,' is a wholly modernist criterion—good intentions and moral means, on the other hand, are the indefeasible expectations of a regime of civility. It is not the getting there; but *how* we get there that is of interest and significance.

Of course, the ruling materialism,[16] expressed archetypically in the drive for endless profits, had to be imposed on a world far from obviously receptive to such criteria. As such, the necessary institutional transformations required the employment of a robust inventory of selective, calculated, violence against various, resistant, social forces. This was directed, firstly, against the peasantry, and subsistence economies generally, so as to usher these reluctant, lumbering, entities into the seamless web of market relations and to render them simultaneously both a market for finished products and the provenance of a propertyless workforce, a process that took its classic form in England from the sixteenth century on with the Enclosure movement (a good portion of classical political economy, the instrumental 'science' of capital, was devoted to *rationalizing* these unedifying policy imperatives).

Secondly, there was violence directed against Nature itself, taking many disparate forms, but perhaps most persistently in the recognizable form of the *technological fetishism* that is still the hallmark of capitalist ideology today, which celebrates machinery as the very embodiment of the heroic 'conquest'—not the pacific harnessing—of nature (and the coeval high ascendance of 'man' as the master of creation). Closely allied to this anile celebration of anthropic 'mastery' was the ubiquitous violence against all nonhuman species, in the arrogant *anthropocentrism* that established (white) 'man' as the lord of the universe, epitomized, and best understood, in the barbaric 'trophy' killing of wild animals (just as much as 'savage' peoples) as 'sport' by conquering Europeans in Africa and elsewhere, still preserved for us, in all their unspeakable ugliness, in the photographic chronicles of the period. The world was, quite simply, being conceived of as the white man's burden, even if the truth, increasingly, lay perhaps in the very reverse of that proposition. Perhaps the most spectacular aspect of this febrile aggression was the rabid violence against ecosystems, expressed in their systematic and ruthless despoliation, today presenting humankind with an entirely 'man-made' catastrophe of the wanton destruction of irreplaceable natural resources vital for its very survival. Thus, complex ecosystems such as rivers and forests, supporting myriads of life forms, were freely and ferociously ravaged and scorched, in order to be made either privately, or publicly, 'productive,' as appropriate given the skewed logic of notions of 'productivity' within a regime of unbridled profit taking. The perversity of the 'benefit-cost' calculations of the economists, still applied willy-nilly to any and all social domains,[17] to this day—say, e.g., to environmental issues—stands testimony to the unscrupulous, asocial, antihuman, and counter-rational calculus of greed. *To imagine, in all stupefying conceit, that costs of one kind, borne by one set of agents, can be written off against putative benefits accruing to quite another set, by means of calculations made by a third (interested) party, is one of the many gross ironies of the regime of capital.*

Thirdly, the age-old tradition of arbitrary violence against women was now canonically restructured in a new division of labor where women were to be legally confined to the domestic sphere (the law, unlike customary restraints that preceded it, being more rigidly conceived, made appeals virtually impossible against the sudden disenfranchisement, quite contrary to the evolutionary experience in this regard), stripped of productive skills, and turned into allegedly 'nonworking' consumers and/or 'breeders' of heirs to men of property—a process best understood in the horrific run of European witch-hunts that singled out productive, property-owning, and/or skilled women, as targets for excommunication, and worse. Lest this appear only a medieval tale of wanton, cruel, iniquity, it must be remembered that even in republican Switzerland (long a paragon of capitalist democracy) women got the vote as late as 1981, a full century after having gained it in the supposedly 'cowboy' state of Wyoming. Indeed, contrary to the liberationist fantasies of colonial historians, the legal imposition of male property rights in the colonies, under European encouragement, worsened, in many regards, (reversing, at times, historical trends of amelioration) the admittedly not enviable status of women.[18]

At another remove, ruthless violence was to be employed against traditional cultures, both European (Irish peasants, for instance) and non-European (the peoples of Africa, Asia, Australia, and the Americas) which offered resistance to the logics of accumulation. It is interesting to note that the manifold objects of this violence could all be, and indeed were, assimilable under the omnibus term of 'nature': women, tribal societies (tellingly called *'naturvolk'* in the German idiom), and, of course, animals, were all 'savage' species to be 'tamed,' civilized and 'domesticated' (another telling phrase) by European, white masters (and enslaved, incarcerated, or killed, when they refused such gratuitous elevation). Shakespeare's *The Taming of the Shrew* can, in this light, be viewed perhaps as symbolizing the European male drive to subdue all that stood in his, now inexpugnable, way.

It becomes clear then, in this reading, that one and the same recidivistic logic united phenomena as far apart as Patriarchy, Imperialism, Colonization, environmental degradation, destruction of the community and social ties, etc. Modernist, materialist 'rationality,' based on the idea that happiness was approximated by the steady and irresistible growth of per capita income (though preferably the by-product of a prior profit inflation) against any and all odds, and that *more is better*—regardless of costs, human, ecological, social, political, etc.—was embraced by Euro-Marxism as well, mirroring the fetishisms of capitalist ideology quite faithfully, as illustrated in almost all of socialist practice to date. European socialism, much as capitalism, inevitably was the fused product of a reckless science and a rabid materialism.

Finally, the material elevation of the new calculus of *exchange value* over the old accounting system of use values (alongside the regressive elevation of the paradigm of alienated labor, viz., endless toil, on the part of the real producers, the dark underside of the mantra of *growth*) to the point of negating the latter altogether was to lead to egregiously self-justifying category errors when applied to non-European and noncapitalist social entities. Resource rich, naturally wealthy, civilizations such as India and China, supporting populations far in excess of European imaginations, were suddenly seen as rag-poor and destitute societies primarily for not being market-led or market-dependent in their direct modes of self-satisfaction of social needs. Subsistence economies were, *ipso facto*, defined as pauperized societies requiring, nay demanding, European uplift and assistance. This analytical category error was then to become a self-fulfilling desperate reality, when Eurocapitalist conquest systematically sundered the organic ties binding social needs to natural resources in these societies, thereby creating vast new domains of *absolute* poverty in place of the preexisting epistemic condition of relative poverty. As such the 'third world' was not 'discovered' but *invented* by capitalist Europe in all canny, deliberate premeditation. Tragically, in this process, the original affluent societies of this world were to be razed and leveled, transformed into the permanently dismal underworld of starvation, beggary, and generalized privation that has been the ill-fated hallmark of the so-called 'third world' in the twentieth century. Not ironic then, but quite typical, that the same Levi-Strauss who could poetically lament the passing of an era, in his justly famous *Tristes Tropiques* (C. Levi-Strauss, 1992), could nonetheless retain the very pivotal premise of that dire holocaust, *rational absolutism*, as his guiding, philosophical lodestar. To first thoroughly extirpate, only to remember it all, much later, in fond nostalgia, is an old modernist artifice.

In sum, given this destructive history of the blind worship of Mammon, the simple antimaterialist truth now demands restatement; humans, outside of the modernist mousetraps that cripple free will and forcibly mold behaviors, are neither driven primarily by material greed (*contra* the delusions of the economic mind-set of modernism, it should be apparent that there is no inherent connection between the paradigm of rationality and the paradigm of materialism), nor are they always mere 'creatures' of material circumstances (anymore than they are placid Benthamite sensors of pleasure and pain)—indeed, their saving grace lies in, periodically, rising heroically above, and against, such material provocations. Even dire economic necessities, in other words, can also be enabling, and inspiring, devices for actions and behaviors that transcend them; (wo)man does not live, perhaps could not live, by bread alone. Indeed, the riches resplendent in the treasure trove of culture(s) represent so many glorious moments of transcendence of the human spirit over, and against, the tawdry wares of materialism. The fact that capitalism hastens to consign any and all culture(s) to history (and/or archival warehouses) is a grim index of its innate, but accurate, fear that *cultural values*—and there are no *other* kind; all else is but so much dross—inherently pose a grave check to its vulgar, debasing, ambitions.

IDEOLOGY: THE CHIMERA OF 'PROGRESS'

The ruling ideology of the time can broadly be described as 'progressivist,'[19] consisting of two rather dubious components. Firstly, it carried the implication that all that had existed prior to the Bourgeois Revolution in Europe was regressive and/or irrational and, therefore, impeachable. Secondly, it assumed, in all insouciance, that all that happened within the new bourgeois mandate was desirable in itself, and better than what the previous epoch had to offer.[20] This was broadly deemed to be true in all spheres of social life: in politics, religion, the economy, medicine, and so on.

The two political founts of this new progressivism were the American and French Revolutions,[21] respectively (although both owed much to the inspiration of the prior English Revolution), wherein the abstract, universal, credo of this ideology was openly declared. Briefly stated, the new catechism of the Enlightenment was built around the (abstract) notions of equality, justice, rule of law, and liberty—ideas that were to inform the reflections of both capitalist and socialist philosophers alike, forever afterwards.

Although stated in piously universal form, and docketed forever as the Bourgeois Progressivist Agenda for the future, it is obvious that these epidemictic notions were mediated by an entire panoply of rigid restrictions from the very start. It is almost absurdly easy to point to the barrage of empirical refutations, that history provides, of the liberal rhetoric. The notion of equality in the U.S. republic—then as much as now—was always circumscribed by restrictions of gender, class, race, culture, and religion. Justice was just as much a mockery, being the preserve of the few, and the despair of the many. After all, in its own terms, how can there be justice amongst unequals? Indeed, to treat unequals equally—the great flourish of capitalist law—is to perpetuate inequality all the more securely. Besides, justice is not the only relevant value in its domain, an argument best understood by counterposing an entire schema of alternative values such as caring, compassion, charity, mercy, etc., to it. In the same vein, the 'rule of law,' such as it was, was always an alien, abstract, imposed, institution; the fact that it falls to some to make rules for others being an obvious, and ever present, danger in any class society (it is useful to bear in mind that the drafters of the U.S. Constitution represented neither workers, women, nor minorities). More trivially, in the case of the contemporary United States, the 'rule of law' boils down only to the dismal (mis)rule of lawyers, which is hardly an edifying corollary. Similarly, liberty is another abstract notion that needs much careful specification. Liberty from what? And, liberty for what? These philosophical speculations aside, in practical terms 'liberty' has come only to mean a negative tolerance for fairly innocuous areas of social activity (such as 'styles' of consumption) kept securely distant from the antagonistic, hierarchical, authoritarian, productivist logic of the economic order. The domain of real liberty is, in both real and ideational terms, an extremely 'bounded' one, carefully structured and circumscribed by the demands of wealth and power.

Thus far, the ideals of progressivism have been dealt with mainly on their own terrain. It is easy to see that, in the domain of their own application, these ideals were almost mortally mediated by the quite antithetical demands of the nation-state, expressed in the various hierarchies of wealth, power, gender, race, culture, and religion, with the empirical residue of validity being quite negligible in the last analysis. But it is quite possible to build a much more daunting critique of their validity. This can be done not on the basis of their empirical record—which is one of unsplendid violation of precept—but indeed at the level of the principle itself. Are the ideals of progressivism—equality, justice, rule of law, liberty, for instance—virtues at all, in and by themselves? It will be argued, in the next section, that human societies have always entertained far more enlightened alternates to these vacuously abstract notions, evolving, as these have, from the regressive premises of an alienated, divided, and antagonistic society.

But first, to complete the critique of the 'progressivist' illusion(s) of the epoch: It is easy, indeed trivial, to see, at the level perhaps of general principles alone, that professed (political) ideals can be quite misleading as a guide to actual practices. Further, it is equally apparent that revolutions, in general, promise much but deliver very little, as the initial fervor gets routinized. Besides, the American and the French Revolutions, despite the resounding rhetoric of universalisms in which they voiced their protest, served, of necessity, rather severely limited social agendas. In the case of the American Revolution, it was a national liberation struggle to end British colonial rule. In the case of the French Revolution, it was the overthrow of monarchy, and associated late feudal socioeconomic practices. It is by no means clear why the inflated rhetoric used to fight these parochial, all-European, struggles should co-opt historical options, in social discourse, for the entire world, and for all time. The hegemony of this mind-set today is less owing to its inherent potency at the level of ideas than with the simple fact of European mastery of the world of political ideals.

At any rate, what belies this progressivist, liberalist, ideology is not so much the ubiquity of empirical deviations from stated high principles (which is almost expectedly *de rigueur*), but rather one hitherto little noticed fact:

that rabid, catastrophic *violence* was always considered an entirely legitimate means to enshrine and defend these wonderful principles. Marx, the declared socialist, was explicit: force, he wrote, is the midwife of history. Robespierre, the budding bourgeois, had even fewer qualms: virtue without terror, he pronounced, was ineffectual! Similarly, Rousseau argued forcefully, indeed passionately, that people can and must be made 'free,' even against their will. Moreover, lest Rousseau seem a predictably French aberration, even the noble J. S. Mill, patron saint of liberalism, in his famous essay on *Liberty*, voiced, paradoxically, exactly the same sentiments. What a grand tradition of 'moral' sanction for outright carnage! Little wonder that two great European wars nearly brought the world, innocent bystanders included, to extinction; and has the United States' record of interventions across the globe not been based on the same logic, however speciously applied? Can despotic means usher in pacific modes of social coexistence? Certainly, the enlightenment ideologues thought it quite eminently possible.

Clearly then, an astonishing emphasis on a catch-all violence was at the epicenter of otherwise pacific European dreams of the good society, a fact linking the liberal progressivists of the Enlightenment solidly and unmistakably with such unedifying agencies as the medieval Church and latter-day Stalinism. Yet it was all quite inescapable; liberal progressivism was built solidly on the basis of State action, much like 'actually' existing socialism—and the violence followed, inevitably, as a matter of course. The truth is paradoxical, but true: liberalism, like practical socialism, was blatantly Statist in the sense that it was 'good government' (whether in the rhetoric of the 'dictatorship of the proletariat,' or of the 'democratic' state) that was to be the facile institutional guarantee of peace and plenty. Amazingly, in the tendentiously naive political catechism of liberalism, it was the sly fox, in effect, that was left to preside, quite genially, if often fatally, over the feeble democracy of chickens!

AGAINST EUROCENTRIC VISIONS

It is now possible to catalogue the legion of problems common to both the philosophy and the programs of the Enlightenment. Eurocentered visions, of this order, were always materialist, androcentric, statist, violent, intolerant, and misogynist. Given their acceptance of the extraordinary idea that society is a *contractual* entity (whether in the liberal Lockean view of a social 'contract' or in the more conservative Hobbesian version of a 'covenant')—the very epitome of alien social relations—it followed that all their quixotic dreams of amelioration of the human condition, as expressed in their ideals (liberty, equality, etc.), could not but be fatally flawed by that original sin of preconceptualization. Moreover, this base error, so to speak, was compounded by the addition of the amazing notion that happiness (personal and/or social) is approximated by the steady growth of per capita access to goods and services. The net result of such a combination of ideas could only be the construction of a rational, material, uniform, yet conflict-driven, universe built on the never-ending misery of rich and poor alike, chained to the treadmill of continuous pecuniary advancement, with the state an ever-present reminder of a lost innocence, and with the arts of life (preserved only in the warrens of the non-European and/or non-capitalist social forms) irretrievably lost forever.

To conclude: firstly, it must be understood that the universalism espoused by the Enlightenment, flights of idealist fancy apart, was always quite spurious. Indeed, Europe tried to pass off its parochialisms, its greeds, and its ambitions as high principles: but it was, in effect, only an ideology, a ruse, that helped it in the conquest of the non-European world and/or domestic forces opposed to it. After all, a genuine universalism respects diversity and demands tolerance—a far cry from Europe's depredations in the non-European world—and does not destroy every vestige of 'difference' it sees in 'other cultures,' as a matter of course. *To be universal is not to disregard differences but to appreciate them, and make allowances.* Besides, to declare universalism as an ideology, or an ideal, is quite vain and superfluous; we are after all, regardless of our different mores, universal simply for belonging to the same family of human society. This is a truth that exists serenely apart from pious, and usually dissembling, declarations of the principle.

Secondly, the objectivity that European science pretended to was for the most part always a fraud; worse, when it was at all real, it reflected only the prevailing state of alienation, for treating people as though they were only *objects* to be studied, analyzed, disposed of, dispensed with, and generally *dehumanized*, as it pleased. Far better, frankly, to opt for *subjectivity* in human relations: because it is honest, it is real, and it is dignified—to be treating human *subjects* (not objects) as human subjects. Subjectivism also carries the important saving grace of not being suitable for godlike, *ex cathedra*, stances on matters of human interest and relevance.

Indeed, it is vital to consider why we need an entity such as an organized social *science* at all to begin with; stated simply, far from being purely an informational entity, as might be supposed, to bring home to all the riches of social knowledge, science has always been, in European constitution, a wilful agent of domination, control, and conquest. *A regime of profit, and a realm of power, require an instrumentalist science as an all important, and continuous, survey tool.* As such, resistance to the dictates of science, quite often, is equivalent to resisting the very structure of domination itself. It comes as a revelation to many to understand that western science does not search for truth, *per se*, but for *order*; indeed, all its reactionary postures, and departures from the spirit of pure inquiry, stem from that fundamental elision. A true humanism must reject a science of society, as currently constituted, altogether. In human society, the need is *not* for analysis (that perjurious instrument of tendentious aims), but empathy.

Thirdly, western 'knowledge', even when stripped of its tendentious nature, has always leaned toward *context-free abstractions*, indeed priding itself on, and idealizing, this form of alienated, dehumanized, abstract discourse. But *wisdom*, a much older idea than this newly instituted norm for knowledge, has always been *concrete and contextual*. It took the genius of a Levi-Strauss to point out that the concrete thinking of the 'savage' mind was not inferior to European flights of reason.[22] However, the truth is even more startling: concrete forms of thought are both more humane, and far wiser, than the free operations of an amorally active, speculative, 'reason,' tied to a predatory 'establishment' wedded to insatiable greed. Abstractions inherently carry the potential for treason and treachery, aside from being ideal vehicles for dissembling and deception, for being couched in an aerial, transhuman metaphysic; contextual arguments remain firmly grounded and are limited in scope, incapable of wild, irresponsible, extension. Abstractions tend to fly perilously, and perfidiously, from the known to the unknown; contextual statements remain confined to the domain of the immediately knowable. Contextual thinking is bounded in its potential for inflicting damage on others; abstract thinking can doom (and has so doomed) entire universes to perdition. It is this perverse facility of *abstract* thinking, howsoever wedded to concrete aims, that undergirded the modernist European resolve—on both sides of the cold war—to risk blowing up the planet to prove their respective platitudes. The rooted, contextual thinking of the 'primitives' is incapable of even imagining such a horrific scale of destruction, let alone acting upon it.

In fact, the treachery of pure reason needs much careful specification. As Arthur Schopenhauer pointed out, decades ago, reason is merely the handmaid of the will, i.e., we can always find (justifying) 'reasons' once we have determined a set course of action. Recently, Prof. Amartya Sen, in a much celebrated essay,[23] pointed out that one can be rational (in the microeconomic sense) and still be, socially speaking, an idiot; but more to the point, in the capitalist scheme of things, one can be rational and be an utter knave as well—even more easily. Reason, therefore, needs to be firmly shackled by moral resolution; better still, we need to appreciate the many alternative ways of knowing, apart from the modalities of reason—empathy, intuition, etc.—that European science has summarily left behind, but which are destined to force their way back into public consciousness, with contemporary research findings in heterodox disciplines, such as parapsychology, being only the thin end of the wedge in this regard. There have always been more ways of knowing than the routinized rote and ritual of the European scientific tradition.

To continue; the Positivist stance, close kin of *Scientism*[24] (that deifies science), which has dominated European scientific discourse for at least three centuries, is quite fraudulent for not recognizing either the fallibility of the observer or the fluidity of the observed (even in Physics, courtesy of the Heisenberg Principle, that observation is an *interactive* process between subject and object that is now almost common knowledge). The empirical tip of the realist iceberg cannot suffice as final data, without reference to the complex multiple layering exhibited by both social and natural ontologies. Also, *contra* the prejudices of Positivism, the search for truth is not negated by normative concerns; indeed, *truth is itself a value and a normative concern*. So, to discard normative concerns as outside the domain of science is to succumb to an antihuman, amoral, instrumental vision of science that can serve, by default, only the masters of the economy and the polity. The fact that positive science was easily recruited to serve the misanthropic ends of miscellaneous oppressive tyrannies from colonialism and imperialism to fascism, Stalinism, and racism, is a powerful indicator of this ever-present danger. The very philosophical premises of Positivism, in effect, are directly contrary to humanism (aside from being 'irrealist,' as well).

Fourthly, the 'law and order' (especially in its imposed form) fetish of the west, with its provenance in alienated society, and its need for various routinized repressive apparati, has always had far saner alternates, represented best in what might be termed the many modalities of *'creative anarchy'* visible perhaps in the congenial workings of an Indian bazaar, or ordinary street traffic in Rome. To believe that society can only be run on the basis of oppressive rules, enforced by ready and resolute guns, is just another European fantasy, insulting the many creative forms of human societal genius that has allowed for cooperative, and mutually sustaining, life-enhancing, forms of behavior for aeons.

The constitutional fetish, too, needs to be seen for what it is; an attempt to confine, and secure, evolutionary questions within the bounds of the imagination (or lack of it) of one set of privileged authors of a given generation (as much as a class, race, religion, culture, etc.) while denying that option to future citizenry, except under near-impossible, exceptional, conditions. The attempt to bound discourse, to regiment, to impose rigidity, and control: in one word, to legislate *order* (*clearly it is conquerors who impose constitutions on the conquered*), but within the guiding frame of modernist outlooks and ambitions, is quite antithetical to the forbearing notion of allowing consensual values to peaceably be allowed to prevail in the fullness of time, mutual contact, and contextual enjoinments. Rather than an *open* discourse, modernism has always preferred a closed one, where the illusion of pluralism is sustained in an essentially monistic framework. For example, it is not as if all the cultures inhabiting the United States have equal rights to prevail, even in their own respective domains—the fact is that all *other* cultures have to bow to the imperatives of Anglo-Saxon institutions. Stated differently, the Great White Way is the hegemonic culture that defines and draws the intercultural boundaries, as it wills; the Native American, on the other hand, to point to but one example, is a *subaltern* subculture, that must take care to live within its fragile, allotted space. At any rate, there is something fundamentally disturbing about a constitution that is merely 'inherited' by those who had no (emotive) part in its original drafting. Cold and dry codification is the very soul of modernism, however, and recondite rules and rotes its driving force. The far more gratifying social form is not the erection of a formal, abstract constitution, usually to the everlasting benefit of the powers that be, but the cordial search for the ever-changing norms and modalities of coexistence as a series of never-ending informal *conversations*, in the plural, where many points of view can be exchanged, and rules and rituals can be freely altered as often as need be, to secure a familial, bonding, social exchange of sentiment, warmth and felicity. Free peoples have never required governance by constitutions; only the artificially, and comperatively, imposed nation-state requires one to enforce its modernist diktats over its hapless subject-citizens.

Fifthly, it is almost an imperative to understand the epistemic basis of the warped genius of European 'modernism,' the force that today threatens to engulf the world. Human society, excepting the 300-year-old aberration of European bourgeois hegemony, dating with the mastery of the capitalist mode of production, has never perceived itself as held together by a fragile *'balance of interests,'* as in all of the 'social contract' formulation(s). It has always been constituted, in contrast, at least in self-perception, as a balance of *affections*. It is easy to see the consequences of such disparate perceptions; in the one instance it leads to society understood as a fragile *balance of terror* (easy enough to visualize New York, or any major modern city, in that light), which is the inescapably 'modern' way; in the other, to society viewed as a warm, convivial entity (still alive in some paradigms of the tribal form),[25] rather than an economic and political war zone. However to not rule by a faceless, unknown *majority* as with the contemporary 'democratic' nation-state, but coexistence through *consensual* norms of mutual affirmation, developed across time, within a matrix of face-to-face relations involving patience, compromise, and goodwill. The metaphor of the family, and the familial, may thus be extended outwards—as in tribal formations—as an antidote to the alien private-public divide of modern society. Cooperative social entities are both just as historically feasible, and humanly possible, as the various antisocial forms quite knowingly organized, by capital, on an adversarial basis.

Sixthly, the preoccupation of western philosophers and moralists of the Enlightenment with '*equality*'—in the face of its ever-conspicuous absence—is simply the vacuous, sometimes disingenuous, search for the holy grail. There are far more convivial alternates that have existed for centuries; *fellowship*, for instance, may be taken as a mediated form of 'equality' but, quite unlike the materialist austerity of the latter term, it is a warm, affectionate, human term involving reciprocities and bondings. One can be formally equal in an alienated society, like capitalism, but feel nothing thereby, remaining distant, aloof, and alone, in the radical isolations of that social form. Indeed, humans seek, instinctively, not cold equalities but warmth and fellowship; easy to see how, say, within the bounds of 'family' and 'home' (no matter how these terms are ontologically defined), we dissolve all manner of very real inequalities (age, gender, wealth, etc.) through 'feelings' of fellowship, caring, and love. Inequality can comfortably coexist with convivial social relations, as in the context of familial relations where the manifest inequality between mother and child (as social roles) does not at all gainsay the striking presence of perhaps the warmest human relationship conceivable. Genuine affective relations can generously, and wholly, compensate for an entire host of obviously asymmetrical roles and responsibilities such as characterize most distributions within all known social forms. On the other hand, to seek only formal equality, outside of such life-giving reciprocities, is only to assure that everyone is *equally* alienated.

The capitalist, and indeed also socialist, fetish with 'equality,' especially in a material context, even if fully realized, would preserve all the misery of the alien social relations of everyday life unchanged. Quite obviously, then, the preoccupation with material, i.e., formal, equality, as in the western tradition, is a chimera, a sop, a decoy, and a detour, from the task of building pacific, nurturing, human relations. *It is high time we realized that all values are not created equal*; indeed, it is worth considering the true, but unfashionable, proposition that in a human society, moral and spiritual values, arguably, *always* rank superior to material ones, no matter how they are derided and debased by the powers that be (the revilement itself, indirectly, being the eternal homage that vice is obliged to pay to virtue).[26]

Seventhly, the notion of 'justice,' in its ominously distal and masculinist tones, could be easily and elevatedly parsed into a still higher order, 'feminine' value like mercy, charity, or compassion, without erasing its rationale—and perhaps actually elevating its diacritical content. Indeed, the evolution of the term bears careful scrutiny; in medieval times justice was simply a collectivist notion of vengeance, or *retribution* (the old 'eye for an eye' idea)—in capitalist terms this became transmuted into the individualist, 'contractual,' criterion of reparation, or *restitution* (to restore, and make up, the—property—loss in question). But there is another, far more satisfactory alternative, again drawn from our trove of 'prehistory': justice as *'reconciliation,'* where the desire is to restore the moral, affective balances of the social bond, rudely ruptured by the unsocial act in question. Only this last conception holds out the promise of a true revival of conviviality, of a real redemption, after the act that has breached it.

It should become apparent the extent to which the false antinomy between 'individual' and 'society,' so profoundly important, for instance, to underscore and situate the differences between the bourgeois and Marxian modes of social theorizing, has been entirely devised by the modernist paradigm itself (of alienated society). This spurious opposition arises only in the context of the 'modern' nation-state and its organization of 'society' at that speciously artificial moment of abstraction. In the worlds ruptured by modernism there could only be social individuals, at once *both* entities, but conjointly, and with no 'separatist' ontology or epistemology that might lead to a permanent contradiction between them. A glance at the internal organization of the 'family' can again make the point clear; the individuals who make up that social form are not aware of any profound contrariety of 'interests' between them, or between them and the totality of the family itself. So it is with the tribal form which is only an extension of that very principle of kinship that dissolves the antinomy in question quite completely. In much the same way that capitalism destroys the peasantry to 'release' the now dispossessed 'working' class into the sphere of the 'economy,' it also destroys the familial moment of the social form thereby releasing dysfunctional 'individuals' into the arena of 'society.' Obviously, capitalist individualism is as much of a caricature as socialist 'collectivism'; neither is a solution to the dilemma of 'modernism'—both are symptomatic instead of an unfathomably deep, and corrosive, rupture of the social form.

It is important to note that all the affective relations that European philosophers have sought, vainly, in their many models of utopia, have always been present within the sphere of the household, primarily directed, and inspired, by the dramatically *contra, affirmative, affective, domestic, social economy of women* (women under Patriarchy, regardless of class, creed, or culture, have clemently retained these traits; far from being an 'essentialist' idealization, this is a readily ascertainable, determinate, and abiding, social phenomenon). As such, the *rediscovery* of utopia consists in an embrace of values that have customarily been derided as 'feminine': caring, giving, nurturance, love, and affection. Utopia, like charity, begins, in this sense, at *home*—concerned not with the *political economy of 'interests*,' as with capitalism and socialism, but with the *human economy of affections*, just as in the simplest forms of 'tribal,' i.e., kinship and kindred-based social forms. The critical distortion of modernism lies in the perverse, late European, penchant for marking off the 'private' sphere from the 'public' one (homologously evoked in the modernist distinction between 'state' and 'civil society'), thereby instituting a permanent schizophrenia in the social consciousness between the 'affective' realm and the so-called realm of 'reason,' leading usually to dual behaviors, norms, and practices, that remain permanently, and divisively, irreconcilable. It is arguably the case that this deep, implacable rift between the 'personal' and the 'public' is at the philosophical base of the many chronically inherent, and irresistible, dissensions of modern society. So-called 'simple' societies have always specialized in *not* bifurcating the social plane into such contradictory dominions, indeed in letting the affective world subsume the material one quite completely. Accordingly, the disciplinary guide to restructuring our lives must come not from economics, politics, or even philosophy—the three sovereign afflictions of alienated society—but from the generous wisdom that has always lain available in our own received heritage of human anthropology. The grave danger today is that we stand poised to wantonly destroy even the very memory of this wondrous legacy.

Finally, and perhaps most importantly, *the essence of European alienation lies in defining social constructs in materialist terms, a phenomenon that definitively marks the era of modernism, inaugurated by the Enlightenment itself.* For the Great Elision, in all of European discourse, capitalist or socialist, is the conspicuous absence of any apprehension of the *primacy of culture* in human society. Various alternative definitions notwithstanding, culture is possibly best understood as both the stock and the process of production, consumption, and exchange of basically *nonmaterial* values. *Both capitalism and socialism are alienated societies because they reverse these normative polarities, much to their everlasting detriment.* It is, accordingly, easy now to see the provenance of their original alienation; *alienation may be deemed to occur when material values are allowed to systematically subvert and dominate the free exchange of nonmaterial values.* Stated differently, it is when the province of exchange value (the domain where subjectively perceived material needs run ahead of the customary trove of real resources) is allowed to extinguish the domain of use values, i.e., when culture is run through, and put paid, by rampant materialism, in both ideology and practice, that the moment of alienation begins (in human society, past or present, *civilization* is the perpetual struggle against the menace of resurgent materialism).

As such, capitalism and socialism are both ineluctably antithetical to the cultural genius of human society, and therefore doomed to certain extinction. A true post-modernism, and not the trite, usurping, philosophy of the interregnum that bears that name today, will arrive only when these alienations are finally overcome; the inspiration for this resolve can come not from any form of wishful thinking but through learning from the practical, lived experience of *pre-modernist* social forms. It would appear that, quite ironically, a satisfactory post-modernism would involve some sort of a return to the guiding spirit of *pre-modernism*. We need to rediscover many of the older civil forms of self-sustenance: *self-provisioning, autonomy, and self-determination*, now in danger of being obliterated forever in the fell swoop of inherently expansionist, and destructionist, European ideologies. The workable microcosms of utopia, wearing necessarily a *feminine face*, lie not in some mythical future that is yet to be revealed, as in all European visions of utopia, but in our own historic past—and present. Inevitably, we may conceive of the entire process perhaps, in practice, as learning—even at this very late stage of rank desiccation and decay—by *undoing*.

A regenerative efflorescence of cultural humanism—civility, grace, and pacifism (the exigent adjuncts of the complacent life)—and the restoration of the convivial social form, must perforce, therefore, await the coming, necessary, even vital, philosophical *break with the Enlightenment*. Modern European philosophy, *the deformed offspring of alienated society*, is utterly incapable of offering any escape from its paradigmatic sufferings, being trapped hopelessly in its own regressive circularities; we have no choice, now, but to *reconstruct a social vision of sympathy and sustenance*, drawn from the bits and pieces of illumination of our forebears still left standing, unnoticed by the modernist tribe of cultural vandals. It is perhaps in the nature of things that women, workers, minorities, and 'primitives,' at the receiving end of its multifaceted, invidious, stratagems of exclusion for so long, will realize, and act upon, this necessity first. However, it is really an imperative for all of us to the extent that organized, corporatist, barbarism, intolerance, and unfreedom, are paralytic conditions not merely for the 'victims' upon which they are inflicted but also for the bearers, and carriers, of the dehumanizing delusions who are similarly racked and reduced by the chains that they forge, albeit for others. Of course, for all of us, in a human society this will ultimately be a matter of *choice*, not necessity; we may choose to break with the Enlightenment—or let it, wantonly, break us.

NOTES

1. Although adopting a stance toward the subject quite different from the one taken in this book, Ernst Cassirer's work (E. Cassirer, 1951) remains the most informative study of the Enlightenment still available. The reader must note that, in this chapter, I am taking two important intellectual liberties: (a) firstly, I am quite deliberately painting with a fairly large brush; there is simply no other way to convey the macro-dynamics of the ideological torrent that was to sweep the imagination of the world for the next three centuries. While exceptions to the general thrust I am detailing did exist, *even within Enlightenment-based metaphysics*, they were exceptions that, by and large, prove the rule of the contrary; and (b) I am consciously merging seventeenth-century and eighteenth-

century European thought, normally distinguished from each other by (European) historians of ideas, under the rubric of the 'Enlightenment,' *for the simple reason that the intellectual commonalities shared between the two periods, relevant to my thesis, far outstrip the many differences between them.* If the brush is inordinately large, it is only because the canvas is appropriately huge, and the critique transcendent.The self-conscious lumping together is, primarily, of the shared premises of capitalist and socialist 'vanguard' thinking, not of the many minor eddies and countercurrents posed by various, still extant, European *oppositions* to these dominant streams. World history was made by the former set of forces, not the latter.
2. It must be noted that all those forces that opposed this confident catechism of modernism—material progress and scientific advancement—were routinely dismissed as deluded, wishy-washy, 'romantics' (who were allegedly impotently 'revolting against reason') who would simply disappear, as irrelevants, under the inexorable march of history. For a generally conventional view of the roots of 'romaticism,' see I. Zeitlin (1968, Chap. 4), and G. Sabine (1950, Chap. 28–30).
3. The inspiration for this chapter is drawn from various sources: its feminism is drawn partly from the work of V. Shiva (1989), its critique of science from the peerless P. Feyerabend (1978; 1987) and S. Harding (1986), and its critical anthropology from Marshall Sahlins (1985). But the overriding influence, combining all these elements, is that of perhaps the kindest, wisest man who ever graced the domain of politics: Mahatma Gandhi.
4. Bacon's writings may be referenced in J. Spedding *et al.* (eds.), *The Works of Francis Bacon* (Reprinted), Stuttgart: F. F. Verlag, 1963.
5. See Paul Feyerabend (1978) for a stinging analysis of this phenomenon. As he points out, today's science operates by ideological *fiat*, dismissive of alternate practices (astrology, e.g.; and the early rejection of acupuncture; homeopathy, etc.) without benefit of even minimum scientific scrutiny.
6. An early critic, from the Right, of this 'historicism' was Popper. See K. Popper (1957; 1962).
7. For alternate visions of anthropological time, see Jonathan Fabian (1983).
8. An important caveat: in this chapter, and indeed throughout this book, the adjectival term 'European' is used historically to exemplify the 'modernist' impulse. This is not at all to imply that Europe began as a 'modernist' entity; indeed the Enlightenment marks the triumph, within Europe, over its own precapitalist heritage. Similarly, while much of the non-European world is still refreshingly precapitalist in its ideology (certainly more so than the white European world), obviously it too is a creature largely given over to the modernist assault, today, though not completely. At any rate, the virtues (and vices) attributed in this book are *not to geography and race but to ideas and norms*.
9. Much useful material on this subject may be found in E. Said's classic work on *Orientalism* (1979). See also, J. P. S. Oberoi (1984) for some notes on the theme of dualism and science, in the European tradition.
10. On this, again, see P. Feyerabend (1978), *op cit.*
11. R. Bhaskar's work illuminates the critical significance of the assumption of 'closed' and 'open' models for science generally. See Bhaskar (1986).
12. Perhaps the most complete critique of Positivism comes from the pen of Oxford philosopher Roy Bhaskar. See R. Bhaskar (1979).
13. Comte and Durkheim represent variants of a positivist *philosophy*, as apart from a mere scientific methodology; the reactionary content of the former is best

understood in Comte's work which assumes the 'best of all possible worlds' approach to capitalist ontology. In more sophisticated versions, like Milton Friedman's (M. Friedman, 1953), the politics, no less reactionary, are left far more implicit.
14. See R. Kanth (1986) for a full rendering.
15. 'It is not from the benevolence of the butcher, the brewer, or the baker that we expect our dinner, but from their regard to their own interest. We address ourselves, not to their humanity but to their self-love...'. (A. Smith, 1986, p. 169.) Thus Stalin, too, thought material incentives the only suitable ones for various forms of 'socialist' drudgery. It is perhaps high time we did appeal to the ample reserves of humanity in people, *contra* Smith, prior to reducing them, by definition, to mean, mercenary, modules of egotism, *but not of course in a world that makes such behavior suicidal*. Capitalism engineers a world where, typically, 'nice guys finish last,' then derides a putatively misanthropic 'human nature' as being hopelessly selfish!
16. Materialism has multiple meanings; here, it is being used to indicate the propensity to attribute all important social drives to underlying 'economic' motivations, functioning therefore as an all-purpose 'explanatory' device. This is quite common to both Marxian and capitalist ideology. This orientation implies that greed is the supreme social (and human) value, and elevates the 'economy' to the very apex of the social pyramid. Enshrined in policy, 'material incentives' become the secure goad to all desirable social action. Yet even capitalist history is rich with *contra* evidence: generations of religious and trade union activists, for instance, who labored sleeplessly for far less than a pittance.
17. In this manifest of amorality, there can be socially 'optimal' levels of any and all 'bads,' ranging from environmental pollution at one end, and rapes and murders at another. No doubt the Star Wars scenario of Ronald Reagan similarly embodied an 'optimal' calculus of directing a first nuclear strike against the USSR.
18. I am indebted to Maria Mies's work (M. Mies, 1986) for illumination in this area.
19. An early critique of 'progressivism' may be found in A. Salomon (1955).
20. This is often referred to in the literature as constituting the 'Whig' view of history. But it was, of course, a viewpoint shared by a much broader constituency than just the 'Whigs.'
21. For a scholarly discussion of these movements, though partly flawed by its Marxist reductionisms, see E. J. Hobsbawm (1962).
22. C. Levi-Strauss (1966).
23. A. Sen (1977).
24. The writings of F. Hayek (1942; 1943) attack Scientism from the Right; Feyerabend (1978; 1987) offers a much more humanistic critique of the pretensions of science.
25. The great philosopher of conviviality, in the western tradition, is I. Illich (I. Illich, 1973). Gandhi, of course, was the spiritual mentor of all such conceptualizations in this century.
26. In the western tradition, the work of German sociologist Scheler (1994) supports this quite premodernist viewpoint; indeed, older German scholarship, quite generally, has been very sensitive to 'eastern' and precapitalist influences.

6

ALTERNATIVE VISIONS: TOWARD CONVIVIALITY

EUROCENTRISM

As noted in the foregoing, the key problem with both the ruling, Enlightenment-based, visions of the world, capitalism and socialism, is their incorporation of the manifestly alien, ideological, and *Eurocentric*[1] blinders of modernism. Though singularly European in provenance, these historically specific orientations of Europe, as the conquering culture, were to become the basis for wholesale idolatry, the world over, for at least the past 200 years. It is quite astonishing that generations of non-European peoples have claimed such visions for their own, despite the violence these (mis)perceptions often did to their own values, traditions, and cultures. Of course, their acquiescence was rarely a voluntary affair (Japan, given its escape from the colonial blight, until very late, is one of the few non-European cultures that received Europeanisms *of its own volition* [though driven by the valid fear of European conquest], without losing, until much after World War II, its own cultural identity and dignity); put simply, it was the net consequence of *colonization* and *conquest*. Whether Marxist or capitalist, colonial elites, educated in European ideologies,[2] and socialized in ways quite foreign to their own societies, always lay at some insular cultural distance from their own traditions.

Within the period of direct colonial rule, such imitative behavior was at least understandable; but after political independence (however nominal), in great part, the vestigial survival of such attitudes could only be the consequence of a lingering *neocolonialism* (like children on the outside of a gaudy shop window, third-world elites continue to salivate at European institutions, ideologies, and practices, even when these are arguably detrimental to their own interests). Of course, the more capitalist socioeconomic relations gain sway in these regions, the more such ideologies appear to the 'localized,' starting to reflect, or rather to be in line with, underlying realities. But it will always remain a conflict-ridden inheritance, dualistic, and prone to many inherent tensions.

Indeed, in the third world today, the principal source of cultural tensions is precisely this tussle between Eurocentrism and *nativism*, the former encountering keen resistance from the inevitable resurgence of long suppressed local ideas, mores, and practices. The extreme example of this revolt against Eurocentrism in our times (aside from the short-lived 'cultural revolution' of Mao) is, of course, clerical Iran (and Islamic resurgence, generally) with its, at least initial, near-total rejection of western ideologies. The BJP (Bharatiya Janata Party), a rising political wave in India, represents the same wave of rejection of non-Indian ideas and practices (even, obviously, where the supposedly antipodal 'Indian' traditions cannot be specified accurately; indeed, perhaps because of it), on the part of a still somnolent giant. Although the West finds the idea not at all palatable, it is possibly only a matter of time before many more European ideological and institutional transplants, always tenuous at best, will be uprooted in most, if not all, of the third world.

It is by no means clear that traditional mores *vis-à-vis* European ones are weaker, ineffectual, or more deficient; in fact, that they are today dismissed wholesale, i.e., uncritically, as 'fundamentalist' by the West suggests only that they are simply *inimical to the development of capitalist (and socialist) modernisms*. The Enlightenment, it must be remembered, was no universal affair: it was a *European*, capitalist, enlightenment, and is no more universal than those two loci. It is ironic that Europe was able to pass off its own native parochialism as a *universalist* ideology, successfully disguising the former under the latter. But non-European ideas have yet to find a similar space under the sun, at least partly because they were savagely suppressed under most colonial regimes. Today, these suppressed practices, products of centuries of cultural evolution, are hesitantly finding their feet and their voices, albeit in distorted form because of the uphill struggle they face to gain only their rightful place in the sun: and in the coming decades, the world, at its peril, will have to learn to listen to them. The Judeo-Christian ideologies survived on, transformed but preserved, in the many variants of Marxism and liberalism—thereby allowing Europe to both eat its cultural cake and have it, too. On the other hand, non-European ideologies have been stuck with the discomfort of being branded as ethnic, parochial, and *retrograde*, i.e., as ideologies necessarily to be left behind in the grand march of (European) history.

Principally, the contrast between Eurocentrism and non-European ideologies, amounts only to the difference between *capitalist* and *precapitalist* orientations. Fundamentally, postfeudal, Eurocentered, ideologies share at least five distinct characteristics: (a) an asocial *individualism*, (b) a *linear* or 'progressive' view of history, (c) a *dualism* that first divides, then conquers the world across various lines of fissure (class, gender, race, etc.), (d) a *materialist reductionism* that renders human welfare subject to material definitions, and (e) a stress on *violence* as the 'midwife' of history. Not merely the precapitalism of non-European societies, but even the precapitalist ideologies of Europe—as in the Paracelsian hermetic tradition that Baconian science displaced—were metaphysically based on a denial of these principles, stressing cooperation not conflict, holism, not reductionism, unity amidst diversity (nondualism), and the social, not the individual. Small wonder that Marx's sanguine vision of the future—*communism*—at its best incorporated these very ideals, hearkening back to his own beloved stereotype of 'primitive communism.' Perhaps most importantly, the notion that (alleged) virtue must triumph over vice, regardless of cost (human or material), has been the enduring, if disastrous, legacy of the dominant variants of Europeanology: liberalism and Marxism (as represented, say, in U.S. imperialist savagery in Vietnam and the corresponding 'socialist' barbarism in the Cambodia of the Khmer Rouge).

A more subtle point is usually lost in critiques of Eurocentrism—that European capitalism fostered, as a general philosophy, the orientation (until then only the prerogative of ruling classes) of *abstract* knowledge, as opposed to the older form of concrete, *contextual* wisdom (that partial knowledge, howsoever rational, can never amount to wisdom, is implicitly illustrated in Sen's famous paper on 'rational fools').[3] In itself, this reflects a fundamental alienation: to think abstractly about people (as with the pseudo-'sciences' of 'sociology,' 'economics,' etc.), with the aid of the vampire of instrumental reason, is to degrade, dehumanize, and depersonalize both subject and object.

As noted, the inherent cynicism of such perspectives was always the preserve of rulers, potentates, and despots (plotting against their own subjects and rivals in the time-honored genre of Machiavelli's *Prince*—to take a European example—and, India's own, Kautilya's *Arthashastra*). However, in Eurocapitalism, this proclivity is generalized as the *total ideology of abstraction* that goes by the name of science.[4] People tied to each other by kinship, affinity, and affection (as, for instance in tribal forms) are incapable, and unwilling, to abstractly demonize their fellows, and rationally dissect their insides; in Eurocapitalist societies, however, this is almost the first axiom of social discourse.[5]

It is not difficult to see how this comes about, for once the cash nexus has, by force, replaced human relations, we are already herded into the Hades of individualist separations; into impenetrable barricades of self-interest; into privately secured and defended poaching grounds. The obviously nondisinterested abstractions are then tied—applied—to canny *calculation*, and the process of, indeed the slide into, dehumanization begins, until we bottom out into the unfeeling neoclassical world of abstract economics, which elevates *context-free knowledge*, supposedly of eternal verities, to supernally absurd levels.

The atomism, and apparent disconnectedness, of capitalist society is then reproduced in theory, as a double error of *reflexivity*. Not only is context-free, abstract thinking ahuman, it is also patently false, producing the urges to delusive grand totalizations, and breathtaking determinisms, which western thought takes such delight in (as with Marxian, or even Smithian, 'stages of history,' and so on). It also nulls the *alternative moral voice*, female in the main, of pity, compassion, caring, and love, in favor of undeniably masculinist metaphors of conquest and triumph. Unlike such distorted visions, feeding the fantasies of the would-be masters of the universe, workers, women, and tribal cultures, with no empires to conquer, have always preferred contextual, local, topical thinking grounded in a simple appreciation of the concrete.[6] Of course, the modernist dismisses such pacific forms of micro-involvements, dyed with exiguous cares and considerations, as reactionary, parochial, and petty. To him, life is not satisfactory until we have acquired, and used, through the sovereign power of detached abstraction, the means to destroy the world and its environs. Both capitalism and socialism, as singular modernisms, build dispassionately unfeeling societal machinery based on the rational, macho slogans of the Enlightenment: 'law and order,' 'equality,' 'justice,' and so on—whereas common peoples, the world over, have yearned only for simple communitarian conviviality, warmth, sentimentality, and affection. The European is, for historical reasons, farthest along this road of depersonalization, in the male voice, which returns to him in the form of a dire philosophical affliction: *angst*, and virulent existentialist despair. Small wonder so many of them prefer to spend their vacations amongst peoples still close to their social genius *not* to be self-directed, atomized, ahuman, atoms of entirely unrequitable greeds, lusts, and desires. Yes, we first world denizens all wish to vacation in Jamaica; do we know anyone who would rather do it, given a choice, in Manchester?

Central to Eurocentric visions has been the reification and genderization of *science* as the vital auxiliary of capitalist patriarchy.[7] Casting their private, parochial, and raptorial inclinations in the superior halo of the Newtonian certainties of *science*, the doughty warriors of the Enlightenment, liberal as much as Marxist, have torched, raped, pillaged, and plundered the world, and all in the name of progress. Both liberals and Marxists have claimed rational science as their own special preserve, seeking thereby to acquire dizzy heights of legitimacy for otherwise thoroughly value-laden, normatively imbued, socially fallible, plans for amelioration. Neither was prepared to admit that citing the authority of science gave no warrant for agency and intrusion in social life, particularly when radical changes were to be imposed, by sufferance, upon disbelieving, and disempowered, groups, classes, and peoples. Both capitalism and socialism, therefore, were lapidary in their intolerance for what they perceived as nonscience and unreason. Thus did handloom weavers perish, in England, because their cottage industry was seen as 'irrational' to capitalist advancement; and quite similarly, peasants in Russia saw their fortunes decline because Bolsheviks (except for the few who rallied around the ill-fated Bukharin) saw their continued existence as 'irrational' for socialist advancement. More recently, many amongst the British Left—Marxians included—extolled the wisdom of Thatcher, as the saint of capitalist efficiency, in letting the hapless miners (their fate consigned to the confident march of 'history') go to the wall. And in the field of medicine, capitalism and socialism similarly assumed that traditional therapies were, *ipso facto*, fraudulent mumbo-jumbo, leading, in the case of newly 'liberated' Maoist China, almost to the complete extirpation of traditional Chinese healings, were it not for a last-minute change of heart on the part of Mao that preserved that near invaluable cluster of traditions for humankind. Indeed, examples of this nature are legion in the short history of modernism where Europeans, and their subservient cronies elsewhere, consecrated the astounding myth that science and civilization were a sixteenth-century European gift to the world. No wonder that science, in the modern era, and with the support of the State, has replaced theology (and the Church) as the new, omnipotent, and terrifying instrument of organized intolerance.[8]

Being driven by deep, dark, dire machinations themselves, Europeans have always, courtesy of their 'materialist' interpretations of everything, assumed the same of other cultures. Thus the genre of putting a spin on everything, of seeing 'wheels within wheels,' of reading 'between the lines,' have led to egregious misreadings of indigenous rites and rituals and practices, for the cardinal failure of not accepting anything at face value. The American sociologist, R. K. Merton's 'manifest and latent' functions notion is quite typical in this regard; if Australian aboriginals meet to put on a rain-dance the western 'anthropologist,' not content with the historical junket that allows him such liberties, finds some other 'hidden' meaning in that innocuous, and quite transparent, tribal activity. European science has always been too clever by far, oblivious of the idea that perhaps in pre-modernist, social forms, appearances and reality might frequently coincide, and that people (unlike canny Europeans) might actually mean what they say. This trait of gratuitous subtlety is carried over by Freudian 'analysis' to suitably absurd limits where the privileged, omniscient psychoanalyst knows more about the internal psyche of a patient than the wretched patient herself. That patients buy into this asymmetric relationship quite resignedly is only an index of the low self-esteem of ordinary people trapped in the modernist straitjacket. To this day, Occam's Razor notwithstanding, confronted with a simple as opposed to a complex explanation, European science instinctively reaches for esoterics (because complexity is what helps empower science and the scientist as against lay people): the pointless jargon that bedevils much of social science is a tribute to this carefully cultivated appearance of superior knowledge. Thereby, the deceptive aura of high science buttresses the inherent insecurities of a corrosive social form.

The most telling index of alienation is the common phenomenon of *objectivication*, a social property wherein human beings unconsciously create a distance between themselves and their own artifacts (rules, norms, etc.), blindly subjecting themselves to the latter—indeed viewing them as, externally given, immutable imponderables (as 'laws of life,' for example). Where genuine reciprocities prevail, as in simple tribal forms, within organic ties that succor and not merely bind, such alienated forms are harmless enough. However, in the context of expropriative, class society, these alienations become dangerously oppressive, turning from social creations to class creations, their content now infused with the tendentious ideology of the ruling strata. Capitalism (to a lesser extent, state socialism) carries these reifications to unprecedented levels, to the point where all societal arrangements take on a 'natural' aspect (so, quite 'naturally': 'life is not fair,' 'time is money,' 'life is a lottery,' etc.). In similar tones, we can speak, 'objectively,' of the 'Supreme Court' having taken a decision preventing Native Americans from smoking mescaline at their religious rituals, instead of the obvious truth: that nine rather rich and powerful white men (or some combination of white men with token women, minorities, etc., sharing a common ideology) decided the fate (well in keeping with the tragic history of Native Americans) of a defeated, subject people. Once again, there is a metacritical loss of content in the dissembling process of abstraction; and much is gained in returning to create—hence emancipatory—understandings of reified phenomena. *Liberation, therefore, involves the critical comprehension of all forms of objectivications; utopia is simply a reversal of their dominance over peoples, so the processes of social life may be recaptured by their makers.* Social forms that permit the renewal and renovation of institutional arrangements, as per the whims of its constituents, hold the key of the promise of a nonoppressive set of social relations. Instructively, in this, as in other respects, it is not modern European societies, but traditional ones, that inherently secrete such benign possibilities.

FEMINISM

There is no gainsaying the simple fact that, taken across history, regardless of geography or culture, men have been the paramount pillagers, murderers, and rapists of history (the many misanthropic urges of patriarchical masculinity are too rabid and obvious to be delicately subsumed under the decorous veilments of social science that apologetically shift the burden of causation on to 'economic' and 'political' forces, thereby effectively disguising it as much as its gentler obverse, femininity. Of course, the same social 'science' has absolutely no explanation as to why, in general, men kill and maim, and women don't.) Indeed, social and personal violence, organized or random, has been such an obviously male monopoly that it is almost silly to argue otherwise. Equally obvious, and related, is the fact that from a European woman's point of view, capitalism, no less than the other 'isms' of the past, entailed *Patriarchy* as well; and socialism, aside from some material and quasi-political alleviations, no less so. The process of primitive accumulation, whose end product was the 'liberation' of the producers from their means of subsistence, involved three distinct modalities of encroachment: campaigns against peasants, tribal and/or traditional societies, and women.[9]

Effectively, over time, capitalism achieved the subordination, of peasants (as workers), women (as breeders), and non-Europeans (as the colonized, *èn masse*, so to speak). While European workers were the last in this process to be completely assimilated into capitalist ways, women and colonies were conquered much earlier. As far as we know, the witch-hunts in Europe, standing at the apex of the movement for redefinition of women's roles, assured that women of property, means, skills, and professions were systematically denuded of all these attributes, such that the only ideal that prevailed was that of woman as a breeder, virtually a housewife prisoner, subordinate to the whims of her father, husband, and sons (roughly in that sequential order). Thus enforced, *housewifization* was one of the complementary planks of proletarianization (all the more astonishing that Marx would have missed this vital concomitant of the process of primitive accumulation): women labored at home and men labored at factories. But the apparent symmetry breaks down readily: for, while capital appropriated the unpaid labor of men and women, women slaved *both* for capital *and* for their male kinfolk, in double jeopardy so to speak. While a host of legal, political, and industrial freedoms were the estate of the male factory workers, unfreedom and chains, albeit under customary restraints, were, for the most part, the gratuities of women houseworkers.

This point is too important to political economy to be ignored or glossed over (though it has been ignored in political economy for the longest time). The assumption of a subsistence wage that characterizes so many schools of political economy—mainstream and Marxian—is simply wrong. No male worker could ever raise a family on the money wage alone; his, and his family's, welfare depended quite critically on the *gratis* labors of women at home.[10] Nor was it the fabled welfare state that shored up the worker's wages in times of business slowdowns; in those wretched times (anymore than today): again, it was the ancient political economy of women (hunting, gathering, foraging; begging, borrowing, stealing) that ensured some measure of survival for the many. Women, thereby, were always the original welfare donors: giving a lot, receiving very little—except systematized abuse and revilement—in return. That economics could conveniently forget these felicitous gratuities of women in the context of the reproduction of the working-class household, vital indeed to any 'mode of production,' is a tribute to its inherent, patriarchical, and all too dogmatic blinders.

While patriarchy was just as prevalent in the colonized world prior to European contact, the dominant strains there were usually slightly different, being *gynocentric* in the main, thereby allowing for important, dignifying roles for women that did not quite render them solely as nonparticipant housewives located in the sphere domestic or, alternatively, in the porn parlor (given the madonna/whore alternates common to patriarchy). This is only to say that precapitalist forms of patriarchy, true to their inherent holism, allowed for some measure of cooperation between men and women, as reciprocating entities, in roles, rituals, and practices, in the economy, polity, and in religion, being less viciously *dualistic* in their orientations. In these contexts, European intrusions into traditional societies were horrific: while depriving women of traditional supports of traditional society, namely the instrumental (but asymmetric) *interdependence* between men and women, Europeans imposed their own perverse, expropriatory, legal definitions of women, as in Burma, within the public household—as *persona non grata* in the main, in a context of a total, legally implacable, dependence on male kinfolk.[11] Thus did a 'progressivist' European ideology, wielded by a brutishly zealous officialdom, visit a heinous regressivism on much of the colonial world.

The socialist movement also treated women as dependent subordinates in the important sense of treating gender equality as secondary to the struggle for socialism.[12] This was eventually to become a permanent backseat, to the point where women's organizations, in the Eastern bloc, independent of party control, were seen as positively reactionary, and the feminist struggle, outside of party mandates, as retrograde and bourgeois—views handed down from Lenin onwards that are still held by many today, even in the radical movements in advanced capitalist societies. Socialist countries routinely pronounced the end of the 'woman question,' while tolerating invidious cultural iniquities, at the same time that they assured better gender parities in the domains of economics and politics. In the obviously extreme case of Romania, for example, abortion was outlawed, and women were *compelled* to have a minimum of three children per family by State diktat. However, thanks to the interventions of the radical feminists in the past two decades, womens' agendas are far less assimilable into the 'socialist' backwash as they once used to be; on the other hand, the *simpliste* rejectionist posture of western radical feminism (reproducing a familiar European dualism) is unlikely to serve as anything more than a consciousness raiser. After all, for practice, of any kind, the human community will eventually have to be dealt with at large, not simply in gender terms.

At any rate, despite the progressivism of capitalism and socialism (or perhaps because of it) women, as the newest—but not the last—colony (as discovered by men, naturally) to be liberated, is perhaps the most profound event/process/movement of this century, being as important as the self-discovery of the working class in England, in the previous one, for the project of emancipation. It is heartening that, unlike the working-class movement, where European ideologists reached out to the third world (Mill, Marx, etc.) as educators and proselytizers, the women's movement is destined to be one where the tail shall wag the dog, with third-world women defining the intellectual frontiers of the struggle today in terms usually more holistic, and integrative, than their first-world counterparts.[13] Perhaps this is only because the most oppressed always occupy the moral high ground. As it stands, despite differences between first- and third-world feminists, there is no doubt that, as a countercurrent, the *femininization of resistance* to capitalism (as opposed to the very masculinist mind-set of old-style socialism) is amongst the most significant, and underreported, political processes of contemporary times. Men have had their turn for millenia, coming close, as they have, to destroying the world; it's time women lent a hand—at saving it. If nothing else, women, like nature herself, have had long experience in repairing the ravages of man.

Ecology

The recent discovery, with suitable dismay, that it is a finite, fragile world we live in is a purely European one; native traditions subsisted on that realization, from the Navaho Indians to the Masai tribals, for aeons. Once again, home truths from precapitalist civilizations are proving their tenacious worth against the tawdry triumphalism of European progressivism, blind to all collateral damage in its drive for accumulation. Of course, such evidence of conservationist tribal wisdom makes a mockery of the linear view of knowledge, where all that is of the past is obscure and worthless, and all that is new (hence European) is revelatory and wonderful. Indeed, this is how European capitalism defined itself, passing its smug, self-validating, propaganda off as but the enunciation of the ineffable axioms of science. Thus, we are led to believe that modern (hence European) medicine is wonderful, whereas, by implication, traditional healings were all the work of charlatans, pretenders, and alchemists. That the truth is precisely the opposite, that capitalism, for the most part, does not produce, but only *appropriates*, the discoveries of other traditions for itself as its own is only now, slowly, percolating into the mainstream consciousness, if still only as an *enclave* wisdom.[14]

At any rate, the newly awakened ecoconsciousness is the inevitable adjunct of centuries of wanton destruction of resources in the name of progress. The consequent poisoning of air and water, destruction of entire ecosystems—whose value, and importance, for human survival may now never be estimated—has reached a point where it threatens human society itself, and Europeans in particular, whence the concern about conservation. In mainstream consciousness, western, 'everyday,' ecological awareness is a splendid fraud (after all, George Bush was the erstwhile environment president), but radical ecologists are making crucial contributions, at least to the spread of a general percipience.[15] Again, while the West intellectualizes, in all political impotence, the third world has seen grassroots movements both take root, and succeed, in practically resisting, if not completely halting, the wanton destruction of nature, if only because ecological degradation is a life-and-death matter (rather than a hip, *'lifestyle'* issue) for agrarian societies critically dependent on the land for survival.[16] The outstanding case in point is the heroic Chipko women of the foothills of the Himalayas (not accidentally, were they *women*, in the main), who managed to stave off government, World Bank, and private developers' depredations, so as to safeguard their forest wealth, representing their own ways, modes of life, and economies, in harmony with their physical environs. It is this harmonious vision of the earth, and its many guests (in which humans occupy no special privileged position), that is defining a whole earth perspective in which the old antagonisms of Eurocentrism may one day be dissolved. The fact that this is simply a precapitalist, tribal, philosophical orientation, come again to life, is of enormous significance, indeed a critical portent of the times.

Successful environmentalism would involve the defeat of both capitalist and socialist visions of the world, given their penchant for pushing growth without limits; as such, it is a formidable project facing formidable odds. Given the experience of Europeans in this regard, it is doubtful that they will give in voluntarily to common sense. Most likely, it will take a catastrophe of gargantuan proportions to halt processes of production, ways of life, and attitudes toward nature that are, ultimately, catastrophically self-destructive. The way things are going, we seem close enough to such events to make the possibility of ecological apocalypse quite imminent, with the litany of problems ranging from greenhouse gas emissions, acidification of lakes, forest depletion, ozone depletion, mounting generation of radioactive wastes,[17] desertification, species extinction, and the general destruction of bioresources.[18] The physical balance sheet, studded, as it must be, with incomprehensible numbers, can possibly only breed aphasia, but facts are still facts: deserts are gaining at the rate of 6 million hectares per year; tropical forests are vanishing at the rate of 30,000 square miles annually; fertile topsoils being lost at 25 billion tons per year; animal and bird species becoming extinct at the rate of one a year; plants and herbs at several hundred annually, and so on. Such, the grim score card of (patriarchical) Man vs. Nature. How can we, then, *not* believe that apocalypse is nigh?

CULTURAL SURVIVAL

The *monocultures* of capitalism and socialism, strikingly European in provenance, have rendered the once opulent diversity of world societies, bare, bleak, monist, unidimensional, and monotonous (where the most recognizable symbol in the world is Coca-Cola or McDonald's); at European hands, culture after indigenous culture was looted, torched, put to sword and extirpated, beginning with Christopher Columbus's egregious genocide of native peoples (and their great civilizations such as the Aztecs, Incas, and so on) in the New World. The U.S. colonists pursued the same logic of calculated misanthropy relentlessly, in North America, rendering the only great civilization of that continent, the Native American one, fit subjects only for museum displays when not banished, *èn masse*, into concentration camps. Europeans carried a similar message of obliteration to their fellow species in Asia and Africa, dulling the vital sparks of a living humanity in their fast and furious wake (the truth almost defies description: astoundingly enough, recreant cabals made up of pirates, privateers, and plunderers [altogether polite euphemisms for 'trading' companies such as the East India Company, for instance] successfully and unblushingly posed as bearers of a loftier, more elevated civilization. However, rationally, i.e., systematically, organized looting still bespeaks only the sway of a regime of looters, no matter how meretriciously, and dissemblingly, dressed up in fine, republican, 'parliamentary,' and 'democratic,' garb)

This scandalous, 'civilization-mongering', extirpation, topping the meager exploits of an Attila, was then taken over by the colonial elites, suitably trained in Eurocentric modes of thought by the departing masters, as third-world governments, after independence, sought to drag their hapless tribal wards forcibly into the cheerless modernisms of wage-labor and taxes. But, sooner or later, such large-scale, state-guided, tyrannies meet up with resistance; and today tribal and nativist cultures, poised on the very abyss of extinction, are fighting back for sheer survival. Sadly, the quintessentially typical military response of modernism, when challenged, ensures that such legitimate revivals of culture take on a regressive, retrograde, form, easily stereotyped, for its own purposes, by the cunning of capitalist reason. However, regardless of the nature of the oppression inflicted upon them by the

Draconian forces of modernism, the alternative cultures still extant today, having passed the bitter acid test of European destruction, are likely not to buckle under. Organizations like Survival International, COICA (Coordinadora de las Organisaciones Indigenas de la Cuenca Amazonia) in Latin American, and the Seventh Generation Fund in the United States, etc., hold promise of the much needed activism to come, thereby keeping alive the hope for a live, noncapitalist, cultural laboratory which may yet be called upon to seed the world anew, into a new renaissance, after the barbarism of the present is only a vanished memory.[19] As such, the trustees of the possibility of civilization are not the wretched economists, ready to plight their troth with the highest bidder, as per Keynes's hopelessly prosaic bourgeois vision, but the eventide reveries of our own forebears, cloaked in the full dignity of their near-extermination. This is only fitting: in human society, affective ideals, in contrast to material inspirations, are, always, *transcendent*.

NOTES

1. Today this topic is in vogue, so the literature, here, is burgeoning. Two, preliminary, readings might be Samir Amin (1989); and G. G. Joseph *et al.* (1990).
2. The term 'ideology' in Marxist parlance refers to false consciousness; in this text it is being used in the simpler sense of 'world-view,' or '*Weltanschaaung*,' as in Max Weber's usage.
3. Amartya Sen (1977).
4. The most cogent critique of western 'scientism' is to be found in P. Feyerabend (1978; 1987).
5. Much of Freudian psychoanalytics represents the very apotheosis of this malefic vision. For a feminist critique of such 'masculinist,' psychological, theorizing, see C. Gilligan (1982).
6. Aeons ago, French Rationalism, in the form of Levi-Strauss, discovered tribal epistemology as, antipodal to itself, wedded to the concrete. See Claude Levi-Strauss (1966).
7. Sandra Harding (1983; 1986) has much to say on this subject.
8. On this theme, Paul Feyerabend's (1978; 1987) lucubrations are simply outstanding.
9. Maria Mies (1986) argues persuasively for this issue, but her remarkable work is devalued by its apparent intellectual opportunism, with its tendency to bypass systematic empirical evidence, and to argue—suggestively—from strong cases alone.
10. My own study of housework in Utah, still awaiting publication, confirms this, quite regardless of the class background of the household.
11. See some explicit accounting, on this theme, by a Mr. Fielding Hall, as cited in Maria Mies (1986, *op. cit.*), p. 111.
12. For a recent assessment, see Maxine Molyneaux (1990).
13. See Chandra Mohanty (1988) and Vandana Shiva (1989) for some referents of this posture.
14. The outstanding western scholar who has made this point in all eloquence is the philosopher, Paul Feyerabend, *op. cit.*

15. For an early sign of a rethinking of such issues, on the part of western radicals, see Andre Gorz (1980).
16. See Vandana Shiva (1989; 1991) for a third-worldist perspective. Also, William Weinberg (1991).
17. On this theme, see K. A. Gourlay (1992).
18. See also P. Blaikie and H. Brookfield (1987), on the general issue of land degradation.
19. For a hopeful account of these developments, see Paul Ekins (1992).

7

THE REVEILLE OF EMANCIPATION: TOWARD VOLITION

BEYOND MARX: TOWARD SELF-DETERMINATION

The world today stands, all but unknowingly, at an enormously portentous, historical watershed: after a 300-year inveterate crusade to vanquish all its foes, internal and external, modernism has now triumphed quite supernally in the late twentieth century, having put paid, quite convincingly, to the (apparently) last 'opposition' worthy of the title—socialism. The old (European) gods of socialist liberation have failed us, quite spectacularly and irredeemably, although the real rationale for the failure has been far from understood, regrettably least of all by the (traditional) Left. The defiant modernist promise of the European eighteenth century, such as it was, stands now ready for deliverance as we approach the twenty-first century consummation of its wildest ambitions. It is the dismal age now, as was feared by the sadly percipient of yore, even as the Enlightenment tolled its dreary bells, given over uncompromisingly to Edmund Burke's lightless entourage of 'sophisters, economists, and calculators.' The burden, accordingly, of the burgeoning revolutionary critique(s), in the making, necessarily from beyond the pale of modernism, must fall as much upon the triumphant regime(s) of capital as upon the domain of its putative, erstwhile archenemy: Marxism,[1] which has posed for over a century as its only sane, credible, humane alternative, despite its very real history of disaster, and/or demoralization, wherever and whenever, it has been practically applied.

Before moving to a critical mining of the Marxian vein of materialism, however, it is quite salutary to remind ourselves of the essence of modernism, of which the former is, after all, but a very small part. *The guiding spirit of the modernist temper is corporatist intervention in all areas of social life aimed at severing the organic links that bind humans to their social nature.* This requires a spate of calamitous intrusions into private, personal, and familial, domains under the spurious slogan of 'rationalization,' which even critics like Max Weber were to ultimately applaud as signifying the immanent ideal of 'progress,' idealized as uniquely innate to western civilization. Amazingly, the wholesale destruction of local autonomies, and the authoritarian, hierarchical organization of all societal institutions (bureaucratization), is seen by the modernist impulse as but so many splendid moments in the exciting ascent of (European) man. To alienate, and then to subject to a craven subordination—that, in a nutshell, is the modernist way (to certain rack and ruin) of catastrophic uprooting of social relations. The disingenuous wiles of modernism, worked through the artful cunning of materialist reason, have robbed humans, of all ranks and races, of even the scantiest memory of the barest dignity, of self-respect, of assurance, of confidence, of joy, of serenity—in short, of their wholly inalienable, ineffable *humanity*. Speaking airily of the age of light and reason, and singing arias to the arrival of humanism and the 'rights of man,' modernism has skewered the human soul with the twisted scimitar of egregious greed.

No one could be left untouched by the grim architectonics of this convulsive plague; institution after institution, role by role, relation by relation, the modernist assault was to drain all social impulses—outside of plunder and spoils—of their affective content, carefully interposing abstract calculation and abstract loyalty to the reified impersonal deities ('law,' 'society,' 'state,' 'order,' etc.), that now stood, as the daunting new collectors of tax and tribute, in their stead. The systematic erosion and denudation of all little traditions, that might still carry the residues of emotive warmth and extra-material affections, implied the consecration of the only Big tradition left permissible: the reign of profiteering in a regime of plutocracy. Family, kinship, affinity, friendship, camaraderie—in short, the very possibility of an empowering 'personalization,' and 'identity,' outside of the tabulations and classifications necessary for *extraction* and *dominion* (such as the issue of number tags, appropriate to gulags) was to be radically expunged. Instead, all power was to be transferred to the lifeless, bureaucratic, machinery of Society and State, both now infused with this distal, imperious, commanding presence reducing the now atomized 'citizenry' to the status of mere insects in an oppressed colony of degraded subjects.

A more efficient penal colony is surely unimaginable; all *internal* struggles within the modernist paradigm (party against party, class against class, gender against gender, nation against nation, race against race) merely strengthen its dominion all the more securely, for participating precisely as required by its logic, for vindicating its apocryphal ideology of pluralism, freedom, and 'open-endedness,' for being forced—sooner or later—to accept the status of becoming just another vested 'interest' in civil society. All such struggles, which usually appeal no further than the system's own sense of justice, law, and constitutionality, are cooptable and controllable for they do not challenge, even remotely, the dictatorial premises of the modernist entrenchment in history; indeed, they are the pliant victims of the great *pretence* of the system (democracy, rule of law, justice, etc.) itself. The tyrant emperor has had no vestment worth the name for centuries; it is we, unknowingly and philanthropically, who have draped him with the enveloping facade of normalcy.

Just one example may, perhaps suffice, denoting the extent of our ideological surrender to the ruling 'political formula': 'democracy,' for instance, is the grand delusion of twentieth-century modernism (despite the fact that it was always imposed on it by dint of force). Certainly, it is hard to imagine a more politically vacuous term; what, in fact, does it mean? One can turn to virtually any institution of modernism to notice that it is conspicuous only by its absence; the army, the bureaucracy, the police, the university, the entire corporate system (factories, trading agencies, banks, etc.)—not one of these major agencies is run democratically in any sense of the word. If we subtract these vast domains from the social fabric, what, indeed, remains that can now claim to be run 'democratically'? So, modernist democracy boils down only to stuffing a near worthless piece of paper in a box once every so many years (to claim, as with Churchill, that it beats its *modernist* alternative, namely 'dictatorship,' is akin to saying that since life is, on margin, preferable to death one should endure *any* version of living no matter how uncongenial; this form of reactionary political logic, which Bhaskar titles the 'TINA [There Is No Alternative] hypothesis' is typical in its confinement of options to the airless, exitless chamber of modernist discourse); besides, majorities need not be 'right'—nor, if they were, could they expect to prevail against money, guns, and propaganda, owned and operated by powerful minorities. Also, if they yet prevailed, they would have effectively won the 'right' only to *impose* their will on weaker segments of the political order. As obvious, the paradoxes of modernism, given its antagonistic internal structures, are thematically endless, and necessarily insoluble. Tragically, however, the rights of self-direction, and self-determination, that entire peoples have lost in this cynical political charade, are today, after decades of indoctrination, almost unimaginable for the ordinary citizen fighting a losing, if daily, battle for bare survival with but a modicum of human dignity. We have been effectively dispossessed of the means, methods, materials—and even the memory—of autonomy and self-governance, though quite paradoxically by a tendentious rhetoric of freedom, rights, and empowerment drawn from a bygone, revolutionary age. Materially, artificially, and antagonistically drawn divisions of social forms are inherently irreconcilable; no 'political formula,' short of rejecting the rules of the game altogether, can ever suffice. Social peace (unless enforced by cannon) and modernist drives are quite simply incompatible.

Marx only paid attention to one of these infamous alienations, where the direct producer is divorced from her means of sustenance; but modernism carries this principle of outright dispossession over, as an encompassing *geist*, to all relations. Thus, the scientist is divorced from the means of her research, the physician from the means and methods of healing, the educator from her means of education, the groom and bride from the means of their marriage, and so on. Instead, corporatism insinuates, and inserts, itself as a licensing, regulating, and extortionist body claiming implicit suzerainty over all domains of social life. So the scientist must now kowtow to an establishment, the educator to a university, the healer to a medical board, the bride to a civil magistrate, and so on. The corporatist dagger aims straight at the very heart of autonomy and self-provision; all must be mediated, within a venal chain of tolls and exactions, through the mechanisms of state. Public (i.e., market and state) appropriation of private domains is the watchword of the system; modernism, paradoxically, first defines *absolute personal space* (a category quite unknown to traditionalism) almost archetypically, only to go on, later, to conquer that space absolutely.

Indeed, the creation of an abject and total *dependency*, and the paralysis of all normal and natural, impulses of self-care, have been at the very heart of the modernist revolution. Contrary to propaganda, capitalism thrives not in the creation of wealth but in the creation of artificial, generalized *scarcities*, for the many, that then become the secure means of a financial transformation into (exploitative) wealth for a few. The steadfast destruction of all native talents, skills, and industry is therefore its very alpha and omega. In this sense, technology is not merely laborsaving and/or cost-reducing, but also a necessary, disciplinary tool for the degradation, and destruction, of any and all average skills that might yet yield some token independence for the worker, artisan, and craftsman. Market and state provision then arrive to substitute, at all times, and at dire cost to economic and political freedoms, for any and all forms of direct self-provisioning. The less we are, the less we know, the less we can do for ourselves, the stronger is the system, the more secure its rule. Everywhere it places its specialized, elite proxies to secure and consolidate its conquests: the intelligentsia thinks for us, the planners plan for us, the physicians prescribe our diets, the priests keep our conscience, the rulers rule us, and so on. As such, the system keeps us not in any 'self-incurred' immaturity, but in deliberately fostered, artificial, egregious ignorance whose sole beneficiary is the structure of domination (and its various hangers-on) itself. How such horrendous, all-total, despotism over social life could come to be seen as the great boon of the Enlightenment, indeed the very acme of a humane civilization, can only remain one of the great, enduring mysteries of our epoch.

The role of 'science' in this relentless struggle for expanding control over the lives of people is especially worthy of note, substituting as it has for religion as a preeminently self-justifying ideology, the sanctity of science, as privileged knowledge, has alway been the preferred shroud for the most sinister of modernist designs (bidding farewell to European science would mean the return, instead, of older traditions of friendship, empathy, curiosity, reflection, and understanding [in one word, *hospitality*, toward all peoples and cultures]; the latter based not on the calculated detachment of the uncaring observer feigning the mask of objectivity, but on the very subjective, human capacity to identify with the joys and sorrows of fellow humanity. It was this very hospitality that the Europeans received [and abused] in abundant measure, quite gratuitously from indigenous peoples, characteristically even during [and after] the moment of ignoble conquest). Contemptuous of lay opinion, jealously resisting public controls, and squanderously wasteful of public funds, the scientific establishment, like the gods of Olympus, have appropriated to themselves a monopoly over the process of production and dissemination of all 'correct' forms of knowledge, carefully weeding out noncorporatist and antisystemic traditions, intimations, and apprehensions altogether. Wielding unmediated—and largely untrammelled—state power, the scientific elite have freely enacted dictatorial mandates for the masses; here, forbidding the teaching of, say, creationism (as a rival theology), there banning the practice of homeopathy (as a rival therapy), and so on. However, knowledge is a local product, the creature of custom, convention, history, and context; no centralized priesthood, from afar, has the right to decide such issues, by force, for sects that do not care to believe in them. *Knowledge, like the knowers themselves, is plural, relative, and multifaceted;* no vulgar absolutism, in this area, must be allowed to hold undisputed sway, fraudulently usurping the license(s) of scientific authority. Possibly, it were best to state the moral now: any and all forms of *absolutist* thinking—involving the deification of one set of values over others—spell little short of extinction for the planet; only relativism, and epistemic pluralism, hold the key to survival.

It still comes as a revelation to some that state Socialism simply carried these atrocious tendencies to a degree improbable even in the most 'advanced' capitalist regimes, creating a passive, dependent, and cowed populace on a scale perhaps unknown to human history. It could not be otherwise; Marxism has always been but a banished *pretender* to the throne of modernism, seeking (when in command of social power), to substitute its own, even more implacable, exactions in place of the extortions of capitalism. How a system that began as a critique of commodity fetishism in turn was to fetishize social labor and its 'productivity,' is a story all in itself. But, as implied in the foregoing, there is much in classical Marxism that merits a quick, if quiet, abandonment,[2] perhaps even a radical excision: (a) its economic reductionism, (b) its assumption of a link between the unveilment of ideology and the revolutionary moment, (c) its notional linearity of historical 'stages' (drawn from a lightning read of European history, and then imposed uncritically on the rest of the world), (d) the implied self-destruction of history/class struggle etc., within the idea of a grand consummation of history (so-called 'communism'), and (e) the highly simplified conceptions of radical social change generally. Speaking broadly, a Marxism divested of its messianic predictions, its vulgar reductionism, its materialism, its reification of 'science,' and its penchant for concentrating the 'political' moment solely on aggregate, macro-entities (state, class, nation, etc.), may still serve as a useful analytical tool in *understanding* certain aspects of contemporary capitalist dynamics.

Nonetheless, there are inherent limits to the efficacy of the distorting biases of economism and materialism. If nothing else, even an amended Marxism would still remain seriously deficient for its apparent inability to directly incorporate collateral social ontologies such as race, gender, culture, ecology, etc., into its social accounts, as legitimate and critical sites of *praxis* in their own right. These autonomous domains are far from being simply assimilable to that of class, as in the old-style base-determines-superstructure logic, despite some obvious overlapping of otherwise separable agendas. The simple Marxian critique of mainstream (neoclassical) economics has always been the latter's neglect of (social) relational entities like class in favor of an (asocial) individualist ontology. Yet, a similar critique could easily be posted of Marxist 'economics': what about race, one might ask; or gender; or culture, as both an explanatory variable and a basis for social action? Why are such nonindividualist, socially defined, and ontologically obvious domains not part of a historical understanding of the dynamics of capitalism? It will not suffice to reject race and gender as ontologically not being primary 'social' categories; enough that they have, epistemically, been granted that 'reality' in social discourse. Marxists must learn that *epistemic fallacies* ['ideology,' or 'false consciousness,' in Marxian parlance] nonetheless have objective, real consequences in social life. The realm of *'appearance,'* in other words, is at the very cutting edge of *reality*; indeed, were not systemic exclusions based on these criteria not significant for the pace, and pattern, of expansion of the realm of capital?

Interestingly, the answer here unites mainstream and Marxist analytics inasmuch as bourgeois materialism and Marxist materialism share a common provenance in the capitalist Enlightenment. *The key concept here is rationality: rationality is assimilated, in both accounts, to self-interest, and then self-interest is attached mechanically to the domain of material motivations alone.* As such, almost by definition, social action based on the putatively noneconomic markers of race and gender, as causally efficacious categories, becomes either a form of *irrational* behavior, in the conservative account, or functions not too far apart from that, as evidence of laggard, anachronistic, precapitalist 'vestiges/residues,' in traditional Marxian renderings. Thus, for instance, it was argued, that erstwhile South African capitalism was simply 'primitive' for being racist, implying that extended—'advanced'—*capitalist* development would, *ipso facto*, lead to an abandonment of explicitly racist policies. In both instances, the progression of a capitalist rationality is seen as 'automatically' dissolving these hangovers from our 'irrational' past, in due course, purely in the fullness of time[3] as though history were a grand and gracious ascent into the ephemera of (capitalist) civility.

Aside from the fundamental error in this reductionist, linear conceptualization (first 'self-evidently' tying reason to material self-interest, and then viewing capitalism as the very apotheosis of an unfolding, historical trend of rationality, *à la* Max Weber), the fact is that quite apart from the context of capitalism, race, and gender (much as religion, kinship, culture, etc.) have not proved readily soluble identities, even in putatively 'socialist' crucibles. Besides, *rationality has to do with the appropriate choice of means contingent upon a specific end; it cannot be defined as encompassing the ends themselves.* Reason, *qua* reason, is independent of self-interest, or any other 'interest.' At any rate, race and gender are independent, sociohistorically defined, culturally loaded, ontological entities: they are real—and *reality may not be reduced, but needs be dealt with on its own terrain.*

Racism and gender oppression predate capitalism (but so, of course, does class exploitation), it is true (though not raised to the level of a 'science' as under capitalism); but capital—when it suits it—utilizes every existing fissure in society, no matter how retrograde, to advance its socioeconomic ambitions (*viz.*, control over its life-process). It is pure delusion to imagine, as with the roseate vision of the *Communist Manifesto*, that capitalism erodes all traditional bondings and identifications, like an all-purpose bleaching agent (that socialism is no more capable in this regard is evident in the survival of, say, anti-Semitism in much of Eastern Europe and the ex-USSR). While this may have been true, but only as a heady impulse, in the heroic, even hasty, epoch of European capitalism (in some moments of the French Revolution, for example), brief as it was, it has never been true since, and, certainly, has not been even remotely plausible in the third world.

The 'progressivist' image of capitalism, carried over into Marxism, is something that *capitalist* ideologues have enshrined in the popular imagination for decades, such that most of us start to identify all good things to be the 'gift' of the Europeans, in line with the idea of the civilizing 'mission' of capitalism. To cite just one instance, even the putatively (Euro)'Marxist' Bill Warren[4] seemed convinced of the egregious myth that capitalism and democracy are 'Siamese twins' (*true only in the negative sense that they are usually swiftly separated at birth*), thereby standing history on its head, not least the history of his own mother country, England, where the worker-based Chartist movement fought bitterly for democracy *against* the conjoint will of the aristocracy and the bourgeoisie. Democracy, even in the purely formal sense of equal electoral rights for all, much like female suffrage, has been won by dint of intrepid struggles, by working peoples (and their allies), *against* the will of capital. Typically, though, once won at the barricades, such rights are quickly co-opted by bourgeois ideology to suggest, in all dissemblance, that these are the benign bequests of capital. One has only to look at the incipient capitalist nations of the third world (particularly the so-called NICs) to realize that dictatorship, and not democracy, has been the prevalent norm in this regard. Neocolonial Hong Kong has still, in the nineties, not fully enfranchised its working class; South Korea, until recently, had the world's longest workweek, with the Korean Central Intelligence Agency (KCIA) serving as industrial relations managers; and Taiwan and Singapore have long impressed the world with facets far less dubious than their democratic pretensions.

Should all of this seem only an Oriental (or Latin American) accident, one only needs to remember the altogether too recent era of European fascist, proto-fascist, crypto-fascist, and other dictatorial regimes: Italy, Germany, Spain, Portugal, Greece, Turkey, etc., that give the lie to such lapidary canards (to say nothing of the recent upsurge of similarly inclined movements all across Europe, east and west). As noted, the fact that Swiss women had to wait patiently until 1981 for the vote (as opposed to the 'primitive' cowboy state of Wyoming that granted it more than a century earlier) provides a telling index as to the supposedly progressive nature of 'advanced' capitalist regimes. Of course, when labor discipline (i.e., the 'class struggle') is not a pressing problem, the democratic political *form* (rather than *content*) is usually advantageous to capital because it allows for capitals, in the plural, to compete without fear of being *politically* expropriated. Dictatorship would give one faction, or one power bloc, of capital ominously omnipotent powers against other capitals (capitals fearing each other just as much as they fear conjoint working-class revolt; this would largely explain the pattern of early, restricted, bourgeois democracy in the preeminently architectonic 'model' capitalist regime of the United States).

It is with this limited notion of purely (class) internal checks and balances that the European bourgeoisie entered the historical arena, *in fretful memory of late feudal absolutism that had exalted the state above capital*.[5] Of course, popular struggles eventually wrested the idea, and practice, of democracy—*this simple artifact of class tactics*—away from, and against, capital, allowing slowly for a gradual extension of suffrage to workers, women, minorities, etc., a process by no means complete today even in putatively 'advanced' Europe (with its recent disgraceful descent into rampant, but entirely modernist, forms of 'tribalism').

The fundamental problem of (orthodox) Marxism can now be succinctly described: *Marxism is hopelessly incomplete in its diagnostics and miserably underspecified, thereby, in its prescriptions.*[6] A guide to analysis? Yes. A program for emancipatory social change? No. One must, accordingly, approach Marxism in much the same way an educated consumer approaches capitalist health care, at least in the United States: make use of allopathic diagnostics, by all means, but always look to alternative therapies for a cure (Marxist surgeries, unfortunately, kill just as efficiently as capitalist ones!) The alternative to capitalism is not only 'scientific socialism,' as Marx, and his epigones, tried to portray it for a hundred years; indeed, there are—as must be—probably as many material, and nonmaterial, utopias as we choose to define, affirm, and fight for (none of this is to gainsay either the reality, or the importance, of traditional notions of class struggle; rather it is to emphasize alternate struggles of equal valency that are becoming the norm today; *contra* Marx, however, it should be absolutely clear that the 'socialist' variants of class rule [the empirical entities masquerading under the myth of 'communism'] cannot—now or ever—be the ready solvents of the malaise of modernism).

Speaking concretely, here is just one small, historically valid, 'example': a society of peasant proprietorships based on small-scale private property, was perfectly conceivable, in Europe of the late eighteenth century, especially in France after the revolution. And yet, for Marxism, this would automatically represent an 'irrational,' even 'regressive' mode of production since economies of large-scale production may not be yielded readily by small farms[7] (notice the coercive, 'economistic,' logic; it is not what peasants may desire; it is what Marxism *prescribes* for them that is 'right'). As such, a peasant society, *ipso facto*, is unfit to produce the communist utopia, aside from having the 'wrong' class base of producers (peasants, instead of workers), for starters. *But, contra Marx, it is obvious that such a society would clearly have been a nonexploitative, classless society, even as per Marxist 'requirements.' Indeed, it would be far more feasible than the mechanistic, linear projection of the standard communism-after-socialism piece of historical fantasy* (regretfully, we now know what comes after socialism . . .). *The Marxist, therefore, offers his private, technicist preoccupation with maximizing social (industrial) productivity as a necessary, historically mandated, goal to those very strata upon whom the burden of the productive labor involved is to be visited*!

Marx's disparagement of 'village idiocy,' in context, and with several caveats, was perhaps barely meaningful; but it surely pales behind the ubiquitous spread of 'advanced' industrial cretinism that is so marked a feature of contemporary western capitalism, where the average citizenry is denuded of all culture, social skills, and information, other than the purely technicist quota strictly necessary for functioning as cogs in the machine. I have never met, despite extensive travels amongst the peasantry of many continents, a village idiot; but the robotized cretins of industry are almost impossible to avoid no matter where you travel. The point could not be clearer: the 'realm of reason' is bare, barren, and bereft of any solace worth the name; it does not nourish, succor, or uplift. It degrades all whom it touches. Thus we are robotized, our deepest instincts buried unhappily under the mantle of function, office, and duty. The miracle is that the human spirit is still alive despite the ubiquity of these degrading structures of repression.

One last example, to underscore the argument: Lenin, in his justly famous *April Theses* (delivered 4 April 1917), thundered to an excited populace that workers could henceforth organize, operate, and run their own state and society. But, only years later, as workers took over factories from their bourgeois managers, in all ingenuous socialist enthusiasm, the very same master dialectician asked them to hand factory governance back over to the managers. Workers run their own factories!: what a fairy tale, said he![8] This is singularly telling, illustrative as it is of standard Marxist practice in state socialist societies to date: workers are merely the tools ('agents of history') to be used for the greater glory of stepped-up production, solidly under the iron rule of the Marxist masters of the polity. However, if they choose to do their own thing, economically or politically, then Marxist governors shoot them down with more impunity than possible even in a capitalist society (short of absolute fascism). Naturally, pseudosophisticated Marxist rhetorics of rejection stand ready to supply a daunting nomenclature of analytical abuse ('Syndicalism,' 'Anarchism,' 'Utopian socialism,' etc.) to be heaped upon such unlicensed, and quite recalcitrant, dissent.

So, despite all the propaganda to the contrary, classical Marxian socialists have always blindly worshipped the advancement of the forces of production (as per Lenin, adjuring politically mature workers to hand over newly liberated factories back to managers), as the key to an ever receding utopia, while repudiating any attempt by workers themselves to take control of the forces and relations of production (as workers indeed tried to do in the early years of Bolshevik dictatorship). *So, worker self-determination, within Marxism, the 'science of the proletariat,' has always been a no-no*: workers are obliged to march according to the tune of the master plan. Small wonder one ends up with gulags like the USSR. Indeed, on this score, it was Bakunin, not Marx, who was by far the better prophet.[9] More importantly, not Lenin nor Mao, but Gandhi[10] it was, *who pointed things in the right direction*, however obscurely, despite his many, perhaps inevitable, insularities and idiosyncracies, of time, place, and personality; certainly (and this is no mean index of an agenda for emancipation), fewer mass murders have been committed in his name.

The modernist understanding of 'work' as *alienated labor*, is not substantially different between its bourgeois and Marxian variants. The alienation of the product of social labor was as thoroughgoing in a socialist, as much as any capitalist, factory with workers seen as but productive 'tools' in either case, under the whip of the masters of society; neither system had any use for the direct production and consumption of use values on the part of self-organized producers. At the material base of the modernist edifice, capitalist or socialist, rests an entire compendium of alien, unhappy, and forced toils of the myriads deprived of their own means, and methods, of sustenance by state power wedded to a putatively 'higher' logic of material rationality (it is time we recognized that the purpose of human existence is simply human existence; not labor, nor consumption, nor the living out of some abstractly specified 'ideal'). All the accumulated cheerlessness of the modern era stems from this baneful dehumanization of work, and the related destruction of the creative, human expenditures of personal and social energies. To heal this stultifying breach of social propriety, *to return work back to the workers*, to transform it into but another species of play, of artistry, and of self-expression, is to repudiate the entire economistic logic of modernism; it is to reject capitalism and socialism—and their repressive 'divisions of labor'—not piecemeal, or hesitantly, but *tout a fait*. Contra Marcuse, Eros *is* civilization.

In his famous '*Theses on Feuerbach*,' Marx could, epitomizing the serene confidence of the all-conquering European, state (*Thesis No. X*) that while the standpoint of the 'old type' of materialism (i.e., 'bourgeois' theory) was 'civil society,' the standpoint of the 'new materialism' (i.e., Marxism) was 'human society or social humanity.' Regrettably, this very universal sounding 'standpoint' was always a rather hollow promise for the myriads who were either women, workers, minorities, or tribal cultures, outside the pale of European-style 'modernisms,' for simply not including them as serious, historical agencies with 'standpoints,' perchance, of their own. It is in this obviously historically conditioned dereliction of philosophical responsibility that Marxism today discovers its inherent, both ontic and epistemic, limits. Not unrelatedly, these limits apply, unreservedly, to the entire paradigm of modernism itself. *The modernists have tried* (often against the will of numerous other constituencies, not always 'reactionary') *to change the world*; *the point now, however* (owing to the very success of their endeavor), *is to save it.*

From Socialism to Self-Determination

The political moral may now be clearly drawn: *workers and peasants, in rejecting capitalist modes (if, as, and when they do) have the right to autonomous social constructions of their choice*, no matter how 'utopian' these may be judged by the scholastics of Marxism—always laying claim, as it does, to an Archimedean, apodictic knowledge—even *when these do not maximize the social dividend in material terms*. Besides, once we break with the absurdity of *a priori* wisdom, as with the confident 'stages of history' epistemics, it is clear that nothing can be dismissed as 'utopian' ahead of the real attempt to put it into practice. History cannot be committed, *by definition*, and *a priori*. *Socialism thereby, in the century to come, will stand simply for self-determination on the part of the real producers; no longer can it be used as the pretext for wielding the whip of iron discipline by a new stratum of nonworkers against the new laboring classes.*

No more fetishism of work and production; no more glorification of the 'motherland' (or, worse, the 'fatherland') i.e., *nationalism*;[11] and no more worship of the all-potent Leviathan of a brutish, 'socialist' state. A free association of *people* (not just *producers*, as Marx, in some moods, visualized it: stated baldly, the universe of humanity is larger than the constituency of the working class; in any case, a true humanism needs be *inclusive*, not exclusive in its orientations.); free, that is in both entry and exit (no absurdly Kafkaesque Berlin walls to keep entire societies in incarceration). All this would seem to follow simply as the lessons of recent socialist history, although the farsighted, like Bakunin, deductively anticipated these discoveries by almost a century. The latter-day Marxian socialist must now comprehend the vital lesson of history: the path to *decommodification* lies in the direct embrace (in production and consumption) of the manifold paradigms of use values, *not* through the fatally mediated *national* path of *state-regulated* commodity production.

In broader terms, social life needs be construed as an organic *whole*, not just as an abstract *totality*, incorporating all the critical moments of social ontology (gender, race, ethnicity, as much as class) as key elements of *praxis*. Human welfare cannot be reduced to a mess of pottage, nor a scheme of prescribed activities: *at its highest, socialism is simply the aspiration of self-determination, an adjunct of the innate capacity, and indeed desire, for freedom of choice in a human community*. The urges of self-determination operating amongst the masses can no longer be roughly, and tendentiously, assimilated into the private, political designs of aspirant ruling classes and elites, as in the past; indeed it is the latter that must now yield their ruling ambitions to make way for the former.

As such, the *nation-state*, an incipient, crypto-capitalist political entity (taken over blindly by socialisms as a given)—dating from thirteenth-fourteenth century Europe, embodying the late feudal reaction to the political crisis of feudalism[12]—is simply an irrelevant unit/realm of final analysis, despite its *de facto reality*, when the welfare of people is the issue under consideration. Peoples and nations are distinctly separable entities, though the former can often be organized (usually to their detriment) in the form of the latter, either by charismatic (including theocratic) or bureaucratic despotisms. Such organizations always reflect top-down initiatives: there is simply no instance of peoples organizing themselves, bottom-up, into *national* entities; indeed, there would be no obvious necessity for such a pointless definition at such a remotely macro level. *Only those classes, strata, and factions that wish to tax, rule, exploit, dominate, and oppress others have an interest in the creation, and maintenance, of such abstract political formations.*

Nation-to-nation relations—as in mainstream parlance, too often uncritically appropriated by radicals—can only boil down to the *agendas* of the ruling classes (and thus is hardly representative of the oppressed, the exploited, and the ruled). *Peoples, fundamentally, are cultural, not economic entities*[13] (contrary to both capitalist and Marxist definitions); as such, self-determination always applies to specific cultures, and ways of life, that must, *ipso facto*, be granted autonomy from the modernizing ambitions of their rulers, taxers, and exploiters. The fundamental alienation introduced into history by the Enlightenment lies precisely in the distorting *redefinition* of human relations in economic and political terms, while simultaneously inventing alien societal forms based on them. Reversing this negative polarity, and thereby restoring precapitalist valuations, is a necessary first step in any drive for human emancipation.

Stated differently, self-determination is primarily a cultural, and only secondarily a political, notion. What the coming era could reveal, as and when people choose to exert their right to reclamation, is the sheer superfluity of the state/nation superstructures, given the resolve of ordinary peoples to govern themselves, yet again, at the microlevels. The state as an imperatively coordinated association, i.e., as an entity imposed upon peoples by force, can, in an appropriately enlightened political vision, be dispensed with. As peoples gain in autonomy, the power of the state will, proportionately, be reduced. Obviously, this can only be the outcome of the struggle on the part of the few, and the many, to recover control over their lives, from both capitalist exploiters and state tyrants.

Contrary to the articles of faith of both capitalist and socialist ideology, *we do not require to be governed*; we do require, on the other hand, to be left alone. That would be genuine *laissez-faire* (allowing people to do 'their own thing' is not tantamount to a free license for Hobbesian anarchy, as the conservative pundits of order are always cautioning us; indeed it is doubtful whether the human nervous psyche is at all conditioned for (prolonged) non-orderly forms of social existence. In that respect, Prigogene's finding, in the molecular universe, of the eventual reemergence of order even in systems characterized by increasing chaos, might be more instructive. The issue, of course, is *not* order versus anarchy but an order evolved spontaneously from the milieu of participatory, affective, ties as opposed to order that is imposed by force. Letting a thousand experimental flowers bloom does not, of course, imply that these experiments will not collide against each other: the collision of wills is but human life as usual; that this collision need not take catastrophic forms—such as latter-day world wars—is given us by the experience of our precapitalist social forms): freedom from economic and political tyranny; freedom from the rule of experts, elites, professionals, and all the other service adjuncts of an alienated, exploitative, society. Those who still think we need a federal bureaucracy, the CIA, and six fleets patrolling the high seas, at taxpayer expense, had better take another look at how the society of African bushmen (before 'progress' destroys them, as well) is able to exist, and thrive, without these costly, and destructive, entailments of affluence.

It is useful to remember that social life did not begin with nation-states; it need not end with them either. On the contrary, most of human society has been based, for aeons, on small, not big, traditions that cannot be totalized, aggregated, and assimilated into some larger designs of the wealthy and the powerful. All of the implacable contradictions of modern society (form of government, mode of justice, etc.) arise from the artificial entity, the state, that inserts rational-legal institutions, of systematized extortion, in lieu of ordinary ways of life, little practices, and simple customs. *We need not produce, consume, nor distribute, across the abstraction of a nation, or even a collection of nation-states.* And this is not at all to fall prey to allegedly 'parochial' visions of so-called autarchy; *world trade, and intercultural exchanges, it will be remembered, flourished long prior to international trade.*

Speaking practically, there is no reason why, say Utah, needs to be governed (or to be held accountable) by Washington; or, to carry the argument further, for a district like Moab, in Utah, to be governed by the Capitol in Salt Lake City, and so on. The top-down nature of administration follows the top-down nature of the capitalist economy (usually the same in 'socialist' regimes, if not even more so): organized from above, by the expropriators, for the expropriators. Peoples can reclaim their patrimonies/matrimonies against the state, nation, alien markets, and the exploiting classes, but only given such a determination. As, when, and where this happens, this will eliminate a very large set of alienations, and irreconcilable contradictions, that have bedeviled the entire epoch of modernism.[14]

Traditions are not right or wrong: they just are (they can, like anything, be judged from the outside, but to what avail?). *Modernism is wrong in that it has always been imposed by modernizers at cost to those being modernized* (a different matter if it were freely chosen by peoples as against their own ways of life: this has almost never happened). Modernism, whether with Ataturk in Turkey, Lenin with Russia, or with the British in India, has always been rammed down a captive/subject populace by force. Indeed, such *civilization-mongers* (to employ a delectable phrase of Engels) have been the very bane of modern history; it is high time that their tendentious plans, for others, were quietly derailed.

Consistent with the theses being advocated here, even 'bad' guys have the right to organize and propagate their views (*so even the modernist's passion for modernism is legitimate*; it is his victims who need to offer resistance), no matter how inhospitable their ideas and however inclement their views; evil (however conceived) may not be banned *a priori*, and by fiat, by one self-ordained set of agents; it can, however, be *resisted* by those who care enough for norms of decency (however defined). Where both socialists and capitalist zealots have erred is in not recognizing this simple precept of true liberty (and in claiming all political virtue for themselves). As noted earlier, human life will always remain, at all levels of social existence, a tussle of wills. Moral orders may not be legislated; they have to be arrived at, repeatedly, allowing for free and open participation, for making and unmaking. This process has neither beginning nor end: it constitutes, in essence, the perpetual continuity of social existence. Both capitalism and socialism try to freeze this process into an end-state (either by force of arms, or by force of rigid constitutions that ban options for all time), as though history were to halt with them. Of course, this has proved a delusion for socialists: capitalists will be similarly distempered.

What nonmodern societies had all along is something denied under both socialism and capitalism: *conviviality*. It still exists amongst those precapitalist peasant and tribal cultures that have not yet been destroyed by modernist intrusions. They, whose notions of value may not be measured in material terms; they, whose aim is not growth, nor power; they, who do not seek to poison the air and water, nor to bore holes in the atmosphere; they, who are not involved in stockpiling unthinkable weapons of mass extermination, or engaged in mad arms races, nor in unleashing holocausts (accidental or intentional) based on the former; they who are more richly and undefinably *plural* and variegated than our cookie-cutter deformities of industrial taste, art, and aesthetics; they, who are more consensual than any capitalist or socialist society can ever hope to be, through centuries of usage, habituation, and consignment. They are the convivials; they have what we lack, what we crave. They are the civilized, the cultured, the peoples at peace with their environment.

In such entities, we must hope to find what 400 years of Mammon worship has nearly permanently destroyed: *the inherent opulence, diversity, and dignity of humankind, averse to all monocultures, whether capitalist or socialist.* To amend the hopelessly Eurocentric Marx, it is far better, perhaps, to worship Hanumana the monkey or Sabbala the cow than to fetishize production and reify things; however suckled in a pagan creed outworn, theirs the enchantment, ours the defeasance—of the wonders of nature, and the nurturance of genuine human relations. The ultimate irony for Marxism is that 'primitive communism' may have more to teach us about utopia than 'advanced' communism; *it is realizable, unlike the latter, because it has been realized* (and still endures in many simple tribal formations not yet deformed by capitalist penetration), across continental and cultural divides, for millenia.[15] The truth is as simple as it is indefeasible: contrary to its 'progressivist' guise, *modernism is alienation*.

Notice that self-determination is not a prescriptive utopia, it is not a determinate state: *it is only a minimal condition for peoples to define their own meanings, invent their own engagements, elisions, escapes, and entertainments*. This will continue to imply *struggle*, between ways and alternate ways: but convivial societies—as in our tribal past—can, will, and must learn to give and take in this regard. Indeed, quite contrary to European fantasies of Utopia, as the very consummations of societal bliss and the expurgation of all morbidities, the vision espoused in this work does not violate the simple axioms of social reality; it is not as if ordinary human ills will ever disappear even in the best of all possible worlds: it is just that they can be, as they once were, 'bounded' within the important, embalming containment of affective, face-to-face, human relations, as within the metaphorical 'family' where much that is bad, ugly, and even evil, continues to happen without (re)producing the chilling alienation of impersonal societal forms, and without threatening, as a consequence, the very existence of humankind. As sentient beings, we will still clash with each other, over various domains, but it could yet be within a framework of values that inherently supports a cooperative, communitarian, resolve to find good faith solutions in the spirit of mutual accommodation. Utopia, in this rendering, is not the European fantasy of the absolutist elimination of all social pathologies but their pacific containment within a benign modus of affective reciprocities, goodwill, and care.

Freedom is always freedom *to*, not freedom *from*; in that sense we, as humans, are always 'free'—free, that is, to struggle for one's beliefs and convictions. All freedoms, capitalist, socialist, and beyond, stem from that fundamental freedom that is always ours in all societies, at all times. *The realm of freedom is, therefore, not some material, historical goal to be realized as in Eurovisions of utopia, but an ideational precondition vested in our own energies and determinations.* Of course, freedom as a precondition given to all does not magically produce a Shangri-La; it points, instead, to a fairly inevitable clash between competing human values and interests as an unavoidable concomitant of free will(s). The 'solution' (that can only be arrived at through trial and error), under such circumstances, can only be a serious commitment to an open plurality of *changeable* norms so people, howsoever organized, can move freely between various value zones, as often as they wish. Clearly, the rigid 'nation-state' of modernism, resting on the predatory logic of *control*, is virulently antithetical to any such fluidity of affiliations seeking to pinion social and physical space under structurally frozen positions, roles, and hierarchies. Thus understood, it should be obvious that modern social evolution, far from increasing the range of choice, has served only to cripple and confine it within arbitrary bounds; in European history, at least since Antiquity, it is almost a case of a straight-line descent to a state of generalized serfdom, in which its erstwhile 'socialist' societies stand at the very nadir of that hapless process.

In line with the foregoing, we must now radically revise our (European) conceptions of 'social change'; 'planned,' sweeping, draconian, 'macro' transformations (as implied in both socialist and capitalist revolutions) only pave the way securely for a new class of potentates (whether in the Iran of the Mullahs or in the Russia of the Commissars), now rendered even more implacable for having swept away the existing residues of customary liberties and enfranchisements. Only the desperately power hungry could ever crave such totalitarian overhauls, and we must not become willing dupes of their depraved dreams of conquest. The altogether human, emancipatory, urges that move us all, consciously and unconsciously, must not be allowed to become the basis for despotism by unscrupulous rulers and power brokers, in much the same way that the simple, common, sentiment of religiosity has been for the longest time the secure and steady basis for the rabid tyranny of popes and priesthoods. Liberation, to be consistent with liberty, must always be *particularistic*, not general and abstract, offering resistance only to the specifics of any given form of oppression. *Not revolution, then, but resistance; not societal transformation, but the select defiance of institutions; not abstract struggles, but personal perseverance; not politics, but morality; not war, but evasion, disobedience, and exile.* It is the open microstruggles of the myriad, not the secret plottings of a few, that give shape and form to lasting, popular momenta for 'social change' that are bottom-up in their thrust. All other grand 'plans' of amelioration, speaking historically, have only been the top-down impositions of ruthless, remote, and alien minorities. 'Society' and the 'state' (as jointly expressed in the modern 'nation'—a degenerate form only of empire—is yet another dubious political gift of Europe), as we know them today, are only the ultimate expressions of the gross alienation of the simpler social ties that have bound humans to each other for millennia—they, that must be undone for humanity to regain its lost autonomies. The species-freedom of human innovation can exist, and flourish, only outside of the grim manacles of Governance (no matter how 'rational,' or benign), whether these shackles are crafted in iron or gold. The moral could not be clearer: *modernism cannot be undone using modernist means, artifacts, and institutional paraphernalia*, for these only strengthen its sway and prolong its dominance; we must find original resolves, from deep within our unmediated species being, nurtured in the purest crucibles of moral energy and spiritual fire. These forces are with us today, for having been our own patrimony until but yesterday when the fell night of the Enlightenment overtook so many of us as we slept secure in our own innocent, primeval serenity. We can, and must, rise again and shuffle off these cancerous, modernist coils.

We must break free from the tyranny of reason, from the myths of modernism that tie us to the wheel and break us on the stone, from false identifications, sham fealties, and sterile relations, forged by others and of benefit to a few, in remembrance of a past where life was not a mere adjunct to social labor, where work was indistinguishable from play, and where time could stand as still as we wished it; where nature was not a tool, people not a means, and joy did not come tumbling, cold and hard, out of a grocer's freezer. We can still rediscover the placid equanimity, and the unspoken reassurance, of the benign social form, its simple nourishments, its guarantee of ready fellowship, and its promise of a life-giving sustenance, regardless of resources and amenities. *We have no need to urbanize, industrialize, westernize, or rationalize our simple, homespun*, time-tested ways, but we do need to categorically reject all of these humbug catechisms of modernist entrapment. Nothing is to be gained by hothouse economic growth, by advancing the scale and scope of regressively inhuman technologies, by robbing the earth of irreplaceable resources. We have mirthlessly supped with the modernist and slept on his cold, Procrustean bed for too long; small wonder most of us are never to wake again, or even to know who we were before being inveigled into the great sleep.

The implications of this stance (of starting over) are little short of a convulsive uprooting of the entire catechism of European modernism, of reopening the floodgates of experimentation, innovation, and variety, across the scale of possible human experience; and supplanting and superseding the received notions of science, politics, freedom, and the human prospect, generally; of thinking, dreaming, and living afresh outside the paralytic crimps of latter-day ideologies and practices of repression, stalemate, and passive surrender. Humans are an astonishingly opulent species, their wealth expressed in the fantastic historical panorama of cultural forms; of means of communication, of modes of entertainment, of mores of art and artifice, music and madness. How this resplendently effulgent plenitude of lustrous light and color could have been reduced to the grisly deformities of the miserable either/or of capitalism and socialism must remain ever the most haplessly sordid enigma of human history. The resulting damage to, and disfigurement of, the very possibility of human imagination must count among the more heinous social acts of calculated, rank desecration.

Of all cultures on earth, the European is the last one to ascend to high civilization; while he yearns for it only imperfectly at the present juncture (the Green initiatives in Europe, and beyond, being the early inklings, prodromes, of this inevitable discontent), it is clear that he too (for being human) shall crave conviviality enough one day to make it happen. Then, in that far future, he would have finally caught up, ironically, with the wisdom of the very worlds he had hoped, in all egotistic arrogance, to leave far behind; the rest of us can only hope—against hope—that his historic tryst with destiny is not too late for the other, humbler, denizens of this planet.

THE REALM OF POSSIBILITY: TOWARD UTOPIA

Given the foregoing considerations, what can we expect to see in the decades to come? Quite frankly, no political economy can answer that question without fudging; indeed, when it comes to *predictions*, astrologers, uniformly, do better than social scientists (despite the fact that positivists, like Milton Friedman, make a huge fetish out of *prediction* as the overriding goal of science). On the other hand, an outline of the transfigurations, both already extant and still to come, has already been sketched; specific outcomes, however, remain to be *experienced*, the fruit of conjunctural determinations and practices.

The only universal, unchanging, datum in human society is struggle: for rights, jurisdictions, ways of life, and modes of discourse. These struggles are not merely at the level of states, classes, and nations (as in the grand materialist visions, whether of Left or Right), the chosen all-encompassing domain of the masculine-voiced, hard-nosed, 'sciences' of economics and politics, but at virtually all fissure points/lines/edges of potential and actual social fractures/divisions: gender, age, race, religion, ethnicity, language, etc. To prioritize any of these frictions over any of the others is to look at matters abstractly, and non-*contextually*; each has its own site, its own practice, and its own negations. None is assimilable to any other, nor can any be seen as a 'sublimated' form of the class struggle. Each of these social ontologies is as real as the economic; and neither the former nor the latter can be 'reduced' to each other.[16] It will remain a Eurocentric enigma as to why, for so long, in secular political traditions, *but* one complex of struggle—class/

nation/state—was seen as preeminently overriding all others.

Traditional emphases on aggregate (social) phenomena vis-à-vis the modalities of social change rest on fundamental misperceptions of the ontological distinction between the individual and social moments. In realist analysis the two levels are not distinguished by an *ontological priority* between the two domains (as reflected in the paradigms both of methodological individualism and Marxism, polar antipodes in this respect) as much as by a radical hiatus between them. *It is almost a law of ontology—both social and natural—that macrophenomena always appear to be 'law governed' and (thereby) predictable while microphenomena seem to be 'free' and less predictable.* An example or two may suffice: any individual worker is potentially capable of turning into a 'capitalist,' given the right collection of attributes, but the working class as a whole cannot turn 'capitalist' without violating the norm of capitalist society. For similar reasons crowd behavior, given someone shouting 'fire' in an auditorium, is more or less predictable, but how any particular individual in that hall will behave (to stay put, or to rush out, being the alternatives) is far less predictable. The point should be clear; individuals are led by apparently 'free' wills, while aggregates of individuals seem more bound to the expectation of normalcy. Stated differently, aggregate behavior is more 'controllable,' (for) being more predictable, (for) being more deterministic; individuals, *au contraire*, can slip through the cracks of the system. Summing up, individuals have more 'options,' more degrees of freedom, than societies. From a dim perception of this truth, the 'reasonable' inference drawn by the sociological minded, in Eurosociology (Durkheim, Spencer, Marx, etc.), seems to be that the social moment is more important, both in terms of the general analytics of a social science, and in terms of the prospects for social change. The unreasonable corollary of this position, on the other hand, has been that the individual placement is an unimportant one in discussing the moment of emancipation.

This, however, is simply false. There is no doubt that individuals can behave *contra* to social norms (be they socialist or capitalist norms; hence the conservative study of social 'deviance' in both social forms), thereby annulling all theories of sociological determinism (conservative or radical). If that's the case, then emancipatory movements can just as easily, in fact are far more likely, to be driven by individual example given the inevitable inertia of aggregate social entities, to initiate the dynamics of social change. If this is possible for any one individual in society it is, ipso facto, possible for all individuals (but only to the extent that they are making individual choices, as against 'constrained' social choices), because society, while a larger organon than the individual, nonetheless also exists at the level of an aggregation of individuals. Individual *delinking* from social norms can just as easily (in point of fact, far more easily) initiate social change as much as the vaunted Marxian faith in conscious class action. Individual delinking from the *logos* of capitalist production and consumption is, therefore, neither reactionary nor retrograde, as the social determinists would have us believe; indeed, in the many instances of the virtual nonexistence of class based resolves, it is the only way to proceed. The truth is quite paradoxical; one has only to examine the role of influential individuals in history, Mohammad or Gandhi or Lenin, to realize that individual determination often prevails over formidable social restraints (rather than the other way around). It is now possible to understand all forms of sociological determinisms (stemming from 'social science,' Left or Right) as profoundly reactionary ideologies, geared to stifling individual initiatives in the area of self-direction, so as to maintain the power and control of mini elites at the head of putative 'mass' movements. Both Marxists and capitalist planners wish only to 'lead' the less-privileged, or the more gullible, 'masses' like so many cattle, into preselected social corrals where they are permanently dispossessed of the will and capacity for self-determination. The mass movement, a herd phenomenon, is quite ideally suited to their purposes, because, being aggregate behavior, it lends itself to both predictability and control. The emancipatory impulse needs to shun all such frenzies: regrettably, it's a lesson of history that mobs will ultimately fall prey to the rule of mobsters.

The epistemic location of politics at the level of the state has given rise to accounts strapped fundamentally to ruling class/elite machinations; as such, the more humdrum, mundane, and down-to-earth struggles of ordinary peoples, in their everyday lives, has received short shrift, being included only when their logic clashes with the logic of statist politics (seen only, therefore, in the wholly negative guise of 'disturbing' factors). Of course, it is true that the era of politics from above has far from ended; indeed, it is perhaps even more securely consecrated now with the absolute dominance of the capitalist mode worldwide. *Indeed, the bad news is that, on the eve of the twenty-first century, we stand on the brink of unimaginable catastrophe as parvenu capitalist Gorgons rear their unsightly heads, looking for worlds to swallow, making the imperial conflicts of the twentieth century seem like so many effete shadow plays.* However, the internal stresses and strains of this very mode, quite endlessly, open up new veins of opportunities for reactive, and resistive, resolves; stated simply, as predators clash, at the level of the state, the prey can now, if they choose to act, bring local matters under their own control.

Just one telling example, of spontaneous human resolve, may be found in the area of the degradation of the environment, a by-product of typically reckless capitalist adventurism in the domain of industrial production. Here is an issue, manufactured by indurate capitalist (and socialist) blindness, that can serve, and is serving, as a rallying point of protest for thousands of ordinary people, across the globe, who otherwise would be impossible to characterize as 'political' animals in any brand of political theory. Yet, faced by a direct threat to their quality of life, such citizenry is organizing and mobilizing to defend itself against intolerable and unacceptable encroachments on their conditions of existence.

Perhaps the most salutary aspect of this new wave of political consciousness and activism is its apparent innate, and untutored, ability to invent and discover novel, and creative, forms of struggle that go beyond the barricades, and bayonets, of traditional norms of European political practices and ideologies. Whether expressed in a refusal to adopt conventional gender roles, linguistic usages, or extant modes of social consumption and production, these movements bid fair to annul the received, antediluvian definitions of the political moment. 'Left' and 'Right,' for instance, are modernist categories indelibly marked with the implacable dualism of European terms; feminist, ecological, and cultural struggles bypass the clutch of these petrified denominations, quite completely disdaining their restrictive one-sidedness. Indeed, in the context of Eurocapitalist societies, the routinized tussles between Left and Right have duly cancelled each other out, strengthening only the center, securely occupied by the wiles of (capitalist) statecraft. Struggles for self-determination defy, and deny, such hoary divides of corporatism, being undefinable, and inexpressible, in the language of modernist politics, therefore being quite unassimilable into its rank designs. Their struggle, to put the matter squarely, is simply *not* for the seizure of *political* power.

Perhaps this brand of politics may simply be called *survivalist*: but it is exactly the kind of movement ('we can't take it any more') that capitalist growth has inspired, in the most diverse cultural contexts, in recent years: rubber-tappers and the Yanomani Indians in Brazil, Himalayan peasants, and Narmada valley tribals in India, Native Americans of the Seventh Generational Fund in America, the Green Belt activists in Kenya, the Village Action Movement in Finland, and so on. All these attempts must be seen as the vital pilot projects in *self-organization*, an old principle all but lost in the modernist invasions of the last 400 years. It is these undramatic, and largely unnoticed, struggles of unexceptional peoples[17] that presage a return to self-directed, *vernacular* values in defiance of the speciously alien industrial ones that have dominated political discourse for so long.

It is sad, but true, that the host of little lamps extinguished by the European Enlightenment were far more profound for human survival than the cheap, gaudy, and illusory illuminations it provided in exchange. Indeed, future historians, paradoxically, will see the so-called Enlightenment itself as a terrible caricature, inaugurating only the New, even Dark(er), Age of 'modernism,' far more menacing to human society than the old. It is doubtful whether a civilization that could first readily consider to calmly manufacture the capacity for nuclear annihilation of fellow humankind (and the earth itself), and then use it, and then go on to stockpile it to the point— and beyond—of rabid insanity, is at all deserving of that flattering appellation. As such, the real barbarians have always lain *within* the grounds of the modernist complex, rather than outside its grisly gates.

At any rate, it is quite true that such autonomous fragmented, and uncoordinated, struggles for self-affirmation and self-validation can and are daily co-opted by the powers-that-be; but, even in that process of co-optation, one can discern ongoing transformations in policies, postures, and politicization. If one breaks with the old Left metaphor of cataclysmic revolution as the only means of amelioration, then it is easy to see that the resistance of the broad citizenry, class-based in some cases, not in others, is now spread across many cross-cutting fault lines in capitalist society. Even within the reactionary context of the nation-state, such struggles can often curb the ploys and pretensions of rulers (as with Die Grünen in Germany, Chipko in India, and the Seikatsu Club in Japan, all quite interestingly the offspring of *women's* initiatives), leaving the door open for building on, and advancing, such people-based prerogatives, one step at a time. One might consider this a form of *micro-social democracy from below*, bypassing the state-inspired institutional structures of managed, and hence trivialized, dissent. Even trapped within the iron cage, as we are, we are yet capable of a fearless faith, of indomitable struggle, of heroic resistance.

Of course, within the first world, such manifestations of people power are still few and far between, with the system still strong enough to beat off, or buy off, oppositional movements. But, in the incompletely capitalized third world, the spontaneous power of the people is still a mighty, untamed force. In heavily statist India, for instance, where the British imperial state survives on under domestic stewardship, but with its repressive arms overgrown, the sudden eruption of the anger of the people is still capable of instantly paralyzing the awesome machinery of state. The fact that much of this populism appears to be reactionary should not daunt the serious observer; indeed, it is not always the populism, but the leadership ready to seize advantage of it, that has been opportunist (as in the anti-Sikh riots, anti-Muslim riots, and so on), *given the structural inability of the traditional, post-colonial Left to embrace the politics of populism.*

Collective bargaining by riot, however, is an old and established principle of social action, in both the European and the non-European worlds, especially when novel impositions, and exactions, upset traditional rhythms and defy common expectations. As such, when not the simple response to the random despotism of oppressive state actions, such explosions are the very specific creature of modern capitalism (European or not), that has done more than any other tyranny in history to decompose and demoralize ordinary ways of life in favor of a regime of permanent disequilibria and permanent insecurity.

In this light, it should be apparent that the seams of capitalist order are not stitched as tightly as imagined; the system is ever vulnerable from within, far more than it ever was vulnerable from without. In the United States, to take but one example, the federalist structure permits permanent tensions between state and federal jurisdictions; and within the state, between cities, regional power blocs, local regimes, and so on. The segmentation principle intrinsic to power blocs knows no real bounds, with communitarian[18] politics capable of securing many more autonomies than currently extant, even as *Corporatist* structures, and processes, try to achieve a regressive, centralist, top-down, integration of the country at large. It is largely up to particular segments of the populace to assert, and then fight for, their rights to autonomy and noninterference by external, outside forces.

This is far from being merely a theoretical assessment: even now, a new populism (whose ultimate trajectory is quite unclear) is on the rise in the United States, admittedly with viciously strong right wing and racist leanings,[19] with the advent of talk-show politicization (a major factor in the 1994 Congressional elections) of a long apolitical citizenry, in a sharp departure from traditional voter apathy (the nucleus of hope within this apparently amorphous resurgence of popular initiative is its spirit of spontaneous resolve and its solidly anticorporatist and antistatist undertones; the enveloping penumbra of darkness is its reactive, often violent embrace of the many systemic intolerances of modernism—sexism, racism, etc. In a social form as depraved by cynicism, materialism, and violence as the United States, it may be inevitable that even *contra* movements continue to reflect their unsightly birthmarks). If revanchist forces can so organize, it is clear that other forces in the spectrum (including, but not restricted to, the traditional, *étatiste*, Left) are capable of following suit, in a humbly bottom-up struggle, to assert critical autonomies.[20] The citadel(s) need not be taken in one swoop (indeed, preferably not, for fear of reproducing, in obverse, the tyranny of the present corporatism); but it may well be transformed, brick by brick, but at the level of microcosms, with checks and balances intact. *Socialism fell from above; capitalism, when it does, will have to be eroded from below, in a form of both ontological and epistemological 'delinking' of ideologies and practices, from the juggernaut of capitalist hegemony* (Modes of origin leave their stamp on modes of extinction: communism, usually empowered in one sudden fell swoop, perished in much the same way, at least in Eastern Europe and the USSR. Capitalism rose to dominance in a much more prolonged, piecemeal fashion; it will erode, probably, likewise). As such, masculinist scenarios of catastrophic revolution will have to yield to the gentler persuasions of piecemeal recoveries of rites, rights, and rituals: indeed, the operative word, both semantically and politically richer in this discourse, is not revolution anymore, but *reclamation*.

All this is not to subscribe to a new form of ancestor worship, revering tribalism for its own sake, idealizing antiquity, fetishizing tradition, and revering custom, but rather to point out some irresistibly important structural principles of its organization, and functioning, that are singularly meaningful, and emancipatory, today, given the modern-day horrors of industrialism. It is to rediscover the wealth of practical knowledge and spiritual wisdom of our forebears, both European and non-European, accumulated over centuries, that were suddenly buried under, or swept away by, the avalanche of capitalist industrialization. It is to understand that history, like culture and civilization, did not begin with the European or with Capital; that the arts of life, social graces, aesthetic delicacies, and cultural revitalization in general, are still possible for the many (as they were, once upon a bygone time), not just the few, once the wheel of alien, oppressive, and exploitative *productions*, upon which millions perish every day, in every corner of the globe, is shut down—for good.

This is not to reject the ingenuity of human industry, but the horrors of modern *industrialism*—the hothouse process of an *impersonal political economy* that subjects the many, lifelong, to compulsory, subhuman, toil, so as to slake the inhuman, insatiate, greed of the few who do not and need not. Tools there will always be, of course; but they could, once again, be 'tools for conviviality,' as Illich[21] puts it, rather than machines that cripple, thwart, and stifle human initiatives. Divested of such extortionist industrial processes, work can still be a species of *play*, merely a creative employment of life's abundance of leisure and the natural talents of humankind. In a human society, any labor process outside of the variable whimsy of the real producer approximates an intolerable imposition of slavery.

Lest all this appear irredeemably 'utopian,' it is wise to recall that women, in the domain of housework, have already shown, for centuries, the possibility of disdaining capitalist (and other expropriative) norms in favor of nurturing *use-values*, within a personal economy of care and consideration, right within the entrails of capitalist society (in fact, the quite stupefying constancy of 'feminine' values under the varying Patriarchies of differing social formations [feudalism, capitalism, etc.] is an ineluctable disclaimer to traditional materialist theories of social behavior; *women represent the triumphal transcendence over such reductionist ideas*). It is time other constituencies learned to profit by their heroic example. What is needed is not the alienating, impersonal, expansion of the *public* household to cover all of society, as in state socialism, but to build outwards on the solid basis of the *private* household, extending the concept/metaphor of *family*, i.e., *personalization*, to one's range of contacts. Integrity, care, and consideration are at first possible only in small groups, with face-to-face relations: these precapitalist norms are the solid, time-tested, well-worn guarantees of conviviality. It is the 'feminine' force of *personalization* that could yet dissolve the alienation of the so-called, antagonistic, 'public sphere,' including the related European distinctions between 'state' and 'civil society.' The public-private divide, of capitalism (and class society, generally) corresponds, in many ways, to the male-female divide instituted by Patriarchy; the assimilation of the two sides of the arbitrary divide, in favor of *unitary* social forms embodying the value of personalization (and femininization) would be yet another major marker in the protracted struggle for the reclamation of utopia.

It might be noted that this is precisely what putatively 'charismatic' interventions have achieved repeatedly, *serving to rebond societal relations with effective, emotional ties*, however briefly and episodically, in human history—pointing to the vital organon of holism and union (but within a cultural matrix) that is almost a species-aspiration in human society, however suppressed by the arbitrary tyrannies of wealth and power. Far from being a hopelessly romantic dream, as ridiculed by modernists, such closely knit, *bonded* social forms were a clear and present species of historical fact, before being swept away mercilessly by the vicious avalanche of modernist invasions.

This rebonding cannot be on the basis of the existing perversions of state and civil society, for that only produces the grotesque deformities of a Hitler or a Mussolini creating artificially 'emotive' unions, by force and propaganda, amongst the various antagonistic separatisms of state and nation. For much the same reasons, Marxian socialist communitarianism, no matter how high-minded, comes to grief similarly. Indeed, what was always spurious about old-style Marxian calls to internationalism was its obvious retention of *nationalism* (subsuming alien forms of the state and society) within it; the more *apropos* slogan, for our times, rejecting the state/nation dyad, is a *universalism*, which *respects, not dissolves, all particularisms*—which are the artifacts, after all, of the human genius in all its evolutionary entirety. We are entirely capable of living again, outside the coercions of state and nation, fief and market, as *human* beings—universal only in our diverse particularisms.

As Herbert Marcuse[22] once suggested, we all carry within us the seeds of anthropic/social 'remembrance' of such warmth and cordiality, now long past; even, perhaps, a deep-felt ache—a forlorn longing, for them. However, far from being a mystical longing for a lost Garden of Eden, as in the Marcuse innuendo, the truth is the thoughtful amongst us can still find them every day—within that magic domain of care and compassion constituted by our 'loved ones,' in the context of 'home' and 'family.' Indeed, if we only knew, we all live in, and come home to, near-utopias—without usually seeing them as such! So-called 'primitive' tribal societies appeared attractive, even to the cruelly cynical eyes of the conquering Europeans, as revealed in their narratives of the 'noble savage,' precisely because they are built on an extension of this very human principle of kinship, and kindred-based social relations, moving in a blessed, 'feminine,' domain of nurturing reciprocity. *The happy family (not necessarily conceived of in 'nuclear' terms), regardless of the depredations of the mode of production, has always been the persistently overlooked metaphorical abode of Marx's 'primitive communism.'* Paradoxical indeed that the search for the holy grail ends precisely where it begins: in that magic circle where we are conceived and reared as human beings. Like lost and misdirected souls we have sought salvation abroad, only to find it, after a long and weary journey, waiting for us exactly where we had left it behind; not in the false promise of the public domain, or in the chimera of the body politic, but within the humble, prior matrix of simple, domestic intimacy.

As such, exits from the bell jar—itself the grand, singularly symptomatic, construction of the Enlightenment—have always been clearly marked, lambently lit up by the grace(s) of femininity until the dark night of modernism choked off its illuminations with the pharisaical glitter of unbounded greed and limitless conquest. Most of us, in this world, still eat, sleep, and live in *micro-utopias* that grant us far more in daily benedictions than any idle communist pipe dream of deliverance. The secrets of emancipation have lain enigmatically buried within that very cell, the original building block of all human social forms, for aeons—high time we understood its meaning, and absorbed its exigent, and restorative, significance. *There has never been anything utopian about utopia*; it is neither a dream, nor a phantom of our imaginations—it is given to most of us almost as a birthright. Indeed, it is time our world-weary wanderings, and anxious meanderings from contentment, brought us all the way back—*home*; it is, and will always be, the simple abode of all our epiphanic social nourishments.

The abundantly resplendent cultural diversity of humankind, the gift of aeons of triumphant adaptation to the vagaries of nature, its incredibly opulent heritage of art and artifact, craft and custom, already much reduced by European annihilation, stand poised to be completely overrun today by the basest impulses of pillage and rapine, greed and empire.[23] The great contribution of modernism has been, and can only be, a seamless *monotony*—flat, stark, rank, cadaverous and cheerless. No Mongol horde, no Attila, has conquered more unremittingly or pitilessly; no vandal in history has ever hoped as much to raze and plough the known world so thoroughly under his tyrant heel as to leave not a trace of the original contours behind. Worse, every step of the scorching way is sealed over with our acquiescence, real or contrieved, to the indefatigable logic of Mammon. More is better, the venal prophets cry, and we are quietly consilient, for being unable to adduce argument; for being bound over, ideologically, into the contrived realm of modernist convenance; and yet the soul, mistress of no one, bestirs, cringes, and revolts. It is in these deep, subterranean veins of the emotive life, that we must hope to find the resolve, wrought in the fiery furnace of suffering, to stem the execrable rot that has overtaken the destiny of humankind. The millennium is upon us; we can and must dare to try again. To *'turn the clock back'* (ridiculous only in linear visions of time) is often savagely satirized, by the modernist, as being an idle, romantic, antediluvian fantasy; and yet this 'fantasy' could well be the very embodiment of a *rational imperative* when the phenomenon in question is a time-bomb ready to blow up the very possibility of civilization.

The real imperative, then, is to shed the crippling baggage of capitalist, and other repressive, corporatist, ideologies (and practices), that have obscured real human relations for so long, by first engineering, and then imposing, *alien* social institutions (state, nation, factory, town, etc.) by either economic, political, or ideological, compulsions on behalf of exploitative/ extortionist strata and classes, upon spontaneously evolved simple societies. *As such, utopia, in societal terms at least, is not a process of invention, but of rediscovery.* Most of human society, across millennia, was less concerned with *having*, or even *doing*, than *being*, in a context of warmth, reciprocity, and fellowship, before the blight of possessive individualism, unmistakably European in provenance, ravaged those simple social relations. Clearly, we have a lot more to learn from the ancients than we already have; indeed, we had better hurry, or else the future *will* belong to Flash Gordon.

The only real resolve needed in this struggle for self-affirmation is the embrace of a new effective *self-consciousness*, stripped of alien allegiances, at once firmly *denationalized* and *destatified*, so that the two critical veils, among many, of the despotism of conventional capitalist (and/or 'socialist') hegemony may be summarily rent asunder. The very language of modernism, which debases past human experience, and decries past achievements of older cultures (even so sophisticated a scholar as Said finds it *de rigueur* to disparage 'nativism,' without pausing to consider what that term really means. Obviously, we accept the 'nativism' of the European blindly but demur our own [equally blindly])[24], in ideological fashion, needs to be systematically challenged, criticized—and abandoned. We are all but cotravellers on a flying planet lost in the emptiness of an unknown universe; the permanent basis of our spirituality, and affective coresponsiveness, is this forlorn, cosmic desolation, intimations of which modernism silences with ceaseless toil, bustle, activity, and noise. Modernism may not stand still, for terror of this hapless condition; but we can, anytime we wish—and that day the giant treadmill will grind to a complete stop, and the follies will come to an end.

It must be borne in mind that the conquering European, as the 'moving' force in recent history, has not only 'made' most of the history of 'modernism,' but has written it as well, in his cortorted political vocabulary, and after his lights (the very notion of treating 'Europe,' part of a continuous landmass, as a 'continent' is illustrative of his ideology of separateness). Given that, it is a truly daunting task to 'deconstruct' and reconstruct the host of real meanings that have been buried and lost in the heavy blitz of 'normal' propaganda. It is this vital, emancipatory function that falls to the critical, scholarly imagination of latter-day liberationists today. Of course, they are likely to be assisted by the self-immolating dialectic of the very forces of modernism; as the System(s) makes ordinary human survival more and more difficult for the many, it is safe to hypothesize that the natural shrewdness of the human race (too often scorned by both capitalist and socialist planners) will discover the means first to defend, and then to emancipate itself from such intolerable exactions.

Rubber-tappers in Brazil and peasant women (and nameless, and countless, individuals, workers and nonworkers, the world over, who have struggled to uphold human dignity against the devouring demands of their governing classes) in India found the political will, without any tutelage from above, under similar circumstances. The peasants of the first world can, surely, take courage from that. *Self-provisioning*, in the economic sense, and self-determination, in the political and cultural sense, are still possible for individuals, groups, and classes, so long as they dare to struggle—and '*delink*' themselves from repressive institutions—for their own choice of cherished immunities and exemptions. *The right to secede, personally and individually, from any, and all, inclement social forms not of our choosing, is inalienably, ours.* The earth is, and has always been, bountiful; we, now, its rather undistinguished trustees, who must decide, as humans, whether we at all qualify for—or deserve—the grace of its almost uniquely 'feminine' largesse of generous, unstinting beneficence.

It is almost impossible not to note that the roster of qualities associated with Patriarchical conceptions of masculinity have, near engulfingly, almost destroyed the very possibility of a pacific social existence across the planet. Yet, oddly enough, it is equally Patriarchical notions of *femininity* that seem to hold out real hope of a truly redemptive revolution in sensibilities today. Ironic indeed, and dialectically richly satisfying, that, all along, but hidden away in the dark shadow of Patriarchical visions, burned a pure flame, all but unnoticed, of promise and deliverance destined, some auspicious day, to dissolve perhaps the very apparatus that breathed it, its delicately nurtured life. It is not too late—*masculinist approaches to the dilemma of existence can yet learn to abdicate in favor of their gentler obverse*. But whether we embrace and nourish this fragile possibility of a more easeful existence, or savagely smother it to extinction, depends entirely on the choices we make today, as sentient and sensual beings, in all aspects of our social, and personal, lives. We can yet adopt, joyfully, the exalted gentility of the feminine principle (in this regard, civilization is simply the extent to which we embrace the felicitous norms of femininity).

The new—*entropic*—world order to come will reflect *such choices* made, both by rulers and the ruled, in sites and practices, located at both *gemeinschaft* and *gesellschaft*, levels of social life. As far as political practices go, no iron laws, but entirely pliable, tractable, and conscious, human wills, will guarantee/disavow our individual and collective fates. Material (but mutable) circumstances erect obstacles and restraints, to be sure, but they also supply enabling, even exciting, opportunities for rising far above them. The mightiest citadels of seemingly intractable power rest but precariously on the will of the governed; thereby, the burden of moral responsibility in these matters is never upon the force of the oppressor (no matter how terrible), but upon the resolve of the oppressed: *apathy, in the twenty-first century, can no longer masquerade as helplessness*. We who have built the cage, through acquiescence, neglect, fear, and venality; we who must dismantle it, or suffer the everlasting consequences of this default. For in politics, and the realm of social action, generally, at least in the long run, it is a truism that one gets, in a sense, what one deserves (*contra* Engels, then, freedom is not the recognition, but the *repudiation* of necessity).

NOTES

1. Lest it appear that Marxism is being singled out for an invidious drubbing, the moral perhaps needs to be stated unambiguously: given the ontological plurality of society no monist, exclusivist, vision can be sustained as a credible *episteme*. The problems of the world cannot, in any prioritization, be defined as exclusively class-based, gender-based, race-based, and so on. We must learn to recognize, instead, the interdependent nature of such struggles, reflecting the interdependent nature of the real world. Secondly, the Marxism being referred to in this book is the kind actually practiced in the erstwhile 'socialist' world; now, the objection might be raised that this invidiously omits the rich traditions(s) of Marxian pluralism in the west—but this ignores the inescapable fact that the 'test' of any ideational system lies in its 'applications.' Liberal European 'New Left' types of Marxism have remained only armchair phenomena, wherein high ideals can be costlessly cultivated; it is highly doubtful whether, once in power, these 'schools' would have behaved significantly differently from the actually existing varieties of socialism. Indeed, all the fatal flaws of 'scientific' socialism are inherent in the works of the classical master, Karl Marx, himself; it is silly, therefore, to blame his epigones for plans gone awry.
2. While this book stresses the need to be critical of Marxian *applications* in the realm of *social change*, it must be remembered that Marx made *two* fundamental contributions to the study of *capitalist* ontology and epistemology that are ineradicable. His ontological contribution lies in his theory of *exploitation*; his epistemological contribution lies in the theory of *ideology*. One cannot begin an analysis of capitalism without reference to these two notions. Finally, his uni-

versal contribution to societal knowledge is in his focus on the class domination of the labor process, i.e., the distinction between those who labor, and those who merely direct labor and appropriate its product.
3. For a lyrical account of the coming farewell to the Enlightenment, see Paul Feyerabend (1987).
4. Bill Warren (1980).
5. See P. Anderson (1979b) for more on the period of state formation in Europe.
6. The great travesty in Marxism is the almost complete absence of a theory of power, and a charter for checks and balances, in a post-revolutionary society—as if the leveling of 'class differences,' and the assurance of plenty, would evaporate all other social frictions. Millions paid a terrible price for this 'omission'. For another perspective on this 'For and Against' position on Marx, see R. L. Heilbroner (1980).
7. In point of empirical fact, matters are far more complex, economies and diseconomies being highly variable depending on the process in question; by and large, in agriculture, they tend to be crop specific.
8. For a full account, see Maurice Dobb (1966).
9. For a synopsis of the anarchist tradition, see James Joll (1964).
10. Certainly, the peace and ecology movements of today owe much to his original orientations; as such, Gandhi was decades ahead of his time. For Gandhi, in his own words, see M. K. Gandhi (1958).
11. On the historical problems of Marxism, vis-à-vis nationalism, see R. Munck (1986).
12. See P. Anderson (1979b), for a lyrical account of this process. More recently, B. Anderson (1991) has written about the state as an 'imagined community'; true, if one remembers that it was 'imposed' first, and 'imagined' afterwards.
13. For a capitalist caricature of this idea, see Kotkin (1993) and Hampden-Turner (1993), where a preanalytic, abstract, concept of culture becomes the simple determinant of 'styles' of capitalism.
14. For more on 'vernacular' ways of life, see Ivan Illich (1973).
15. Perhaps the most insightful self-criticism within western Marxism ever penned is by Perry Anderson (1979a); the fact that his study, nevertheless, does not come even close to considerations of such issues shows up the inherent limitations of Eurocentrism quite dramatically.
16. For a host of corrections to Marxian orthodoxy, in favor of a critical, indeed *transcendental* realism, see the incomparable Roy Bhaskar (1986).
17. For a catalog of such current grass-roots movements, see Paul Ekins, *op. cit.* (1992).
18. Communitarianism is fast becoming a buzzword in academic parlance, with the recent work of Amitai Etzioni (1993); however, this is still more ideologically, than practically, inspired, intended to sit 'midway' between capitalist individualism and 'socialist' collectivism.
19. For a more benign populism, much less noticed by the press in the United States, rediscovering the bounty of village life, see Richard Critchfield (1995).
20. All popular, and populist, struggles *against* the logic of modernism are routinely either ridiculed or demonized as reactionary, 'nativist,' and romanticist, by the modernist intelligentsia. Thus, Gandhi was laughed at as an errant fakir by the Indian establishment of his time, and contemporary Islamic struggles for self-respect are similarly painted black by the western press. By now, this rhetoric of debasement must be understood for what it is—a nervous, fearful, insecure,

     expression of the inherent fragility of the modernist edifice despite its impressive paraphernalia of repression.
21. Ivan Illich, *op. cit.* (1973).
22. H. Marcuse (1964).
23. The many fertile *subcultures* that are often thrown up, at least originally as ramparts against the advancing decay of modernism such as rock, reggae, etc., are no part of modernist culture, but constitute revolts against its monotonic anticulture. Of course the system co-opts them to the extent it can.
24. The paralyzing impact of modern Europe on the political imagination(s) of the non-European world, though of recent provenance, was to be extraordinarily complete as culture after culture was forced to capitulate, surrendering its own social, cultural, and political genius—including their sovereign right to dream their own dreams—to the relentless juggernaut of European innovations. Non-Europeans, playing with European institutional acquisitions, clumsy and ill at ease, pathetically and desolately out of touch with themselves, conscious of the dispiriting spiritual rift between their instinctive apprehensions and the awkward masks that concealed them—what a recipe for disaster! And yet, it is all too easy to shed these ill-fitting imports and rediscover the sources of the sheltering matrices of their own splendid cultural identities within which they may reconstitute themselves, but with their own, self-determined 'modernisms' of invention and innovation, not as second-class subjects of a European world but as first-class beings of a moral universe of their own creation.

POSTSCRIPT

The European Enlightenment, capitalist and materialist in provenance, has provided the dominant paradigm of social relations, and social change, for the past 300 years, slowly extending to the world at large by virtue of the all-total triumph of European ideologies (capitalist or socialist) in the twentieth century. Through the conduits of trade and investment, ideology and terror, treachery and subterfuge, a hapless world was fashioned in the image of this paradigm, destroying, in its wake, the natural and social diversity of peoples, cultures, and modes of civilization evolved over millennia. Worse than this despoliation itself was the widespread diffusion of the extraordinary belief that this was, contrary to the lived experience of multitudes, the best of all possible worlds. Even the Marxist, putatively opposed to capitalist ideologies, was to acquiesce to the 'progressive' nature of this world system, thereby closing the gate on the opposition of millions—peasants, tribals, women, and autonomist working-class activists in the main—who refused, for generations, to capitulate to this near-total expansion of alienated society. Worse than this acquiescence still was the inherently reactionary Marxian notion that 'historical' and 'material' constraints preempted all the creative modalities of change advocated by the disparate logics of resistance embraced by these simple, oppositional forces.

Today, this expansionist paradigm of growth and domination is at its all-time zenith, even as abject despair and impuissant misery are the lot of the majority who live under its insensible yoke. Fortunately, in keeping with a hoary lineage of revolt, a few have now risen in protest (largely self-organized women, disgruntled tribals, and sensitive people generally, the world over) against the very metaphysical foundations of this inveterate culture of death, and its grotesque philosophy of materialism. In all naive 'voluntarism,' they have shown that there is only one 'science' of social change—*struggle and resistance*—that is valid in all epochs, past and present. Nothing that cannot be changed, that is fought for; nothing that may not be evaded through intelligence, guile, and exile. This book confirms that simple intuition of the untutored mind: that human volition can overcome the very institutions that are its own artifacts. In one phrase: apathy confirms and conserves, while activism emancipates and liberates. Indeed, this is true at *every* ontological level, in all epochs: at the level of the individual, the family, the group, the class, and so on. True, society as a whole does not succumb, except rarely, in one fell swoop; but discrete interventions at all of the meaningful sublevels of social life are always possible and, more to the point, always extant, constituting precisely the vital processes of evolution and change. *We may be shackled by Society; but we are free in its subjurisdictions, the ontological hiatus between the two domains (unnoticed in all variants of social theory to date) offering the critical possibility of transition.* So, there is no historically ordained 'revolution' (other than one people choose to make), or officially designated standard bearers and vanguards of emancipation, to *wait* for (like Godot); we can '*delink*' to the limits of our ingenuity. There is no terror of organized despotism that the natural shrewdness of the human race cannot surmount, given the will. All we have ever needed, to make a difference, is volition; and all we have ever needed to act is to care enough (by dint of suffering and compassion) about the specifics of oppression. This was true of Spartacus, it was true of Wat Tyler, of Danton, of Lenin, of Gandhi, and of the many more nameless, humble heroes and heroines who dared to struggle, however haphazardly, to defend their cherished autonomies. So, let it now be *written*; so let it now, more aptly, be *done*—lest the reveille of emancipation from the recreant enjoinments of modernism lapse into a subdued quietus of defeat.

BIBLIOGRAPHY

Ahmad, A. *In Theory* (London: Verso, 1992).
Altvater, E. et al. (eds.) *The Poverty of Nations* (London: Zed Books, 1991).
Amin, S. *Imperialism and Unequal Development* (London: Monthly Review Press, 1977).
———. *Eurocentrism* (New York: Monthly Review Press, 1989).
———. *Delinking* (London: Zed Books, 1990a).
———. *Maldevelopment* (London: Zed Books, 1990b).
Amsden, A. 'Third World Industrialization: Global Fordism of a New Model?,' *New Left Review*, No. 182, July–August 1990, pp. 5–31.
Anderson, B. *Imagined Communities* (London: Verso, 1991).
Anderson, P. *Considerations on Western Marxism* (London: Verso, 1979a).
———. *Lineages of the Absolutist State* (London:Verso, 1979b).
Arrighi, G. *The Geometry of Imperialism* (London: Verso, 1983).
Bahro, R. *The Alternative in Eastern Europe* (London: New Left Books, 1978).
Baran, P. *The Political Economy of Growth* (New York: Monthly Review Press, 1957).
Bell, P. 'Gender and Economic Development in Thailand.' In *Gender and Development in Southeast Asia*, edited by Penny and John Van Esterik. Proceedings of the Twentieth Meetings of the Canadian Council for Southeast Asian Studies. CCSEAS xx vol. II York University, 18–20 October 1991. (CASA: Montreal, Canada, 1992).
Bernal, Martin. *Black Athena*, Vol. 1 (London: Free Association Books, 1987).
Bhaskar, R. *The Possibility of Naturalism* (Brighton: Harvester, 1979).
Bhaskar, R. *Scientific Realism and Human Emancipation* (London: Verso, 1986).
Blaikie, P. and Brookfield, H. *Land Degradation and Society* (London: Routledge, 1987).
Blaut, J. M. *The Coloniser's Model of the World* (New York: The Guilford Press, 1993).
Bluestone, B. and Harrison, B. *The Deindustrialization of America* (New York: Basic Books, 1982).
Bowles, S. et al. *Beyond the Wasteland* (Garden City, N.Y.: Doubleday, 1983).
———. *After the Wasteland* (Armonk, N.Y.: M. E. Sharpe 1987).
Branford, S. and Kucinsky, B. *The Debt Squads* (London: Zed Books, 1988).
Brewer, A. *Marxist Theories of Imperialism* (London: Routledge, 1980).
Broad, D. and Foster, L. (ed.) *The New World Order and the Third World* (Montreal and New York: Black Rose Books, 1992).
Brus, W. *Economics and Politics of Socialism* (London: Routledge and Kegan Paul, 1973).
———. *Socialist Ownership and Political Systems* (London: Routledge and Kegan Paul, 1975).
Bukharin, N. *Imperialism and World Economy* (London: Merlin, 1972).

Cassirer, E. *The Mind of the Enlightenment* (Princeton, N.J.: Princeton University Press, 1951).
Chomsky, N. *World Orders Old and New* (New York: Columbia University Press, 1994).
Cleaver, H. *Reading Capital Politically* (Austin: University of Texas Press, 1979).
———. 'Close the IMF, Abolish Debt, and End Development: a Class Analysis of the International Debt Crisis,' *Capital and Class*, No. 39, Winter 1989, pp. 17–30.
Corbridge, S. *Capitalist World Development* (Totowa, N.J.: Rowman and Littlefield, 1986).
Critchfield, R. *The Villagers* (London: Anchor Press, 1995).
Crow, B. et al. *Third World Atlas* (Milton Keynes, United Kingdom: Open University Press, 1983).
Davidson, B. 'The Ancient World and Africa: Whose Roots?,' *Race and Class*, Vol. XXIX, No. 2, 1987, pp. 2–15.
Dobb, M. *Studies in the Development of Capitalism* (New York: International Publishers, 1963).
———. *Soviet Economic Development Since 1917* (London: 1966).
Dornbusch, R. *Stabilization, Debt and Reform* (Englewood Cliffs, N.J.: Prentice-Hall, 1993).
Emmanuel, A. *Unequal Exchange* (London: New Left Books, 1972).
Etkins, P. *A New World Order* (London: Routledge, 1992).
Etzioni, A. *The Spirit of Community: The Reinvention of American Society* (New York: Simon and Schuster, 1993).
Fabian, J. *Time and the Other* (New York: Columbia University Press, 1983).
Feyerabend, P. *Science in a Free Society* (London: New Left Books, 1978).
———. *Farewell to Reason* (London: Verso, 1987).
Fornann, A. *Femininity as Alienation: Women, the Family in Marxism and Psychoanalysis* (London: Pluto, 1977).
Frank, A. G. *Capitalism and Underdevelopment in Latin America*, (New York: Modern Reader Paperbacks, 1967).
———. *World Accumulation 1492–1789* (New York: Monthly Review Press, 1978).
———. *Critique and Anti-Critique* (New York: Praeger Press, 1984).
Friedman, M. *Essays in Positive Economics* (Chicago: University of Chicago Press, 1953).
Frobel, F. et al. *The New International Division of Labour* (New York: Cambridge University Press, 1980).
Gandhi, M. K. *The Collected Works of Mahatma Gandhi*, 50 vols., to date (Delhi, 1958–).
Ghai, D. *The IMF and the South* (London: Zed Books, 1991).
Gilligan, C. *In a Different Voice: Psychological Theory and Womens' Development* (Cambridge, Mass.: 1982).
Gordon, D. 'The Global Economy: New Edifice or Crumbling Foundations?,' *New Left Review*, No. 168, March–April 1988, pp. 24–64.
Gorz, A. *Ecology as Politics* (Boston: South End Press, 1980).
Gourlay, K. A. *World of Waste* (London: Zed Books, 1992).
Hampden-Turner, C. and Trompenaars, A. *The Seven Cultures of Capitalism* (New York: Doubleday, 1993).
Harding, S. *The Science Question in Feminism* (Ithaca: Cornell University Press, 1986).
Harding, S. and Hintikka, M. (eds.) *Discovering Reality: Feminist Perspectives on*

Epistemology, Metaphysics and the Philosophy of Science (Dordrecht: Reidle Publishing Co., 1983).
Hayek, F. A. 'Scientism and the Study of Society,' *Economica*, 1942–1943.
Hecht, S. and Cockburn, A. *The Fate of the Forest* (London: Verso, 1989).
Heilbroner, R. *Marxism: For and Against* (New York: Norton, 1980).
Hilferding, R. *Le Capital Financier* (Paris: Editions de Minuit, 1970).
Hinton, W. *The Great Reversal* (New York: Monthly Review Press, 1990).
Hobsbawm, E. *The Age of Revolution* (New York: Mentor, 1962).
Hobson, J. A. *Imperialism—A Study* (London: Allen and Unwin, 1902).
Illich, I. *Tools for Conviviality* (New York: Harper and Row, 1973).
Jalee, P. *The Pillage of the Third World* (New York: Monthly Review Press, 1968).
Joll, J. *The Anarchists* (London: Eyre and Spottiswoode, 1964).
Joseph, G. G., et al. 'Eurocentrism in the Social Sciences,' *Race and Class*, Vol. 4, No. 31, April–June 1990, pp. 1–26.
Kaldor, M. et al., eds. *The New Détente* (London: Verso, 1989).
———. (ed.) *Europe from Below* (London: Verso, 1991).
Kanth, R. *Political Economy and Laissez-Faire: Economics and Ideology in the Ricardian Era* (Totowa, N.J.: Rowman and Littlefield, 1986).
———. (ed.) *Explorations in Political Economy: Essays in Criticism* (Savage, Maryland: Rowman and Littlefield, 1991).
———. *Capitalism and Social Theory: The Science of Black Holes* (Armonk, N.Y.: M. E. Sharpe, 1992).
———. (ed.) *Paradigms in Economic Development: Classic Perspectives, Critiques, and Reflections* (Armonk, N.Y.: M. E. Sharpe, 1994).
———. *Against Economics: Rethinking Political Economy* (London: Avebury Publishing forthcoming, 1997).
Kornai, J. *The Economics and Politics of Socialism* (1973).
———. *The Economics of Shortage* (Amsterdam: 1980).
———. *Contradictions and Dilemmas* (Budapest: 1985).
Korner, P. et al. *The IMF and the Debt Crisis* (London: Zed Books, 1986).
Kotkin, Joel. *Tribes* (New York: Random House, 1993).
Lakatos, I. *Philosophical Papers*, Vols. 1, 2 (Cambridge: Cambridge University Press, 1978) ed. Worral, J. and Curry, G.
Lenin, V. I. *Imperialism, the Highest Stage of Capitalism* (New York: International Publishers, 1939).
Levi-Strauss, C. *The Savage Mind* (Chicago: University of Chicago Press, 1966).
———. *Tristes Tropiques* (Harmondsworth: Penguin Books, 1992).
Lipietz, A. *The Enchanted World* (London: Verso, 1985).
———. *Mirages and Miracles* (London: Verso, 1987).
Loewenson, R. *Modern Plantation Agriculture* (London: Zed Books, 1992).
Lutzeler, P. M. (ed.) *Europe after Maastricht* (Providence and Oxford: Berghahn Books, 1994).
Luxemburg, R. *The Accumulation of Capital* (New York: Monthly Review Press, 1968).
Magdoff, H. *Imperialism* (New York: Monthly Review Press, 1978).
Mandel, E. *Europe versus America?* (London: New Left Books, 1970).
———. *Late Capitalism* (London: Verso, 1978).
———. *The Second Slump* (London: New Left Books, 1978).
———. *Long Waves in Capitalism* (New York: Cambridge University Press, 1980).
———. 'In Defense of Socialist Planning,' *New Left Review*, No. 179, 1989, pp. 5–37.

Marcuse, H. *One Dimensional Man* (London: Routledge and Kegan Paul, 1964).
Marx, K. *Critique of the Gotha Programme* (Moscow: Progress Publishers, 1971).
———. *On Colonialism* (New York: International Publishers Co., Inc., 1972).
Marx, K. and Engels, F. *The Communist Manifesto*, Huberman L. and Sweezy, P., eds. (New York: Monthly Review Press, 1964).
Mendes, C. *Fight for the Forest* (New York: Monthly Review Press, 1989).
Michelmann, H. J. and Panayotis, S. (ed.) *European Integration: Theories and Approaches* (New York and London: University Press of America, 1994).
Mies, M. *Patriarchy and Accumulation on a World Scale* (London: Zed Books, 1986).
Mohanty, C. 'Under Western Eyes: Feminist Scholarship and Colonial Discourse,' *Feminist Review*, Vol. 30, Autumn 1988, pp. 65–88.
Molyneaux, M. 'The "Woman Question" in the Age of Perestroika,' *New Left Review*, No. 183, Sept.–Oct. 1990, pp. 23–49.
Mukherjee, R. *The Rise and Fall of the East India Company* (New York: Monthly Review Press, 1974).
Munck, R. *The Difficult Dialogue* (London: Zed Books, 1986).
Nove, A. *The Soviet Economic System* (London: Allen and Unwin, Inc., 1986).
Oberoi, J. P. S. *The Other Mind of Europe: Goethe as a Scientist* (Delhi: Oxford University Press, 1984).
Offe, C. *Disorganized Capitalism* (Cambridge, Mass.: MIT Press, 1985).
Owen, R. and Sutcliffe, B. (eds.) *Studies in the Theory of Imperialism* (London: Longman Press, 1972).
Parboni, R. *The Dollar and Its Rivals* (London: New Left Books, 1981).
Payer, C. *The Debt Trap* (New York: Monthly Review Press, 1975).
———. *The World Bank: A Critical Analysis* (New York: Monthly Review Press, 1982).
———. *Lent and Lost* (London: Zed Books, 1991).
Piore, M. J. and Sabel, C. F. *The Second Industrial Divide* (New York: 1984).
Popper, K. *The Poverty of Historicism* (London: Routledge and Kegan Paul, 1957).
———. *The Open Society and Its Enemies* (New York and Evanston: Harper Torchbooks, 1963).
Rustin, M. 'The Politics of Post-Fordism: Or, The Trouble With "New Times",' *New Left Review*, No. 175, May–June 1989, pp. 54–78.
Sabine, G. *A History of Political Theory* (New York: Holt, Rinehart and Winston, Inc., 1950). Revised Edition.
Sahlins, M. *Tribesmen* (Englewood Cliffs, NJ: Prentice-Hall, 1968).
Said, E. W. *Orientalism* (New York: Vintage Press, 1979).
———. 'Orientalism Reconsidered,' *Race and Class*, Vol. 2, No. 27, 1988, pp. 46–54.
Salomon, Albert. *The Tyranny of Progress* (The Noonday Press, 1955).
Scheler, M. *Ressentiment* (Milwaukee, Wisconsin: Marquette University Press, 1994).
Schumpeter, J. A. *Business Cycles*, 2 vols. (New York: McGraw-Hill Co., Inc., 1939).
Seligman, C. G. *Races of Africa* (London: 1929).
Sen, A. 'Rational Fools: A Critique of the Behavioral Foundations of Economic Theory,' *Philosophy and Public Affairs*, 6, Summer 1977, pp. 317–344.
Shaikh, A. 'An Introduction to the History of Crisis Theories,' *U.S. Capitalism in Crisis*, (New York: Union of Radical Political Economists, 1978).
Shaikh, A. and Tonak, E. *Measuring the Wealth of Nations: The Political Economy of National Accounts* (New York: Cambridge University Press, 1994).

Shanin, T. *Late Marx and the Russian Road* (New York: Monthly Review Press, 1983).
Shiva, V. *Staying Alive* (London: Zed Books, 1989).
———. *The Violence of the Green Revolution* (London: Zed Books, 1991).
Shiva, V. and Mies, M. *Ecofeminism* (Halifax, Nova Scotia: Fernwood Press, 1993).
Smith, A. *The Essential Adam Smith* (New York and London: W. W. Norton, 1986) ed. by R. L. Heilbroner.
Spedding, J. et al. (eds.) *The Works of Francis Bacon* (Reprinted) (Stuttgart: F. F. Verlag, 1963).
Sweezy, P. *The Theory of Capitalist Development* (New York: Monthly Review Press, 1942).
Thurow, L. *Head to Head* (New York: William Morrow & Co., 1992).
Tsetung, M. *A Critique of Soviet Economics* (London: Monthly Review Press, 1977).
Turner, Bryan. *Marx and the End of Orientalism* (London: Allen & Unwin, 1978).
Warren, B. *Imperialism: Pioneer of Capitalism* (London: New Left Books, 1980).
Weinberg, W. *War on the Land* (London: Zed Books, 1991).
White, G. et al. (eds.) *Revolutionary Socialist Development in the Third World* (Lexington: The University Press of Kentucky, 1983).
Wolf, E. R. *Europe and the Peoples Without History* (Berkeley: University of California Press, 1982).
Zeitlin, I. M. *Ideology and the Development of Sociological Theory* (Englewood Cliffs, N.J.: Prentice-Hall, 1968).

INDEX

abortion, 123
absolute capitalism, 23
absolutism, 3, 96, 97, 102, 133, 136
abstract economics, 118–19
abstraction, 107, 118, 121, 130
abstract universalism, 50
academia, 58, 63
accounting system, 89
accumulation, 52, 84, 91, 98, 122
activism, 19
affection, 109, 111, 112, 119, 130, 142, 144
Afghanistan, 49
Africa, 2, 5–6, 12, 33, 44, 51, 126
African National Congress, 12, 35
agenda, bourgeois, 103
agenda perspective, 16–19, 61, 74, 78
agent, in theory, 78
Age of Capital, 98
Age of Capital, 99
agrarianism, 41
agriculture, 4, 13. *See also* land reform
'aid,' 29
Alaska, 7
Alexandria, Egypt, 6
Algeria, 45, 49
alienation: and abstraction, 118; and capitalism, 83; and class, 121; and corporatism, 129–30; and Enlightenment, 141; and family, 144; and industrialism, 153; of labor, 87, 102, 139; and law, 108; and Marx, 132; and materialism, 112; and modernism, 130, 144; and *objectification*, 121; and state, 145–46; through trade, 1
Allendé Gossens, Salvador, 34, 38, 45, 51
Alliance for Progress, 21
American Revolution, 103, 104
Amin, Samir, 51, 73–75

Amsden, Alice, 66
anarchy, 141–42
ANC: *See* African National Congress
Anglo-American economy, 13
Angola, 49
anthropocentrism, xiii, 92, 100
anti-capitalism, 49
anti-imperialism, 49
antimodernism, 49
Antinomial Dichotomy, 96
April Theses (Lenin), 138
Aquino, Corazon, 46
Arab people, 12
Arbenz, 34, 51
Argentina, 12
aristocracy, 6
Arthashastra (Kautilya), 118
ASEAN: *See* Association of Southeast Asian Nations
Asia, xv–xvi, 2, 44, 47, 51, 65, 67, 70, 126. *See also specific countries*
Association of Southeast Asian Nations, 47
atomism, 95, 119, 130
Auto industry, 70

Bacon, Francis, 92, 94, 118
Bahro, Rudolf, 93n. 5
Baker, James A., III, 30
Baker Plan, 30
Bakunin, Mikhail Aleksandrovich, 138, 140
balance of interests, 109
Bandung Conference, 45
Bangladesh, 44
bank, 29, 30
Belgium, 4
Bell, Peter, 61, 81n. 4
'benefit-cost' calculation, 100
Bengal, 4
Benin, 49

Bentham, Jeremy, 102
Berkina Faso, 49
Bharatiya Janata Party, 117
Bhaskar, R., 131
BJP: *See* Bharatiya Janata Party
Black Africa, 5–6. *See also* Africa
Bolshevik Revolution, 74
Bolshevism, 87
bourgeois economics, 83
bourgeoisie, 12, 31, 91, 96, 103, 134, 136
Bourgeois Progressive Agenda, 103
Bowles, Samuel, 59–61, 69
Bradley, Bill, 30
Brady, Nicholas F., 30
Brady Plan, 30
Brazil, 12, 33, 45, 47, 49
breeder, woman as, 122
Brenner, Robert, 66
Bretton Woods Conference: and crisis of capitalism, 26; and economic integration, 10, 65; and imperialism, 18, 20–24; objective of, 30; replacement of, 71; suspension of, 61; and third world, 34, 46; and United States, 20–24, 75
Britain: *See* United Kingdom
budget, balanced, 22
Bukharin, Nicolai, 8; *Imperialism and World Economy*, 9
Burke, Edmund, 129

Cambodia, 49, 118
Canada, 33
Cape Verde, 49
capital: competition of, 79; export of, 63, 64; metropolitan, 32, 68, 74; migration of, 65–66; and society, 6; *vs.* state, 136
Capital, Age of, 98, 99
capitalism: *absolute*, 23; agenda of, 14–15; and alienation, 83; alternative to, 137; and Asia, 47; and bourgeoisie, 136; and Bretton Woods Conference, 20–24; and center *vs.* periphery, 73; and China, 67, 76; and class, 8, 11; and colonialism, 1–6, 52, 122; crisis of, 26, 27, 62, 77, 84–85; critique of, 82–85; and culture, 126; and democracy, 136; and determinism, 97; dominance of, 161; and Enlightenment, 96, 98, 119; and environment, 100, 125, 149–50; and equality, 110; and Eurocentrism, xiv, 116, 120; and Europe, 79; fall of, 152; and fascism, 69; and feudalism, 48; and freedom, 87, 132; and Germany, 9, 79; and growth, 101; and India, 46, 67; and individual, 149; *international*, 20; and investment, 79; and Japan, 79; and knowledge, 124–25; and Latin America, 12; leadership in, 10; and Lenin, 8, 9, 14; and liberty, 87, 132; and market, xiv, and Marx, 158n. 2; and Marxism, 82; and mass consumption, 13; and monopoly, 7–8; and morality, 143; and neocolonialism, 116–17; and oppression, 135; order of, 142; and patriarchy, 122; and peasantry, 111; and political economy, 58; in post-World War II era, 16–35; and production, 52; productivist *vs.* consumerist, 31–32; and progressivism, 124, 135–36; and rationality, 135; revolt against, 156; and Russia, 42, 67, 76; and *scarcity*, 132; and socialism, 10–11, 37, 87, 88–90; stability in, 76; and state, 23, 79; and Taiwan, 47; and theory, 78; and third world, 44–46, 48, 50–52, 102; and United Kingdom, 10; and United States, 10, 23, 59–60, 79, 84; and USSR, 13–14; and violence, 92; *vs.* precapitalism, 117; and women, 83, 122, 153–54; and working class, 11, 83, 111. *See also* imperialism; modernism
capital surplus, 29
capitulationism, 46
cartel, 7
cash crop, 4
cash-nexus, 83
Castro, Fidel, 39
center *vs.* periphery, 73–74
Central America, 2, 44, 45
Central Intelligence Agency, 34
Chartist movement, 136
Che: *See* Guevara, Ernesto "Che"

Index

Chilé, 12, 38, 45, 48, 51
China, 6; and Africa, 33; and capitalism, 67, 76; and colonialism, 2; containment of, 47; data on, 88; economy of, 40; and Hong Kong, 65; and imperialism, 65, 71; independence of, 14; and industry, 33; and International Monetary Fund, 88; Maoist Revolution in, 74; and market, 102; and medicine, 120; and self-government, 11, 12; and socialist agenda, 37–39; and South Korea, 46; and Taiwan, 65; and trilateralism, 34; and USSR, 10, 38; and World Bank, 88
Chipko women, 125
Chomsky, Noam, 86
Christian ethic, 99
circularity, 96
civilization, 147
civil rights, 42, 49
civil society, 111–12, 130–31
class: and alienation, 121; and capitalism, 8, 11; and colonialism, 2; governing, 17, 19; and individual, 149; and Marxism, 17, 19, 73, 134; and Mies, 73; in United States, 31. See also working class
'class-in-itself' *vs.* 'class-for-itself,' 19
class struggle, 17, 62, 63
Cleaver, Harry, 17, 61, 62
COICA: See Co ordinadora de las Organisaciones Indigenas de la Cuenca Amazonia
cold war: and Bretton Woods Conference, 36; and hot wars, 42; and imperialism, 14, 20; and Newly Industrialized Country, 70; and third world, 46, 48
colonialism: and Bretton Woods Conference, 22; and capitalism, 1–6, 52, 122; and class, 2; development of, 1–6; and Eurocentrism, 126; and Europe, 2, 5, 116–17, 123; legacy of, 45; and Lenin, 9; and migration of capital, 65; and patriarchy, 123; and self-government, 11, 12; and women, 101, 123. See also imperialism; third world
Columbus, Christopher, 126

commerce, 1, 6
commercial monopoly, 32–33
commodity fetishism, 133–34
commodity price, 29
commodity production, 84, 87
communism, 14, 20, 134, 137, 144
communitarianism, 152, 154, 159n. 18
competition, 8, 70–71, 79
comprador, 4, 5, 12
Comte, Auguste, 97, 114n. 8
confederated autonomy, 30
Congo, 4, 49
consensus, 108, 109
conservation, 124. See also environment
conservatism, 25
constitution, 108–9
consumerism, 31–32
consumption, 41, 91
consumption-led growth, 12
context, 107, 118
contract, 105, 109
control, 145
conversations, 109
conviviality, 119, 143, 153
Co ordinadora de las Organisaciones Indigenas de la Cuenca Amazonia, 127
Corn Laws, 98
corporation, 59–60, 61. See also Trans National Corporation
corporatism, xv, 54, 98, 129–30, 132
creationism, 133
crisis, of nineteen seventies, 24–26, 61, 68, 69, 70–71, 72, 73, 75, 76, 77
Cuba, 35, 39, 40, 47, 61
cultural movement, 49, 50, 150
culture, 141; of death, 90, 161; and Marxism, 134; and social organization, 90; and third world, 117; in United States, 103; violence against, 101; *vs.* modernism, 57, 112, 126–27; *vs.* nature, 96. See also tradition
currency, 22, 24–25, 26, 29

debt crisis, 29–30, 61, 75
debt-peonage, 29
decommodification, 140
deficit, 61

delinking, 73–76, 148–49, 157, 162
demand, 73
democracy, 60, 86, 87, 131, 136
dependency, 66, 132–33
depression: *See* Great Depression
Descartes, René, 95, 96
despotism, 35
determinism, xiii, 91, 97
devaluation, of currency, 22, 29
development, uneven, 74
dictatorship, 66, 136
'difference,' 106
discourse, 108–9, 119, 156–57
'Disproportionality,' 85
dollar devaluation, 29
domestic market, 45
domestic sphere, 101
domestic strife, 26
dualism, 96, 117–18
Durkheim, Émile, 114n. 8

Eastern Europe, 66, 83
East Germany: *See* German Democratic Republic
East India Company, 126
EC: *See* European Community
ecological movement, 49, 50
ecology, 124–26, 150. *See also* environment
economic empire, 35
economic reductionism, 51, 77, 134
economics, 19, 53, 83, 89, 97, 118–19, 134. *See also* political economy
economism, 74, 85, 134
economy, 159n. 7; capitalist *vs.* socialist, 88–90; and colonialism, 4–5; *entrepôt*, 44; and Marxism, 39; political, 57–80; and socialism, 39–40, 91; and state, 6, 11
ecosystem: *See* environment
Egypt, 5–6, 11, 12, 44, 48, 51
Einstein, Albert, 97
Elitist tendency, 95
emancipation, xv, 53, 80, 93, 121, 129–58, 155, 161–62. *See also* freedom
Emmanuel, A., 74
employment, 25, 27, 60
Enclosure movement, 100
ends *vs.* means, 99

Engels, Friedrich, 55n. 22
English Revolution, 103
Enlightenment: and alienation, 141; approach to, 113n. 1; characteristics of, 94–113; and dependency, 132–33; discourse of, 119; dominance of, 161; and Europe, 114n. 8, 117; and Marx, 93n. 8; and modernism, 90–93; and social science, xiii; and traditional culture, 150–51
entertainment industry, 32
entrepôt economy, 44
environment, 83, 89, 90, 100, 124–26, 149–50. *See also* ecology
environmentalism, 49
epistemic pluralism, 133
equality, 103, 104, 110
equity *vs.* growth, 41
étatisme, 22, 75, 87. *See also* state
ethics, morality, xv, 99, 107, 119, 143
Ethiopia, 49
Eurocapitalism, 52
Eurocentrism, xiv, 116–21; and colonialism, 126; and economics, 93n. 8; and Enlightenment, 94–113; and environment, 125; and history, 153; and Marx, 144; and Marxism, 73; and materialism, 120; and non-Europeans, 160n. 24; and socialism, 87; and struggle, 147; and third world, 50
Eurodollar, 29
Euro-Marxism, 66, 101
Europe: and capitalism, 52, 79; and civilization, 147; and colonialism, 2, 5, 116–17, 123; and culture, 126; divisions in, 32; and Enlightenment, 96, 117; and environment, 125; and language, 156–57; and materialism, 92–93; and modernism, 114n. 8; and productivism, 31, 32; and third world, 43, 46; and violence, 105
European Community, 24, 30–31, 32, 34, 76
European Union, 32
exchange rate, 25
exchange value, 101–2
ex-colonial world: *See* third world
experience vs. experiment, 95
export, 4, 7, 8, 22, 29, 63, 64, 74

extraversion, 45

Fable of the Bees (Mandeville), 91, 99
family, 109, 111, 130, 144, 154–55
fascism, 10–11, 69, 136, 154
Fed: *See* Federal Reserve Board
Federal Reserve Board, 28
fellowship, 110
female *vs.* male, 96, 110, 119, 154, 157–58. *See also* men; women
feminism, 71–73, 121–24, 150. *See also* women
feudalism, 48, 78, 136
finance capital, 8
Finance Capital (Hilferding), 9
fixed exchange rate, 25
floating exchange rate, 25
Ford, Henry, 12
Fordism, 12–13, 26–27, 68–71
France, 7, 9, 31, 33, 34. *See also* French Revolution
Frank, Andre Gunder, 32, 51, 73, 75
freedom: and capitalism, 87, 132; defined, 144–45; and Enlightenment, 103; and progressivism, 104; and rights, 143; and self-determination, 140; and socialism, 41; and USSR, 85–88. *See also* emancipation; liberation; self-determination
'free enterprise,' 21, 22
free exchange rate, 22
free market, 41
free trade, 21
free trade zone, 26
'free' will, 148
French Revolution, 103, 104
Freud, Sigmund, 97, 120

Gaddafy, Moammar, 34
Gandhi, Mohandas, 43, 139, 159n. 10, 20
GATT: *See* General Agreement on Tariffs and Trade
gender, 134–35
General Agreement on Tariffs and Trade, 21
German Democratic Republic, 40, 88
Germany, 136; and capitalism, 9, 79; and competition, 30–31; and economy, 6; and imperial rivalry, 24–25, 71; and industry, 33; and National Socialism, 10–11; and productivism, 32; and Roosevelt, 12; and trilateralism, 34; and United States, 59; and USSR, 9
Ghana, 49, 51
Global Fordism, 68–71
Global Organization of Production, 63–67
GNP: *See* gross national product
gold parity, 29
good *vs.* evil, 91, 99
GOP: *See* Global Organization of Production
Gorbachev, Mikhail, 42–43
Gordon, David, 59–61, 66, 69
governing class, 17, 19
grant, 29–30
Great Britain: *See* United Kingdom
Great Depression, 11, 12, 14, 20, 27, 59, 69. *See also* stock market crash, of 1987
Greece, 6, 136
greed: *See* materialism
Green initiative, 49
Grenada, 49
gross national product, 84
growth, 12–13, 27, 37, 41, 68, 101, 102, 106
Guevara, Ernesto 'Che,' 39
Guinea, 49
Guinea-Bissau, 49
gynocentered production, 72
Gypsy, 11

Hawaii, 7
Hegel, Georg Wilhelm Friedrich, 5, 95
hegemonic overreach, 24
Heisenberg Principle, 108
hermeticism, 118
heroic aggregation, xiv–xv
Hilferding, R., 8, 10; *Finance Capital*, 9
historical materialism, 91
history, 90, 95–96, 117–18, 134, 153
Hitler, Adolf, 10–11, 14, 19, 154
Hobbes, Thomas, 96, 105, 141–42
Hobson, J. A., 8, 9
home, 111, 154, 155
homeopathy, 133
Hong Kong, 14, 47, 64, 65, 136

hospitality, 133
housewife, 122
housework, 72–73, 153
humanism, 107, 108, 113
Hussein, Saddam, 34

ideology, 5, 32, 90, 134
IDL: *See* International Division of Labor
Illich, Ivan, 153
IMF: *See* International Monetary Fund
immiseration, of proletariat, 73
immunizing stratagem, 74
imperialism: and China, 65, 71; and colonialism, 12; and conservatism, 14; defined, 18; growth of, 6–10; and loan, 29–30; and NIDL/GOP perspectives, 65; and periphery, 74; in post World War II era, 16–35; and socialism, 35, 38; in Social Structure of Accumulation view, 61; and third world, 34, 46; and world government, 21. *See also* colonialism
Imperialism and World Economy (Bukharin), 9
import control, 22
import substitution, 45
income growth, 101
India, 6; and *antimodernism*, 49; and capitalism, 46, 67; and cold war, 48; and colonialism, 2, 5; economy of, 43–44; and import substitution, 45; independence of, 14; and industry, 33; and market, 102; and *nativism*, 117; and self-government, 11, 12; and United Kingdom, 43, 92, 151; and USSR, 38
individual, 96, 111, 117, 118, 148–49, 156
Indonesia, 48
induced inflation, 27–28
industrial capital, 8
industrial monopoly, 32–33
industrial revolution, 2, 74
industry, industrialism: and alienation, 153; and China, 33; and colonialism, 4; and environment, 90; and imperialism, 6; and socialism, 41; and technology, 33; and third world, 44, 63; and west, 65

inflation, 27–28, 61
integration, economic, 10, 21, 30, 65
intentionality, 19
interest, xv, 87, 109, 111
international capitalism, 20
International Division of Labor, 71–72
International Monetary Fund, 21–22, 78; and Bretton Woods Conference, 36; and China, 88; and debt crisis, 30; and India, 46; and third world, 34–35, 52
International Monetary Fund Plan (1982–1985), 30
'international political economy,' 53
interwar period, 9–15
intra-imperial conflict, 24–29
investment, 41, 79
investment-led growth, 12
Iran, 51, 117
Iraq, 11
Islam, 159n. 20
Italy, 33, 40, 88, 136

Jamaica, 45
Japan, 14; and capitalism, 79; and colonialism, 5; and competition, 30–31; and Europe, 116; and European Community, 32; and imperial rivalry, 24–25, 71; and industry, 33; and NIDL/GOP perspectives, 65; and North American Free Trade Agreement, 76; and productivism, 31–32; and third world, 47; and trilateralism, 34; and United States, 59
Jew, 11
justice, 103, 104, 110–11

Kalecki, Michal, 79, 81n. 19
Kautilya: *Arthashastra*, 118
Kautsky, Karl Johann, 21
KCIA: *See* Korean Central Intelligence Agency
Kenya, 45, 49
Keynes, John Maynard: anticipations of, 9; and capitalist decline, 18, 20; and culture, 127; and 'Great Depression,' 11; and reconstruction, 20; and White plan, 21

Keynesianism: accounting system of, 89; failure of, 61, 65; military, 23; and *underconsumption*, 69; and wage, 12
Khmer Rouge, 40, 118
knowledge, 94–95, 107–8, 124–25, 133
Kondratieff cycle, 17, 19, 76
Korean Central Intelligence Agency, 136
Korean War, 70
Kornai, Janos, 41
Kronstadt, 86

labor: alienation of, 87, 102, 139; and colonialism, 3–4
labor union, 12
laissez-faire, 22, 141
Lakatos, I., 74
land parcellization, 4
land reform, 46, 47
language, discourse, 108–9, 119, 156–57
Laos, 49
Latin America, 7, 9, 12, 39, 44, 45, 136
law, rule of, 103, 104, 108
League of Nations, 11
Lenin, V. I., 10, 80; *April Theses*, 138; and capitalism, 8, 9, 14; destructiveness of, 92; and *Ultra-imperialism*, 21; and 'uneven development,' 74; and women, 123–24
Levi-Strauss, Claude, 96, 107; *Tristes Tropiques*, 102
liberalism, 105, 118, 119–20
liberation, 5, 145. *See also* freedom
Libya, 49
linearity, 91, 95–96, 117–18, 134
Lipietz, Alain, 33, 68–71
loan, 29–30
Locke, John, 95, 105
Lumumba, Patrice Emergy, 51
Luxemburg, Rosa, 23

Machiavelli, Niccolò di Bernardo: *Prince*, 118
machine, 100
macrophenomena, 148
Madagascar, 49

male *vs.* female, 96, 110, 119, 154, 157–58. *See also* men; women
Mali, 49
Malthus, Thomas Robert, 74
management, 12, 68
Mandel, Ernest, 76–77
Mandeville, Bernard: *Fable of the Bees*, 91, 99
Manley, Michael Norman, 45, 51
manufacture: *See* industry
Maoist Revolution, 74
Mao Zedong, 37–38, 120, 139
Marcuse, Herbert, 154
market, xiv, 78, 102
market dependency, 84
marketing, 32
market relation, 100
Marshall Plan, 10, 29, 34
Marx, Karl, 3, 55n. 22; and alienation, 132; and *anthropocentrism*, 92; and capitalism, 158n. 2; and colonialism, 1; and consumption, 91; and Enlightenment, 91, 93n. 8, 94, 97; and Eurocentrism, 144; and family, 155; and linearity, 95; and materialism, 37; and peasantry, 138; and precapitalism, 118; and production, 91; and proletariat, 73; 'Theses on Feuerbach,' 139; and 'uneven development,' 74; and violence, 105; and women, 122
Marxism: and capitalism, 82; and class, 17, 19, 73, 134; and colonialism, 4; and commodity production, 84; critique of, 134–39; and 'economics,' 77; and economy, 39; and Enlightenment, 90; and Eurocentrism, 73; and growth, 101; and Italy, 61; and Mandel, 76–77; and Mao Zedong, 38; and materialism, 139; and modernism, 133; and monopoly, 7; and nineteen seventies crisis, 70–71; and pluralism, 158n. 1; and political economy, 61, 80n. 1; and power, 159n. 6; and production mode, 8; and progressivism, 161; and reductionism, 91; and science, 119–20; and self-determination, 140; and socialism, 41, 58–59, 158n. 1;

Marxism *cont.*
  and state, 87; and third world, 50; and trade, 78; and USSR, 85; *vs.* state, 79
mass consumption, 13
mass movement, 149
mass production, 12–13, 68
materialism, 57–80, 91, 115n. 16; and alienation, 112; dominance of, 161; and Enlightenment, 98–103; and equality, 110; and Eurocentrism, 120; and European ideology, 92–93; and Marxism, 37, 134, 139; and modernism, 130; and socialism, 87; and USSR, 85; and women, 153
materialist *reductionism*, xiii–xiv
materialist reductionism, 118
Mechanistic tendency, 95
medicine, 120, 124
men, 121–22. *See also* male *vs.* female
merchant capital, 1
Merton, R. K., 120
metropolis, and colonialism, 4
metropolitan capital, 32, 68, 74
Mexico, 4, 12, 33, 45, 47
microphenomena, 148
Mies, Maria, 71–73
military, militarism, 22–23, 25, 33, 34, 35, 57–58, 126
'military Keynesianism,' 23
Mill, John Stuart, 4, 60, 105
mind *vs.* body, 96
minority, 59, 61, 139
modernism, 5; agendas of, 14–15; and alienation, 130, 144; and *control*, 145; and culture, 127; and discourse, 108–9; and ends *vs.* means, 99; and Enlightenment, 89–90; epistemic basis of, 109; and Eurocentrism, 116; and Europe, 114n. 8; language of, 156; and militarism, 126; and monotony, 155; and political economy, 53–54, 57; and populism, 152, 159n. 20; resistance to, 146; and subculture, 160n. 23; and subjugation, 143; triumph of, 129–33; and work, 139. *See also* capitalism; socialism
monetarism, 28
monopoly, 6, 7–8, 32–33

monopoly capital, 7–8
monotony, 155
'Monroe Doctrine,' 7
morality: *See* ethics, morality
Mossadegh, Muhammad, 51
Mozambique, 49
Mussolini, Benito, 154

NAFTA: *See* North American Free Trade Agreement
Nasser, Gamal Abdel, 45, 51
nationalism, 140
National Socialism, 10
nation state, 140–41, 142, 145
Native American, 7, 109, 121, 126
nativism, 117, 156
NATO: *See* North Atlantic Treaty Organization
nature, 83, 96, 100. *See also* ecology; environment
needs *vs.* resources, 89
Nehru, Jawaharlal, 45
neocolonialism, 43, 44, 48, 49, 116–17
neo-Taylorism, 33, 70
Netherlands, 2, 33
New Deal, 12
new international division of labor, 63–67
New International Economic Order, 45
New International Order, 65
Newly Industrialized Country, 33, 34, 47, 63–65, 67, 68, 70, 136
NIC: *See* Newly Industrialized Country
Nicaragua, 49
NIDL: *See* new international division of labor
nineteen seventies crisis, 24–26, 61, 68, 69, 70–71, 72, 73, 75, 76, 77
Nixon, Richard M., 25, 29
Nkrumah, Kwame, 51
nonalignment, 44–45, 48
Non-Alignment Initiative, 45
North American Free Trade Agreement, 33–34, 64, 76
North Atlantic Treaty Organization, 10, 19, 21
North Korea, 47, 49
north *vs.* south, 63, 68
Nove, Alec, 37
nuclear weaponry, 31

OAS: *See* Organization of American States
objectification, 121
objectivism, 17, 96, 97
objectivity, 96, 106, 132
observation, 108
Occam's Razor, 120–21
OECD: *See* Organization for Economic Cooperation and Development
oil, 29
OPEC: *See* Organization of Petroleum Exporting Countries
oppression, 71, 80
order, 142
ordinary person, 71, 79–80
Organization for Economic Cooperation and Development, 21, 72, 78
Organization of American States, 21, 48
Organization of Petroleum Exporting Countries, 26, 29, 62
orient *vs.* occident, 96
overproduction, 76

Pacific Rim, 34, 64, 65
Pakistan, 45, 48
Palestinian people, 35
Pan Africanism, 12
Paracelsus, 118
'Paris Club,' 29
particularism, 154
patriarchy: and capitalism, 122; and colonialism, 5, 123; critique of, 73; and female *vs.* male, 154, 157–58; and feminine values, 111, 153; Mies on, 72; and science, 119
Pax Americana, 20, 21, 65, 71, 75
Pax Britannica, 20, 21
Peace of Utrecht, 2
peasantry: and accumulation, 122; and capitalism, 111; emancipation of, 157; and Enlightenment, 100; and Marx, 138; and property, 137; in Russia, 86, 120; and self-determination, 140; and third world, 44, 49; and working class, 122
peonage, 29
periphery *vs.* center, 73–74
personalization, 154
Philippine Islands, 7, 11, 12, 46

Piaget, Jean, 96–97
plantation economy, 4
play, 153
pluralism, 133, 158n. 1
Poland, 62
policy *vs.* theory, 77–80
political economy, 53, 57–80, 80n. 1, 81n. 19. *See also* economics
political empire, 35
politics, 19, 141, 152
Ponzi, Charles, 29, 30, 55n. 12
populism, 12, 151, 152, 159n. 20
Portugal, 2, 3, 136
positivism, 97–98, 108, 114n. 13
postcolonial stance, 43, 48, 151
'Post-Fordism,' 68
post-modernism, 112–13
poverty, 89, 102
power, 159n. 6
precapitalism, 53, 117, 118, 124, 153
pre-modernism, 112–13
price, 13, 27, 29
Prigogene, Ilya, 142
Prince (Machiavelli), 118
private sector, 11
private *vs.* public, 111–12, 132, 153
production: and capitalism, 31–32, 52; of commodity, 84, 87; cost of, 65–66; crisis of, 84; decentralization of, 64; and Lipietz, 68; and Marx, 91; mode of, 8, 78, 83; and third world, 45; and underconsumption, 85
productivism, 31–32
productivity, 28, 60, 61, 62, 69, 74, 87, 91
profit, 66, 69, 73, 84, 100, 106
profit-motive, 83
progress, 87, 91, 103–5, 130
progressivism, 5, 117–18, 124, 135–36, 161
proletarian internationalism, 60
proletariat, immiseration of, 73
property, 83, 137
public *vs.* private, 111–12, 132, 153

quadrilateralism, 33

race, 134–35
racism, 5, 152
rational absolutism, 102

rationality: *See* reason, rationality
Reagan, Ronald, 11, 22–23, 25, 35, 59, 64, 71
realization, 52, 71, 73, 84
real poverty, 89
reason, rationality: and affection, 111–12; and Eurocentrism, 118; and Levi-Strauss, 102; and Marxism, 134–35, 138; and modernism, 101, 130; and morality, 107; resistance to, 146
reclamation, 152
'reconciliation,' 110–11
reconstruction, 20, 21
reductionism, xii–xiv, 87, 91, 94–95, 118, 134
reflexivity, 119
reform, 8–9
regenerative circularity, 96
regulation, 78
Regulation School, 68
relative poverty, 89
relativism, 97, 133
rentier, 8
reparation, 20
resources *vs.* needs, 89
restitution, 110
retribution, 110
revolution, 151, 152
Ricardo, David, 18, 74, 97, 98
'robber baron,' 7
Robespierre, Maximilien François Marie Isidore de, 105
Romania, 123
romanticism, 53, 114n. 2
Roosevelt, Franklin D., 12
Rousseau, Jean Jacques, 105
rule, of law, 103, 104, 108
Russia: and capitalism, 42, 67, 76; and imperialism, 65; and imperial rivalry, 71; and peasantry, 120; and trilateralism, 34. *See also* USSR
Russian Revolution, 19–20, 74

Sadat, Anwar el-, 48
Said, Edward, 55n. 29, 156
Saint Simon, 97
Sartre, Jean Paul, 98
Saudi Arabia, 45
scarcity, 41, 132

Schopenhauer, Arthur, 107
Schumpeter, J. A., 56n. 31, 84
science: and abstraction, 118; Baconian, 118; and Enlightenment, 94–98; and Eurocentrism, 119–21; and knowledge, 133; and Marxism, 134; and objectivity, 106; and state, 120, 133
Scientism, 108
SDI: *See* Strategic Defense Initiative
Seaga, Edward, 45
SEATO: *See* Southeast Asian Treaty Organization
secession, right of, 157
Second International, 9
security, 41
self-determination, 50, 87, 131, 138, 140–47, 157
self-government, 11, 12
self-interest, 87, 91, 99, 115n. 15, 118, 134–35
self-organization, 150
self-provisioning, 157
Seligman, C. G., 5
Sen, Amartya, 107, 118
service, on debt, 30
sexism, 152
Seychelles, 49
Singapore, 14, 44, 47, 64, 65, 136
singularity, xiii
'slump-flation,' 76
Smith, Adam: and Enlightenment, 91, 94, 97; and linearity, 95; and materialism, 37; and vice, 94; and world market, 2
'social contract,' 109
social democracy, 42
socialism: agenda of, 15, 35–43; and capitalism, 10–11, 37, 87, 88–90; case against, 85–88; collapse of, 67; and culture, 126; and democracy, 86; dominance of, 161; and economy, 39–40, 91; and Enlightenment, 119; and environment, 125; and equality, 110; and Eurocentrism, xiv, 87, 116, 120; fall of, 58–59, 152; and growth, 101; and imperialism, 38; and industrialization, 41; and Marxism, 41, 158n. 1; and materialism, 87; and modernism, 133; and morality,

xv, 143; and National Socialism, 10–11; and productivity, 87; and progressivism, 124; and self-determination, 140; and state, xiv; and theory, 78; and third world, 49, 51; and violence, 92; and women, 122, 123–24; and working class, 138. *See also* modernism
social moment, 148
social science, xiii–xiv, 106, 121–22
Social Structure of Accumulation, 59–61
society, 96; and capital, 6; civil, 111–12, 130–31; traditional, 101, 122, 123, 124, 150; tribal, 49, 139, 153, 154–55
Sukarno, 48, 51
Solidarity movement, 62
Solow, Robert, 92
Somalia, 49
South America, 2, 7
Southeast Asian Treaty Organization, 21, 48
South Korea, 33, 34, 45, 46, 47, 64, 65, 136
South Yemen, 49
Spain, 2, 7, 33, 136
Spice Islands, 2
SSA: *See* Social Structure of Accumulation
stagflation, 27, 29, 76
Stalin, Joseph, 11, 37, 38, 42–43, 115n. 15
Stalinism, 83, 87
Standard Oil, 7
state: and alienation, 145–46; artificiality of, 142; and capitalism, 23, 79; and colonialism, 1–2; and economy, 6, 11, 13; and Marxism, 79, 87; and modernism, 130; revolt against, 156; and science, 98, 120, 133; and self-determination, 140–41; and socialism, xiv, 35; and United States, 59; and USSR, 87–88; and violence, 105; *vs.* capital, 136; *vs.* civil society, 111–12. *See also* *étatisme*
stock market crash, of 1987, 28. *See also* Great Depression
Strategic Defense Initiative, 22–23, 35

struggle, 147–48
student protest, 61
subculture, 160n. 23
subjectivism, 17
subjectivity, 106, 132
subordination, 130
subsistence wage, 73, 122
Suharto, Raden, 48
Sujugationist tendency, of science, 95
surplus, 7, 29, 43, 84
survival, 35
Survival International, 127
Sweden, 33
Switzerland, 33, 101

Taiwan, 34; and capitalism, 47; and China, 65; and communism, 14; and industry, 33; and NIDL/GOP perspectives, 64
talk-show politicization, 152
Tanzania, 49
Taylorist management, 12, 33, 68, 69, 70
technicist perspective, 18
technological fetishism, 100
technology, 32, 33, 132
Thatcher, Margaret, 11, 59, 64, 79, 120
theory, xiv–xv
theory *vs.* policy, 77–80
'There Is No Alternative hypothesis,' 131
'*Theses on Feuerbach*' (Marx), 139
think tank, 54n. 2
third world: agenda of, 15, 43–54; and Bretton Woods Conference, 34, 46; and capitalism, 44–46, 48, 50–52, 102; creation of, 3; and culture, 117; and debt crisis, 29–30, 61, 75; and environment, 125; and export surplus, 29; and imperialism, 34; and International Monetary Fund, 22, 34–35; invention of, 102; and migration of capital, 65–66; and nineteen seventies crisis, 73; revolts in, 61; and United Nations, 65; and women, 72, 124; and World Bank, 34; and world economy, 34
third-worldism, 26–27
'TINA hypothesis,' 131
Tito, Josip Broz, 45

TNC: *See* Trans National Corporation
'Tobin's Q,' 59
trade, 1, 21, 25, 26, 65, 68, 77, 78
tradition, 90, 130, 142–43, 153. *See also* culture
traditional medicine, 120
traditional society, 101, 122, 123, 124, 150
Trans National Corporation, 10, 64, 79
tribal society, 49, 139, 153, 154–55
Trilateral Commission, 54n. 2
trilateralism, 30–31, 32, 33–34, 65
Tristes Tropiques (Levi-Strauss), 102
trust, 7
Turkey, 136

U. S. Steel, 70
Uganda, 49
Ultra-imperialism, 21
underconsumption, 69, 85
'Unequal Exchange,' 74
union: *See* labor union
United Kingdom: and Bretton Woods Conference, 20; and capitalism, 10; and Chartist movement, 136; and colonialism, 2, 3, 4; and competition, 31; economy of, 6–7, 40, 88; and Great Depression, 11; and imperial rivalry, 24, 71; and India, 43, 92, 151; and industry, 33; and 'Post-Fordism,' 68; and United States, 21; and USSR, 9; and working class, 120. *See also Pax Britannica*
United Nations, 11, 21, 34, 45, 65, 75–76
United States: agenda of, 18; and Bretton Woods Conference, 20–24, 75; and capitalism, 10, 23, 59–60, 79, 84; and class, 31; and colonialism, 9; and competition, 30–31; conservatism in, 25; and constitution, 108–9; and consumerism, 31–32; and Cuba, 39; and culture, 126; and democracy, 136; and domestic strife, 26; economy of, 6, 7, 25–26, 59–60, 69–70; and Enlightenment, 103; and Fordism, 69; and Germany, 59; and Great Depression, 11, 14; and imperialism, 65; and imperial rivalry, 24–25, 71; and industry, 33; and Japan, 59; jurisdictions in, 152; and marketing, 32; and Marshall Plan, 29; and mass consumption, 13; materialism of, 152; and 'Monroe Doctrine,' 7; and nineteen seventies crisis, 24–26, 68, 69, 70–71, 71, 73, 75, 76; populism in, 152; and 'Post-Fordism,' 68; productivity growth in, 28; and socialism, 42; and third world, 46, 47, 51; and trilateralism, 33–34; and United Kingdom, 21; and United Nations, 75–76; and USSR, 88; and violence, 105; and working class, 26, 31, 59–60, 62. *See also* American Revolution; *Pax Americana*
universalism, 50, 96, 106, 117, 154
use value, 101–2, 112, 153
USSR: and capitalism, 13–14; and China, 10, 38; collapse of, 13–14; economy of, 40, 42; failings of, 85–86; and Hitler, 10–11, 14; and India, 38; and inter-War period, 9–10; and Roosevelt, 12; and socialist agenda, 35–37; and state, 87–88; and third world, 48, 51; and United States, 88. *See also* Russia
usury, 30
utopia, 111, 113, 137, 144, 147–58, 156

value, xv, 101–2, 103, 110, 112
Vietcong, 62
Vietnam, 34, 38, 47, 49, 61, 62, 118
Vietnam War, 70
violence, 92, 100, 101, 104–5, 118
virtue *vs.* vice, 99, 118
Volume One analysis, 74, 77

wage, 60, 65–66, 73, 74, 122
wage-led growth, 12
wage-price control, 22
Warren, Bill, 136
Warsaw Pact, 36
Weber, Max, 130, 135
Weisskopf, Thomas, 59–61, 69
welfare, 39
welfare state, 40–41, 65, 122–23
welfare subsidy, 22

White plan, 21
Wilde, Oscar, 23
Wilson, Woodrow, 11
wisdom, 107, 112, 118, 153
witch-hunt, 122
women: and accumulation, 122; as breeders, 122; and capitalism, 83, 122, 153–54; colonial, 123; emancipation of, 157; and Enlightenment, 100, 101; and Lenin, 123–24; and Marx, 122; and Marxism, 139; and materialism, 153; and patriarchy, 111, 122; and political action, 151; and socialism, 123–24; and third world, 44, 49, 50, 124; and tribal society, 154–55; in United States, 31, 59; and utopia, 113; and welfare state, 122–23; and working class, 72. *See also* female *vs.* male; feminism
women's movement, 61
work, 139, 153
working class, 26; and capitalism, 11, 83, 111; and class struggle, 17; and Enlightenment, 100; and European society, 6; and Fordism, 12, 68; and Marxism, 139; and nineteen seventies crisis, 25; and peasantry, 122; and political economy, 61–63; and reform, 8–9; and self-determination, 140; and socialism, 138; and third world, 44, 49, 63; in United Kingdom, 120; in United States, 26, 31, 59–60, 62; and women, 72
World Bank, 21–22, 30, 34, 36, 52, 88, 89, 125
World Court, 75–76
world government, 21
world market, 2, 3
world trade, 68
World War I, 2, 9, 10, 67
World War II, 10, 14, 19, 64, 67

Yeltsin, Boris, 41, 86

Zaire, 45
Zimbabwe, 49